Symbol of Creation

SYMBOL OF CREATION
AN EXPLANATION

Like many people when I first saw the Symbol of Creation, which has been adopted by the Society of Servants of God as it's own symbol, I thought that it was a clever artist who tried to work up a symbol that combined aspects of some of the major world religions.

When I asked Dr. Dinshah K. Mehta about this, he answered that the Symbol was revealed to him in meditation and that it is a symbol of Creation. The Star of David, the Holy Hindu mantra 'OM,' the Cross and the Swastika, which is a very important Hindu symbol, were not included in the symbol to reflect Judaism, Hinduism and Christianity, although they did do that. Rather the Star of David, the 'OM,' the Cross and the Swastika were all part of the symbol because they each reflect a state of Creation.

Given below is Dr. Mehta's explanation of the symbol as understood by me.

In the beginning there was only the "All Pervading Nothing, which is the Source everything." It is not really nothing but from the point of view of human beings it is as if it is nothing because it is beyond human perception. The vibrations are so intense, so fast, that it is just as if there is nothing. This All Pervading Nothing, which is the Source of everything, is mentioned in some of the major world religions. In the Zarathusti (Zoroastrian) religion it is called "Zarvane Akarne." The Hindus refer to it as "Sarva Akarnum." In the Kabala it is called the "Ayn," out of which emerged the "Ayn Sof," or that which is endless. Buddha called it the "Antim Shunyata" or the Ultimate Nothing or the Ultimate Zero.

Within this "All Pervading Nothing," spiritual energy, for lack of a better expression, started concentrating on a point. That was the First implosion. When all this energy continued to concentrate, it reached a point beyond which it could not concentrate any further and it had to go somewhere. So there was an explosion. This was the first movement and this movement was in the counter-clockwise direction. In the Bible this is symbolically called the First Day. Out of this implosion and explosion, the Word came into existence. In the Bible, It is called the Word of God. The Hindus call it the 'OM' and other religions call this

3

Word by different names. There were a total of six implosions and explosions until the Word finally stabilized. There was a seventh implosion followed by an explosion, which is still going on. This is reflected in the Biblical statement, "God created the universe in six days and on the seventh day He rested."

The series and implosions and explosions were contained and limited within the "All Pervading Nothing which is the Source of all Sources" including the Word of God and God. The circle around the Star of David reflects the containment within Itself of these implosions and explosions by the "All Pervading Nothing." This is reflected in the fact that movements of all creations are contained within their source.

Out of the Word emerged God the Creator Principle. This is reflected in the Biblical statement, "In the Beginning there was the Word. The Word was with God. The Word was God."

After God the Creator Principle emerged, God the Creator, God the Sustainer and God the Re-Creator became. Together they make up the Holy Trinity. In Zoroastrianism they are referred to as Asha, Vohu Mano and Kshatravairyo. In Hinduism they are called Brahma, Vishnu and Shiva, who is also called Mahesh. In the Old Testament the Arch Angels making up the Holy Trinity are known by the names of Raphael, Gabriel and Michael and in the New Testament they are referred to as The Father, The Son and The Holy Ghost. Out of the Holy Trinity emerged the remaining four Arch Angels. Out of these first seven created Arch Angels, one separated from its Source and became what is commonly known as Satan.

The Star, or Shield of David, represents the six Arch Angels that remained with the Word, which is central to their Creation. Therefore the Word, as represented by the Hindu symbol 'OM," is placed in the centre of the Star of David.

The top half of the Symbol represents Spiritual Creation. Matter had not yet come into existence.

When Lucifer separated from God and the other Arch Angels, he lost his luminescence and became dark. He was falling indefinitely. To limit his fall and prevent him from sinking further, bedrock was created below which he could not sink. The bottom end of the long arm of the cross represents the domain of Lucifer commonly called hell.

To help Satan and the many souls that fell with him to ascend back to the Spiritual Planes, from time to time, High Beings descend from the Spiritual Planes. This is reflected in the symbol by the rays that emanate from the Star of David. These rays represent the descending High Beings. These High Beings descended all the way to hell to create a pathway for the fallen souls to climb toward the Spiritual Plane. The fallen souls ascend along a straight path 'til they reach the earth plane. The material plane, which is earth in our solar system, is the filter through which the ascending souls have to pass to work out their shortcomings and prepare themselves for the ultimate journey to the Higher Spiritual Planes. Until souls reach the material planes of consciousness, they have no liberties and are totally under the thraldom of Satan.

Once they reach the material plane, which, as explained above, is earth in our solar system, for the first time they experience a free will. Having a free will after the bondage of hell and the planes below the earth plane, most souls go astray. They no longer continue on the straight and narrow ascent. Instead the many desires they experience on earth sidetrack them as they strive to enjoy their new-found freedom. This then causes them to move laterally. This lateral movement by souls that have ascended to the earth plane is what collectively creates the Cross of God. These individual crosses that souls create for themselves is what binds them down to the cycles of birth, life and death. The Swastika within the Cross represents the rounds of birth, life and death to which all souls are bound until such time as they work out their Karma. The need to work out one's own karma is reflected in the Bible, which tells each individual to bear his/her own cross. Unless one works out one's karma one cannot again walk the straight and narrow path up the long arm of the cross towards the Spiritual Planes of Light which is reflected by the top half of the symbol. The Rays of Light ascending from the Cross reflect the souls that are liberated from the material plane and are ascending toward the Spiritual Planes.

This ascent of the fallen souls back to their Source is reflected in the Biblical story of the Prodigal son.

The arms of the Swastika are pointing clockwise. This reflects the fact that the movement of Material Creations is opposite that of Spiritual Creations. As mentioned above, after the first implosion and explosion, the first movement happened counterclockwise out of which the Word of God came into Being.

From the above explanation one can see that the Star of

David, The Word "OM," the Cross and the Swastika are all important symbols and represent only a part of the movement of Creation. They are complete unto themselves for that part of Creation that they signify but do not represent the complete Symbol of Creation as His Guiding Mind disclosed it to Dr. Dinshah K. Mehta.

The above is a simple explanation of the Symbol and what it represents. Much more can be written about this subject and perhaps it may be done in another book.

THE JOURNEY OF LIFE ETERNAL

From The Source Unto The Source

by

Bahram Rashid Shahmardaan, Ph.D.

CONTACT INFORMATION:
176 Los Altos Avenue,
Walnut Creek, CA 94598-3141
Tel: 1(925) 934-8467
Fax: 1(925) 934-8468
Email: Bahram@cyberwebglobal.com

This edition dated June 2003
The Journey of Life Eternal
Published by New Age World Publishing
ISBN: 1-59405-034-1
Copyright © 2003 by Bahram Rashid Shahmardaan, Ph.D.
Cover design © by C'Ric Mose
(Used with Permission)

The Journey of
Life Eternal

LORD ZARATHUSTRA: PROPHET OF PERSIA
CIRCA 8,500 B.C.E.

DR. DINSHAH K. MEHTA IN MEDITATION
CIRCA 1967

WHAT IS A SCRIPT?

Script is the Word from thoughts that are heard
By the earless ears that know no birth;
The Source of all and brightest of bright.

This gives not full scope of the Word *Script*
Rather its limit for finite human minds.
For full scope, outgrow unto Divine that shines
With faith deserve that Blessed Gift.

For another explanation of Script and the Source of the messages
revealed in the Scripts please go to Page 273.

I AM LOVE

I AM LOVE and also Beloved. I take any form that MY OWN choose. I AM the water that descends in rain and falls on all evenly, whether the place is clean or dirty. Even when I fall on dirty places, I cleanse them because I AM Love. I become dirty thereby Myself, but I take up the dirt and purify it. I AM the Sun that shines on all evenly, whether good or evil. I scour out the dirt by My purifying rays of Love. In places where purification is not needed, I give My bounty of Love for My own to use and spread the sunshine of Love that is Me. But I am also very particular to whom I give My Love to use at their will. If one is not prepared by becoming one with Me, I withhold from him the gift of using Love, though I give it freely when he takes Me as the Beloved. I draw all his love, polluted or otherwise, to Me first, and after purifying, I give it back to be used as I guide. In that trial, if he succeeds, I give the right to use Love that is Me at the will of My beloved, and not until the purification is achieved, is the trial passed by the chosen one.

This is general for all. But there are times when I allow My Love to be used by the dirty ones also according to their discretion with a purpose. That purpose varies according to My Plan, but when the Plan is fulfilled I withdraw the sanction if the one who so uses My Love does not become pure. These are exceptions...

From the *Scripts* April 19, 1955

DEDICATION

This book is dedicated to –

The memory of Dr. Dinshah K. Mehta who is the author's Spiritual Master and without whose teachings the author would have undoubtedly continued to flounder in his search for the Spiritual Principles that enable each one of us to complete the Journey of Life Eternal.

Lord Zarathushtra, whose teachings enabled the ancient Persians to achieve greatness and spawned a great civilization with many Persian dynasties and Kings such as Darius the Great, Khashiyar Shah (known as Xerxes amongst the Greeks) and Koorosh (Cyrus) the Great.

"Society of Servants of God" – the Spiritual Organization founded by God through Dr. Dinshah K. Mehta.

All Servants of God appearing anywhere, in any form, race, sex, religion, or creed.

My late parents Goolbanu and Rashid Shahmardaan who endured many hardships to give their six children a good formal education and served as living examples of moral fortitude.

And Hazrat Hassan Pathan, my first spiritual teacher.

ACKNOWLEDGEMENTS

All the people whose lives have crossed my path have each contributed in their own way to help me reach my present state of being. I am grateful to them all, especially my siblings and many cousins. I apologize to everyone for any discomfort they may have experienced because of my actions during shared situations.

This book could not have been written without the support and encouragement of several people. Special mention must be made of my Spiritual brothers and sisters Ardeshir D. Mehta, Bohman Shamardan, who is also my older sibling, Bruce Welinski, Dr. David F. Sucher, Desh Ramchandar, Dr. Larry J. Meyer, and Ron and Melodie Greenblatt, each of whom have made a special contribution. Others who need special mention are the Amici in Germany, Anne and Burton G. Greenblatt, Edna C. Martin, Richard and Debbie Hobin and Loren and Sandy Rhodes for their continued faith in me despite my many failings.

To Colleen who has forgiven my many trespasses and Shirin who by her devotion inspires me to continue to focus on eliminating the blocks within myself that prevent the Divine Light and Love that abides within us all from shining through.

Dr. Mark Bartel and Dr. Frank Krakowski of New Age World Publishing must be acknowledged for selecting this book for publication and seeing it through to its final form. Phil Hall and David Nagler of Open City Communications should be mentioned for ensuring that the Public got to hear about it and Ms. Victoria Vandertuin for ensuring it's placement in bookstores.

Finally my niece, Ms. Farzeen F. Moogat, has to be acknowledged because she insisted I write the book. Farzeen is from Dahanu Road, a small farming community about 70 miles north of Mumbai (formerly Bombay), India. The farmers of Dahanu Road are a tenacious bunch with a lot of initiative. There my older sister Ms. Nergis B. Irani successfully led local environmentalists in court battles against the State of Maharashtra and Multinational companies to save the natural environment.

The battles continue.

INTRODUCTION

The Journey of Life Eternal is an unusual narrative of the author's efforts to determine if there is a purpose to life and, if so, the principles one can live by to realize it. The author also examines one's role in creation, which he views as ongoing and not just ancient history.

The author grew up initially in the multi-religious-cultural-ethnic-racial city of Bombay, India during the British occupation of India, and subsequently in newly independent India. In this environment, he was exposed to conflicting value systems that competed to control his mind and influence his outlook. He tried to understand what was being taught and ended up rejecting the superficiality of the dogmas and rituals of the prevailing belief systems that focused on externalizing rather than internalizing spiritual practices. He felt that such dogmas and rituals caused people to become superstitious rather than enlightened. Instead of embracing them, he embarked upon the quest to discover the underlying truth that was the foundation of those belief systems. This led him through a winding journey with many conflicts, which ended when he met his spiritual master, from whom he learned certain principles by which he chose to live.

For more than thirty-three years, the author has strived to live by these principles in his daily life. This effort has given him deep insights, which are both unique and highly useful in clarifying the universal issues all of us face in sorting out the conflicts we experience in our daily lives. His gift of expressing these insights with clarity and simplicity can help us as we navigate our own journeys through Life Eternal.

Ron Greenblatt

PREFACE

I have known the author of this book, Bahram Rashid Shahmardaan, for many years now. As a result, I can say the following two things with confidence:

First, though not foremost, this book *comes straight from the heart.* Bahram is not a writer in the professional sense. He does not write for the sake of turning a phrase, being eloquent, or swaying the reader with flowery language. He writes only because he has something very valuable to say. And this alone should make the book well worth reading.

But secondly, and perhaps much more importantly, it is *what* he has to say that is of such great value.

This book is basically a "How-to" book. It is not, like a book on philosophy, one that is meant to be *read and understood.* Rather it's more like a cookbook, or a book on making beautiful furniture: it has to be *actually put into practice.*

Just as one does not profit from a cookbook if one buys it or takes it home from the library, but does not actually *cook* and *eat* the delicious recipes mentioned therein; or just as one does not profit from a book which shows one how to create beautiful furniture unless one actually *makes* the furniture as the book advises; so, too, one will not profit from this book unless one actually *practices* what it suggests.

Just as a cookbook, or a book on furniture making, shows you, step-by-step, how to create wonderful and delightful things (*viz.*, meals or furniture, as the case may be), so, too, this book shows you, step-by-step, how to create something wonderful and delightful.

But this "something" which this book shows you how to discover is the most valuable reality you can have access to–namely, *yourself!* This book shows you, step-by-step and in considerable detail, how you can go about getting in touch with the real you who are more wonderful than you can imagine. Indeed that wonderful *you,* your real self, is beyond imagination because it is beyond the human mind. However, if you will steadfastly practice the exercises this book reveals, I do believe that you will eventually realize your real self.

Let this book be the beginning of *your* Journey of Life Eternal—a journey that will take you so far in even a few years that you will be amazed that you could travel that distance.

Ardeshir Mehta
Ottawa, Canada

CONTENTS

CHAPTER 1
THE ART OF LISTENING

For the past 25-odd years, many friends of mine have requested that I write a book so that a wider audience may have a chance to share what I have learned about life and its purpose. I resisted their suggestions because I felt all along that the world does not need another book. I eventually succumbed to the persistent insistence of my niece, and hence this book got written. The subject dealt with in this book is one that has confused society for millennia. Due to the confusion, wars have been fought between societies in the name of Truth and Righteousness. Due to a lack of understanding of the purpose of life, and the process of conducting and completing the journey, ignorant people in positions of power, who obviously thought that they were right, have destroyed civilizations and persecuted innocent and good people. This is still happening today and the world is constantly in a state of upheaval, if not war. I hope that through this book, you, the reader, will be able to grasp the purpose of life and the Universal Principles, which if practiced, will enable you to participate in the Journey of Life Eternal rather than get trapped in the blind lanes of existence.

This is not an easy book to read. The book is not meant to entertain you and enable you to escape reality, as you define and accept it, for a brief period of time. The entertainment industry, the news media and various drugs, both legal and illegal, do a good job of that. The book is meant to show you how you can recognize that what most people think of as reality is really an illusion. The book also reveals hard-won Spiritual principles, which, if learned and practiced on a daily basis, will enable you to see through the illusion of our daily life experiences and experience reality that is more fulfilling than any illusion.

Although each chapter can be read independent of the others, the subject will be easier to grasp if the chapters are read in succession. To prepare the reader to get the most out of this book, it would be good to briefly describe the art of listening. We are taught the mechanics of reading in our schools but hardly anyone teaches the art of reading or listening.

Listening is more difficult than speaking. In order to speak you have to get in tune with yourself and then project your thoughts in words. In order to listen, you have to first silence your mind and then get in tune with the mind of the speaker. In order to absorb what the speaker says, you have to prevent your thoughts from getting in the way. Quite often, instead of listening to the speaker and absorbing the ideas being presented, we use our thoughts as a filter. We reject the thoughts we disagree with and only allow the thoughts we agree with to enter our minds.

The result of this is that we really have not listened to the speaker at all but have merely heard him. This is further compounded by the fact that, quite often, because our minds wander, we do not even hear the speaker fully. In fact, even as you are reading this it is possible that your mind wants to drift into other thoughts and you are editing out those thoughts you may disagree with.

The chapter entitled *Value of Opinions* explains why we hear with our ears but listen with our mind, and look with our eyes but see with our mind. Our attitude and what we have learned from past experiences influence what we absorb through listening and seeing. It shapes our present experience, which in turn influences our whole being. It is most important that we have the right attitude.

Now what is the right attitude?

It is said that Almighty God who has created the Universe can create and/or do anything, and nothing is impossible for Him. We can conclude from this that God must have an open Mind, a Mind that is open to all possibilities. Why? If God's Mind were closed to any possibility, then that possibility would not be possible for Him. But since we accept that nothing is impossible for God to achieve, He must have an open Mind. The Limitless Source of all sources cannot have limited possibilities and yet be Limitless. Therefore It has to remain open to all possibilities.

You can only receive new ideas and grow if you have a mind open to all possibilities. It should be obvious that, unless you have an open mind to receive what is being witnessed, you cannot experience the witnessed situation and certainly cannot learn from it. A closed mind thus limits your possibilities. Therefore, the right attitude is to listen with an open mind. This also applies to reading.

To help overcome the resistance in his own mind, Rev. Dr. Dinshah K. Mehta, Founder Chairman of the Society of Servants of God, received a Principle from the Spiritual Planes of Consciousness that crystallizes this attitude beautifully. To deal with difficult subjects, the Principle Revered Dr. Mehta received is, "Accept what is acceptable but do not reject what is not acceptable." When reading this book, I ask you to accept what you can accept, and not reject what you cannot accept. As Rev. Dr. Mehta has often indicated, with time, changed circumstances and inner growth, what is not acceptable initially, will not only be accepted, but may be the very Thought or Principle which will create the opening in your mind, through which the Higher Consciousness can descend into your mind.

Chapter 2
The Search

The main purpose of this chapter is to share with other searchers and seekers of the Spiritual Path the fact that even when one grows up in a pluralistic society that is a democracy, it is very difficult to find the Path. One has to continuously seek and never give up. "Seek and ye shall find" is the injunction given by the Lord Christ. It is much more difficult to find the Spiritual Path in a society where only one religion or code of conduct predominates.

If one is interested in the esoteric aspects of life, then one is indeed fortunate to be born in India. India is a country that supports a sea of humanity. All the races and most of the religions and cultures of the world thrive in India. This is amazing when you consider that India has about sixteen regional languages, and, I read once, about 600 dialects. Unlike Europe, which has distinct languages, most of which share the Latin script, many of the languages of India have their own script. India is often erroneously described as a country of Hindus. The fact is that India has the second largest Muslim population in the world—about 200 million—and within it the different sects of Islam are also represented. If one is interested in comprehending the unity in the diversity of Life, India is a wonderful laboratory to research the field.

While India was still a British colony I was born in the year 1942 in Mumbai (formerly known as Bombay) into a Zarathusti (Zoroastrian) family. I am the youngest of six brothers and sisters. It may interest the reader to know that many scholars now acknowledge that the three wise men that brought gifts for the infant Jesus were Zarathusti Magi's from Persia. Still others consider the Zarathusti religion to be the mother religion for Judaism, Christianity and Islam because, among other things, it is the first of the Monotheistic religions and had a major influence on other cultures during the height of the Persian Empire under monarchs such as Koorosh (Cyrus), Darius and Khashiyar Shah (Xerxes) and others. Indeed to this day, the name of Xerxes lives on in Greece in the form of a body of water called the "Straits of Xerxes."

My mother was fairly orthodox in her beliefs while my father was very spiritual. While mother recognized that there were other religions, she was committed to educating her children to believe that the Zarathusti religion is the oldest and best religion in the world, especially since it is generally accepted to be the first monotheistic religion. Mother was not very concerned about studying the other religions that thrived in India. She did not have to. Her mind was made up. She was born into the oldest and best religion in the world. She was secure in her beliefs and would pray every day and that was enough. Father on the other hand was a true Spiritual seeker and he studied the texts of various religions and during his life was, and still is, recognized as one of the leading scholars of the Zarathusti Scriptures and history. Father would rise every day around 4 a.m. and pray for about two hours before leaving for work and would also pray every evening for about two hours. Because of their different attitudes towards religion, there was a lot of conflict in our home. Witnessing this as a child made me wonder what and who is right. When I was about five years old, I decided that I would find God and ask Him.

Of course, that is much more easily said than done.

India is an ocean of religious beliefs and all the religions of the world thrive there. Traditionally the people of India are very tolerant. Lately, though, there have been outbursts of religious intolerance, which is really uncharacteristic of the citizens of India and is motivated by political miscreants who fan the flames of bigotry to support their own agenda.

When I was a little boy, due to the partition of India, there was a lot of conflict between the two major communities, *i.e.,* Hindus and Muslims. Hindus and Muslims were at each other's throats. In sections of neighborhoods that bordered the two communities there were frequent murders. Generally, people who were not Hindus or Muslims were not subject to attack. To protect ourselves from the possibility of being kidnapped and/or killed, we were told to proclaim that we were Zarathustis. Being non-Muslim and non-Hindu protected us from attacks and thus we could enthusiastically proclaim that it was our Good Religion that protected us. All the more reason to be a proud Zarathusti.

The Author's parents Rashid and Goolbanu shortly after they were engaged, circa 1929.

The Author's parents shortly after they were married.
Circa 1929

Although I was born into a Zarathusti family, I was educated in a Catholic school, with good reason. The Christian missionaries in India and the Zarathustis established world-class institutions of learning from the elementary level all the way to universities of higher education. The school my brother and I were enrolled in was St. Joseph's High School. We had a very good Principal by the name of Father D'Souza. The school was located right on the border of a Hindu and a Muslim neighborhood. Ninety percent of the student body belonged to the Muslim faith. The rest of the student body was comprised of Christians, all of who were Catholics, Zarathustis and a handful of Jews and Hindus. We began the day with prayers. Our teachers, who were mostly Catholic, along with Catholic students, recited the Hail Mary. Other students were also encouraged to participate in reciting the Hail Mary but were allowed to recite their own prayers if they so chose, or to remain silent.

The school had an intercom system and around 10 a.m. every day for a half hour, Father D'Souza, true to his calling, would preach Catholicism to us.

He would narrate various stories from the Bible and generally try and inspire, some may say brainwash, us into accepting Christianity, if not converting to it. In addition, once a week each Wednesday, the entire student body had to assemble in the School auditorium to be tutored again on the Bible. Father D'Souza would have a skeleton hanging from a frame. He would point to the skeleton and tell the audience that we would all one day become like the skeleton. "Dust thou art and to dust thou shalt return" is the quote he would recite from the Bible. He would then exhort us again and preach to us about living a God-fearing way of life, and would quote the Apostle Matthew: "What does it profit a man if he gains the whole world but suffers the loss of his soul?" Father D'Souza was a very good human being.

Thus after being taught at home about the Zarathusti religion being the straight path to heaven, in school, my child's brain was being exhorted again to accept the easy salvation offered by the Catholic way of life. Easy because, according to my Catholic friends, all one had to do was confess one's sins and be absolved of all responsibility. Compared to the Zarathusti religion where one had to atone for one's transgressions, the Catholic religion was much better because as my Catholic friend Charlie, who was about three years older than me, explained, one could sin all week long and then come Sunday, be absolved of all responsibility by confessing one's sins. Thus a place in Heaven was assured to all Catholics. We Zarathustis had no such luck. I noticed that my friend Charlie was as secure in his Catholic faith as my mother was in our Zarathusti faith. I was not as secure. I wondered why Zarathushtra did not choose an easy out for his people as Christ did for the Catholics. I did not know at the time that there were other denominations of Christianity, each of which considers itself a separate religion. As a result of my limited exposure to Christianity I felt that we Zarathustis had a harder load to haul. Charlie suggested that I could make it easy on myself by converting to Christianity. Although it was a tempting thought, I felt that I could not be disloyal to Zarathushtra and it would be a cowardly thing to do. Charlie meant well and was a good childhood friend as were Joseph, Aloysius, Richard, Stanley and Daniel.

Unfortunately, I have lost track of all of them.

The disparate religious teachings at home and those given in school by Father D'Souza and Charlie's influence was not the end of the conflicting religious signals to which my child brain was being subjected. Since ninety percent of the student body was Muslim, there was a backlash amongst the Muslims to Father D'Souza's preaching. The Muslims would ridicule Christianity and assert that Mohammed was the last and best of all the Holy Prophets and the Holy Koran was the Final Word of God. In other words, Islam was a new and improved version of both Judaism and Christianity. The Prophet of Islam acknowledged and accepted Abraham and the Prophets of Israel and also Christ, and then expanded on and improved their teachings. Of course, Islam is not only the latest and the best but also the Final Word of God. There is to be no other Prophet. Now my child brain had to contend with a third claim to religious righteousness. My Muslim friends also meant well and I miss them, especially Saifuddin Dohadwala, Zainuddin Aarsiwalla and Zoeb Tayebji, who was a lovable scoundrel.

From the above, one can begin to get some idea of the cultural crosscurrents my child mind was being subjected to. But there was more.

36

We lived in a Zarathusti neighborhood, which was surrounded by Hindus of many different castes and creeds. Most educated people know that the Hindus consider the cow a holy being. Even today many cows are permitted to roam freely on the streets of Mumbai and other major cities of India. This Hindu belief that the cow is sacred has a good basis and serves as a unifying factor among the Hindus. But I doubt if Westerners have any idea of the extent to which the cow is considered Holy. As a boy I had a personal experience that, more than 50 years later, is still as vivid in my mind today as the day it happened.

When I was about six-years-old, my older brother Bohman and I were on our way to school. To go where the tram (*i.e.*, streetcar) stop was, we had to cross a very wide street full of cars, buses, horse-drawn carriages, bicycles, pushcarts, pedestrians and such. We were holding hands so as to safely cross the street, which was in front of the building in which we lived. All of a sudden there was pandemonium. All traffic came to a screeching halt and from every direction people started running towards something. When we got our bearings, my brother and I realized the cause of the commotion. What happened was that a cow had begun to urinate in the middle of the street. A Hindu man rushed to the rear of the cow and started to wash his hands and face in her urine. Other people also barged in to do the same. A Hindu lady came with a large tin can to collect as much of the cow's urine as possible.

When I witnessed this event, my child mind was confused. Should we now wash with urine?

Some Hindus consider the cow's urine holy and cow dung is used for plastering the walls and as fuel. Although I have personally not witnessed it, I am told that some folks even apply cow dung on their bodies to cleanse themselves. In June 2000 it was reported by *ABC* on *World News Tonight* with Peter Jennings, that some young adults who grew up in one of the Centers of the International Society for Krishna Consciousness movement, popularly known as the Hare Krishna sect, are suing the Hare Krishna Center for child abuse because as children they were made to apply cow dung to their bodies before showering. The Hare Krishna sect has centers in many parts of North America.

As reported in the same story, the leaders of the Center have acknowledged that some mistakes were made and that steps have been taken so that they are not repeated.

One can imagine what all the cultural crosscurrents could do to a sensitive child who is trying to understand how to live a life that is in keeping with the Will of the Almighty.

But that is not all. As we grew older, my brother Bohman—who grew up to become one of India's best fighter pilots—and I preferred to walk to school and use the tram fare as pocket money. Our walk to school took us through a Jewish neighborhood. We had the benefit of some Jewish influence as well.

And finally there was the profound influence of the Lord Buddha. India is the land that Buddha was born in and where Buddhism originated. In school, some of us were fortunate enough to be taught about his life and a bit about his teachings. I was seven-years-old when I first read about the Lord Buddha in class. I distinctly remember where I was sitting in class and the thoughts that went through my child-mind at the time. The text narrated the condition of the world when the Lord Buddha was born in words to the effect, "He was born at a time when the world was plunged in Darkness. He brought Light into the world." When the teacher read these words, the thought crossed my child mind—"We have electric lights now so we do not need Buddha's teachings." I laugh when I think about that now. Nevertheless I was very impressed with the story about the life of Buddha and wanted to know more about the Four Noble Truths and the Eight-Fold Path. At the age of seven I could not do much about learning what Buddha taught. I was already exposed to enough religion. Besides I had to also cope with homework from school, as well as the other things that occupy a child's mind.

Having this multi-cultural background had its plusses and minuses. If one can maintain one's sanity and not become skeptical, with time, one can begin to see the common thread in the diversity of religions. Yet there are obvious differences, and each group of religionists asserts that theirs is the best way if not the only right way. To someone who is interested in doing what is right, such assertions made no sense. All of them cannot be right and all of them cannot be wrong. If all of them are partially right, then it follows that they are also partially wrong; and a partially right solution certainly is not *the* right solution. So, what to do?

Bohman Shahmardaan on a battlefield somewhere in Lahore, Pakistan, circa 1965, during the war between India and Pakistan.

I pushed all these thoughts away to be dealt with at a later date while I dealt with the pangs and urgency of growing up.

My parents had less than a perfect marriage. Father was a very strict disciplinarian. He did not believe in sparing the rod. He was a very good provider. However, when I was about nine-years-old his business took a turn for the worse. As a family, although we were still financially well off relative to many other people, mother complained a lot. Father had more than one source of income. When one of Father's businesses took a severe downturn, he gave it away to his long time manager, Kassam, who was a Muslim. Mother did not like Muslims and was quite upset. Due to mother's carping, I mustered up enough courage to ask Father why he gave away his business when we were experiencing financial hardship. To my surprise, instead of scolding me, Father explained his decision, and I am still grateful to him for doing so. Father asked me the following questions: "Do you have enough to eat? Do you have a roof over your head? Do you enough clothes to wear? Are your school fees paid each month?" I answered yes to each question. Then Father asked, "What is your problem?" I told him that I had no problem but mother was complaining. Father replied, "Let her complain. Kassam, too, has a family. They, too, need to live, for which they need an income. There was not enough money in the business to support two families. We have other sources of income so I decided to give the business to Kassam." I thanked father for answering my question and was very glad with his decision. His explanation left a lasting impression upon me and helped formulate my sense of values.

The increasing tensions in our household, and the confusion caused by so many cross-cultural experiences, took their toll. Between the ages of twelve and thirteen, I experienced fear. One could call it a nervous breakdown, except that it was not really a breakdown. I was fully functional in every sense of the word but for no particular reason, I was full of fear—not mere anxiety. I was not afraid of anything in particular—just fearful and tense. After living with this tension for more than a year, I finally approached Father. To eliminate the fear, he gave me a three-syllable mantra and told me to recite it 64,000 times a day. As a result of this exercise, I realized why prayer beads were invented. It used to take me four hours a day to recite the mantra the

The author's mother
Goolbanu
at about age 55.

Circa 1964

The author's father
Rashid
at about age 60.

Circa 1965

64,000 times. Here I was at age thirteen and fourteen reciting the mantra for two hours in the morning and two hours in the evening. After doing this for about six months, I did experience peace and the fear left me. I continued to recite the mantra though for many more years.

When I was fourteen years old, things came to a head between mother and father. Father had had enough. He transferred all his financial holdings and business to our mother and decided to concentrate on his research.

Father was a world-class scholar on the history of the Zarathustis and, to this day, his work is being used as references by many universities worldwide. He is recognized as one of the pre-eminent scholars in his field. The Government of the late Shah of Iran recognized Father's work and sponsored some of his research. They also invited him for many official celebrations. Two of them stand out in my mind. In 1954 the Government of Iran celebrated the centennial of Avicena, the great Persian Physician. Four people were invited from India. Father was one of them. Again, around 1972, essentially to glorify himself, the late Shah of Iran celebrated the ancient monarchs of Persia beginning with King Cyrus the Great. Political Leaders from the world over were invited. Vice President Spiro Agnew represented the USA. Father was invited to that party, as well. I did not fully realize how well-known and respected Father was academically until about five years ago when scholars from Denmark and Sweden contacted me because they were writing his biography as part of their Doctoral dissertation. The name Rashid Shahmardaan is very much revered by people who are interested in the subject he spent his life researching and writing. A remarkable achievement for any individual, and much more so when you consider that he had only three years of formal schooling. Father was self-taught. Since he himself did not have the opportunity to finish high school, with the full support of Mother, he made certain that all his children, including his daughters, got a college education. This was very unusual. At the time, because of the prevailing social values, women in general, were discouraged from getting a college education. Ovnai, the firstborn had not prepared to go to college because she was sure our parents would not allow her to do so. But two of my sisters

The author's father Rashid (second from left) with delegation from India that went to attend the Avicena Centennial in Iran.

Circa 1954

Rashid Shahmardaan leading a Zarathusti religious ceremony called Jashne Sade in Naghsh Rostam, Takht-e-Jamshid (Persepolis), Iran.

Circa 1977

graduated from college. Sarosh, the oldest son, was born deaf and so at the time did not have an opportunity to go to College. But our parents did enroll him in a school for the deaf and mute. Sarosh graduated from the school and in my judgment was the most brilliant of all the siblings.

Both my parents were very progressive in their thinking and very responsible socially.

Mother was also a superior person in her own right. She was an accomplished artist in every sense of the word. She was an excellent painter working with oils, watercolors, pencil and charcoal. She loved the movies, music and theater and encouraged her children to participate. She hired a music teacher to teach us to sing even though it was obvious that I was unable to even hum a tune. Mother was an excellent seamstress and cook. She taught all her daughters how to sew and knit and all my sisters sewed their own dresses, knitted sweaters and items. Mother was also socially very conscious and conducted classes in which she taught other women some of her many skills for free. She also organized tours for Zoroastrian women and children within her sphere of influence. Mother loved music, social activity and crowds. Father found such activities very annoying. He was into books, research and spirituality—and preferred silence and solitude. Father and mother had very little in common socially. Consequently, there was always tension in the household.

It is amazing that they produced and raised six children.

The rift between mother and father certainly did not help clarify things for me.

When I turned fifteen I graduated from high school and entered college. No one was available to guide me. Typically four professions were presented to students, *viz.* engineering, medicine, the law and accounting. Of these, medicine was considered to be the best, by far. Although I had no real pull towards medicine, I decided to study science when I enrolled in university. I studied hard in my first year of college and was among the top of the class. The second year of college was the most important academic year. That was the year when students had to decide whether they wanted to study mathematics or biology. Also the grades of that year determined whether one made the cut and got admitted to medical college or engineering college. If one was interested in going to medical school or engineering school, one

The author's siblings:

Seated Front row (L-R) Sisters Nergis, Ovnai and Pervin.

Standing (L-R) The author, brothers Sarosh and Bohman.

Pervin & Nergis' graduation photo

had to study especially hard during the second year of college to ensure that one had grades good enough to gain admission.

When I entered the second year, I realized that although I was good at reading and retaining words written in a book, I knew very little about life in general. Everyone around me seemed to be very confident about the direction of his or her life. I was still very confused. About that time, I read an interview given by the late Prime Minister Indira Gandhi, which appeared in one of the leading English newspapers printed in India. At the time, Mrs. Gandhi did not hold any public office and her father Pundit Jawaharlal Nehru was Prime Minister of India. During her interview, Mrs. Gandhi was asked to name the single greatest contribution made by her father in her life. Mrs. Gandhi replied with words to the effect, "He taught me what was important in life." This answer by Mrs. Gandhi strengthened my resolve to try and figure out what is important in life.

At about the same time, I read a statement about wealth made by Sri Aurobindo Ghosh, a contemporary of Mahatma Gandhi and one of the revolutionary Freedom Fighters of India who became one of the great Spiritual Leaders of Modern India. This is what Sri Aurobindo said:

> All wealth belongs to the Divine. Those who have it are mere trustees and not possessors. It is with them today. Tomorrow it will be elsewhere. All depends upon how they discharge their trust while it is with them. With what consciousness in their use of it, to what purpose.

The statement appeared in one of the English dailies. I was so impressed by the saying that I clipped it and carried it in my billfold for the next seventeen years. Sri Aurobindo's statement also supported the statement attributed to the Apostle Matthew who was oft quoted during the weekly assembly meetings held by our school principal, the Reverend Father D'Souza, *viz.,* "What does it profit a man if he gains the whole world but suffers the loss of his soul?"

During my second year of college, instead of focusing on my studies, I decided to try and figure out what life was all about.

Throughout my schooling I went straight from home to school and from school to home. Except for joining the boy scouts while in school, and the National Cadet Corps while in college, I had very little social interaction. Father did not encourage any other extracurricular activities. To become worldly wise, I decided to spend time with our neighbor, Mr. Siavakhsh Mody, who was a bachelor about 54 years old at the time, and another neighbor Nariman Rabadi who was about two years older than I. Siavakhsh taught me a bit of culture but could not shed any light on the purpose of life. Nariman, who comes from a priestly family and who himself is an ordained Zarathusti priest, barely scraped through high school. He decided not to go to college. Instead he became a bank clerk. He and his friends, some of whom were bootleggers and had done time in jail, would roam the streets of Bombay city most of the night until the wee hours of the morning. I accompanied them in the hopes of becoming worldly wise.

After reciting the mantra that Father had given me during the day, I spent the rest of most every evening going out with Nariman and his friends, who soon became my friends. We would start around 9 p.m. and return around 3 or 4 a.m. After doing this for almost a full year, I realized that although I did not know the purpose of life, these guys were not any wiser. I decided to focus on my studies. Since I had really not studied all year long, I knew that if I took the final exams, I would not get a grade good enough to enter medical school. Nonetheless, I decided to take the final exam so as to gain the experience and thus be better prepared when I would take it in earnest the next year. To make sure that I would not get a passing grade, I deliberately did not answer all the questions to make certain that I would have a failing grade.

I was surprised with the results. I passed with Second Class Honors. It was quite a blow. My grades were not good enough to join medical college and under the rules, I could not repeat the class. The die was cast. No medical college in Bombay would accept me. I concluded that there were forces at work that were influencing the course of my life. Rather than continue further studies aimlessly, I decided to get some professional counseling.

I learned that the University of Bombay offered free student counseling through the Vocational Guidance Bureau. A friend of mine and I decided to go for counseling. They put the two of us through four days of tests to gauge our psychological profile and such. At the end of the four days, we were both called in together. The counselor's name was Mr. Kotwal, a fellow Zarathusti. Mr. Kotwal first addressed my friend, "How do you think you did on the test." My friend said he thought he did okay. Mr. Kotwal replied that the average student who is admitted to the Elphinstone Technical Institute, which was then the premier engineering college in Bombay, if not India, averages 67% on the test. To be accepted to the Elphinstone Technical Institute, a student must average straight A+'s throughout his/her student career and then, on top of that, have several letters of recommendation, *et cetera.* My friend who had never really applied himself academically and therefore averaged a B- grade had scored 83% on the test—a very impressive score indeed. Mr. Kotwal then proceeded to suggest various career options that my friend could pursue.

He then turned to me and asked, "And how do you think you fared on the test." I replied that I thought I did okay. Mr. Kotwal informed me that I had scored 67.5% on the test. I felt good because I equaled the score averaged by the engineering students. I now waited with anticipation for the guidance Mr. Kotwal would give me. Instead Mr. Kotwal looked me straight in the eye and said, "Mr. Irani, you are one of those very rare individuals who knows exactly what he wants. No one can guide you. You know what you want to do. Go out and do it. Why did you waste our time?" I was incredulous. I thought Mr. Kotwal was trying to be funny. I protested, "You are joking, aren't you?" to which Mr. Kotwal replied, "No, I am not. I am very serious. You know exactly what you want. No one can guide you." I was speechless. My friend and I both got up. We thanked Mr. Kotwal and left his office. As we were descending the long flight of stairs leading out of the building, I turned to my friend and asked him, "What are you going to do?" He replied, "I am going to study microbiology." I said, "I will study microbiology with you." We both enrolled to study microbiology at the St. Xavier's College.

Mr. Kotwal was right. I did know what I wanted to do. Except that I did not know how to go about doing it. The year was 1960. That spring, before college was to start, I was involved in a scooter accident. Fortunately, I did not break any bones but was laid up in bed for about two months with a swollen knee and thigh. While I was recuperating in bed at home, Father gave me a very small book written by Madame Annie Besant entitled *The Ladder of Lives*. Mrs. Annie Besant was a very elegant and distinguished British Lady who was one of the founders of the Theosophical movement. She was a prolific writer and worked tirelessly for the emancipation of women and also for the freedom of India.

The only books I ever read were books that were part of the school/college curriculum. I did not like reading books, particularly fictional books. I set the book aside. Finally boredom overtook me and I started reading *The Ladder of Lives*. I was absolutely fascinated by the subject. I finished reading it in one day and asked Father for more books. The next book Father gave me was also written by Annie Besant entitled *Thought Power*. It is an excellent book. The next book was by Bishop C. W. Leadbeater entitled *The Hidden Side of Things*. I had been introduced to authors who were dealing with the topic that interested me the most. I became an avid reader of Theosophical literature because I felt it would help me gain a deeper understanding of the Universe and how to reach its Maker.

Madame Annie Besant had declared that a boy from South India, J. Krishnamurti, whom she had adopted, was the Messiah that the world has been waiting for. There is a small book entitled *At the Feet of the Master* written by J. Krishnamurti in which he shares the teachings given to him, when he was around fourteen years old, by the Master Kuthumi in the astral planes of consciousness. Madame Annie Besant wrote the preface to the book.

During the 1960s, Mr. J. Krishnamurti was still alive, and was so in the early 70s as well. He traveled around the world giving lectures on spirituality. Around the month of March each year, Mr. J. Krishnamurti would come to Bombay (now called Mumbai) to give lectures for about three weeks. Beginning with the year 1961 I attended his lectures, which were free to the public. There was usually a very large crowd. Mr. J. Krishnamurti is the most eloquent speaker I have ever heard. He spoke with a very deep soulful voice. I was very impressed, and continued to attend his lectures for the next four years.

Mr. Krishnamurti was quite a contradictory person. Theosophical literature and indeed most Spiritual literature emphasize the need for a Spiritual Master. Without a Spiritual Master one cannot become free from the shackles of this world. Indeed Madame Annie Besant and many Theosophists declared that Mr. Krishnamurti was the Messiah the world had been waiting for. Yet not only did Mr. Krishnamurti repudiate the claims made by Madame Besant but in his lectures exhorted people to not go after gurus and not to seek a Spiritual Master. His message was, "Listen to yourself." However, the "How" of listening to "oneself" was not explained.

During the course of the year, I would also attend lectures given by other Hindu Spiritual Leaders. My interest in the Spiritual way of life was very real and I was very eager to be on the path. Late in the year 1960 when I was in my third year of college, at the age of 17, Father introduced me to a Spiritual teacher whom I came to know as Hazrat Pathan. Pathans are from the North West Frontier Regions of British India. Hazrat Pathan was around 69 years old when I met him. He was a Muslim, a non-Zarathusti. Mother would be very upset if she knew I was learning spirituality from a non-Zarathusti and that, too, a Muslim. The fact that Hazrat Pathan was not a Zarathusti and did not have much formal education was unimportant to me. What was important is that he came across as a truly holy man and one could see that he was in touch with some deeper source of knowledge and knew what life was all about.

I was aware that all the great Masters of the world whose teachings have been the foundation of religions and civilizations that have endured did not have any formal education, as we know it. The list includes Zarathushtra, Abraham, Moses, Jesus, Buddha, Mohammed, Guru Nanak and others. I found it very natural to learn about life from a person who was much older than I and who was willing to teach me for free. After college classes were over for the day, I would go to visit Hazrat Pathan and spend several hours with him trying to learn all I could about the Spiritual way of life and life in general. He endorsed the mantra that Father had given me a few years earlier and so I continued to recite it 64,000 times a day.

Hazrat Pathan was my first real Spiritual Teacher. I liked being with him and I still remember the times we shared very clearly. Since I was thinking in terms of a career, Hazrat Pathan told me, "Bahram, all the money you will ever earn in this life is based upon your destiny. It really does not matter what you do.

Hazrat Hassan Pathan, the author's first Spiritual Teacher

"You will reap what you have sown in the past. When it comes to selecting a career, select it not because you think you will earn more money if you become an engineer or a doctor or do this business or that. Rather the one criterion you should use when selecting a career is, 'Will it take me closer to God or away from God.' If it will take you away from God then shun it. Only do those things that will take you closer to God."

Since I was young, hardworking, ambitious, and, if I may say so, also intelligent, I could not accept Hazrat Pathan's statement about destiny determining my monetary success or failure. I did not reject it either because I had no real basis to reject it. However I did like the second part of his advice and decided to follow it.

When I was in my final year of college, about a year after I met Hazrat Pathan, he died. I was saddened by his departure and did not know how to continue on the Spiritual path. On Father's recommendation, I visited Hazrat Pathan's grave to pray twice a week—once every Thursday and Sunday. Each trip would take about four to five hours. An hour to hour and a half to reach the cemetery, two hours of reciting the Mantra at his graveside and an hour to hour and a half to return. I did this for the next few years.

In the year 1962, I graduated from College having completed my Bachelor's Degree with a major in Microbiology and a minor in Zoology. At that time, it was the vogue for young students in India to go abroad for further studies. The countries of choice were the United Kingdom, the USA, and West Germany. I applied to various universities in those countries and sent them my transcripts. The University of Glasgow, Scotland accepted me for any field of my choosing including medicine. Everyone expected me to leave. But I was not ready to leave India.

I went back to basics. I reasoned that every country, no matter how advanced or backward, and every individual, no matter how exalted or foolish, had some lesson to teach. Why was I born in India? Why was I not born in Iran, the country of my ancestors, or one of the other countries that I was seeking to go to for higher education? I concluded that I was born in India because India had some lesson that I needed to learn. I had not yet learned the lesson India had to teach me. That meant that I lacked the ability to learn.

If I lacked the ability to learn from India, I would also be unable to learn what other countries had to offer. Besides, if I left India without first learning what it is that India had to teach me, then I would miss the opportunity of learning that important lesson for which I took birth in India. Based upon that line of thinking, I decided to not leave India until I learned what it is that I was supposed to learn from India. I also concluded that I would not continue with my college education but rather continue learning from the University that is Life itself.

I reasoned that if I have to spend my whole life doing things that pleased God and avoid doing things that were against His Will, then the first thing I should do is to find God and ask Him what it is that He would like me to do. My resolve to find God was strengthened even further.

Then a peculiar thing happened. I noticed that when I told people that I wanted to find God and ask Him how I should live my life, most thought I was crazy. I was not surprised by their reaction but found it very strange.

These were people who lived their whole life based on how they thought God wanted them to live. They admitted that they had no real clue. However, it did not seem odd to them that even though they admitted that they were not sure what it was that God wanted them to do, they vehemently defended their values and thought that I was crazy because I first wanted to find God and ask Him how I should live my life. The reason they thought I was crazy is because, according to them, "No one can talk to God." A few people who were sympathetic to my cause suggested that if I wanted to find God, I should join a monastery or what the Hindus call an ashram. However based on my experience in school with Father D'Souza and the other Catholic priests, it appeared to me that although they were very decent people and could quote the Bible, they certainly did not know God. They had embraced a way of life that promised heaven after death. Similarly the Zarathusti priests and Hindu Brahmins only had Scriptural knowledge and did not know God. I concluded that joining any church or ashram or studying Scriptures would not help me, because I wanted to find God while still alive on earth.

After graduating from college, I spent some time looking around trying to decide what to do. I gave up reciting the mantra that Father had given and eventually stopped going to Hazrat Pathan's grave. Although these activities had made me peaceful, they did not give me any insights into creation. I also stopped reading theosophical literature and going to listen to Mr. J. Krishnamurti and other gurus because I found that all I accomplished was create a mental image of the universe that was really based on my own point of view and not necessarily what was so.

I said a silent prayer, telling God that if He wanted me to find Him then He was going to have to show me the way because I did not know how to find Him.

Having left my fate to God, I decided to engage in activities that were considered normal for a man of my age. However I always kept an eye out for anything that would show me the way to God.

For the next two years I did business with various cousins. I realized that I was not using my college education in the business my cousins were engaged in and wanted to do something that was intellectually more challenging.

Eventually in the year 1965 I went to work as a sales representative for an American pharmaceutical company in India. Sales and marketing were interesting fields and so I decided to study marketing.

Coincidentally in the year 1967, the St. Xavier's College started the St. Xavier's Social Institute of Industry. It focused on management with a human face. It appealed to me so I enrolled in the Institute to study marketing In the meantime, Father, who never went out in the evenings, started going out every Saturday around 6 p.m. After observing this for several weeks, I asked him what he was up to? He told me that he was attending Spiritual lectures given by a Parsi (Zarathusti) gentleman in a state of trance. I told him that I would like to accompany him. Father told me that if I wanted to accompany him, I should be ready at 6 p.m. the next Saturday. After Father reminded me several Saturdays in a row, one Saturday, I finally accompanied him.

I had no idea who I was going to see or what the meeting was all about. All I knew was that I was going to meet a Spiritual person. I believe that a Spiritual being should be able to look past one's dress code. I deliberately wore outlandish clothes to see if the clothes I wore would negatively affect this person who I was going to meet.

The meeting was in a flat in one of the most affluent sections of Bombay, *viz.*, Malabar Hill. There were many people in the room and the gentleman asked everyone to be silent for a few minutes so that he could tune his mind with the Mind that guides him to speak. After about three minutes of silence he started speaking. He spoke for about an hour. I do not remember the topic but it held my attention.

After the lecture was over, I was introduced to him. He was known as "Dadaji," which means Elder Brother in Hindi. I did not know his name and had no idea who he was but it was obvious that he was an eminent individual.

It is the custom in Spiritual circles that when one meets a Spiritual person, one should take a gift. I offered Dadaji the gift of my service, within the limits of my capacity. He told me that he would let me know if he wanted me to do anything for him.

Off and on, I attended several more lectures given by Dadaji. During this period I learned Dadaji's name was Dr. Dinshah K. Mehta, and that among other things, he was the founder of modern naturopathy in India and a personal confidant and personal physician of Mahatma Gandhi. Even before I found out who he was, it was evident to me that Dr. Mehta was a very special human being, unlike anyone else I had heard or met.

What was unique about Dr. Mehta was that before answering any question, he would examine the underlying Principle that controlled the particular situation we were discussing. Dr. Mehta said, words to the effect, "Behind every manifestation there is a Principle which supports the particular manifestation. Emanating from the Principle are laws and rules and based upon the Principle, laws and rules are systems that control the manifestation." Whenever I asked him a question, he would first explain the underlying Principle, point out the laws that emanated from the Principle and then proceed to answer the question.

Dr. Mehta answered all my questions and more. I understood from him that most people are trapped in the day-to-day struggle for existence–oblivious about the purpose of life. A few strive to understand the purpose of existence. When they begin the search, they grope for the Truth. Many give up after a bit. Some of the gropers continue until they become searchers, many of these give up the search. A few searchers become seekers.

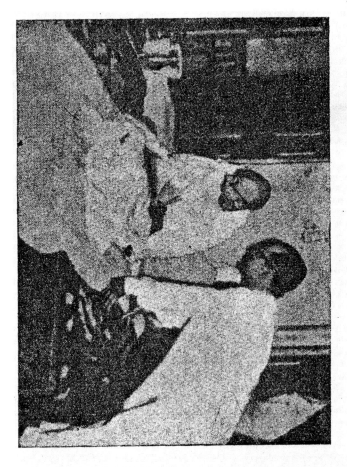

Dr. Dinshah managed Mahatma Gandhi's fast in 1947 in Calcutta. He also manage the epoch making 2nd and 3rd 21-day fasts of Bapu, besides many smaller fasts.

Mahatma Gandhi marked his 78th birthday with the words: "Today I am a lone voice in India and have lost all desire to live long." Behind Mahatma Gandhi and to his left is Dr. Mehta.

Circa 1945

Mahatma Gandhi descending prayer platform resting his arm on Dr. Dinshah K. Mehta's shoulder.

Circa 1946

Mahatma Gandhi leaving a political meeting with Indira Gandhi. Dr. Mehta is in the background.

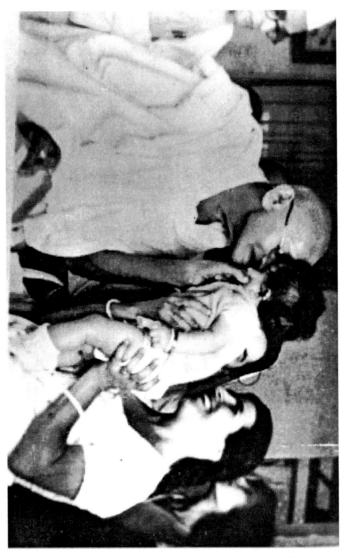

Mahatma Gandhi playing with Dr. Mehta's daughter Shireen, whom he had named, while Mrs. Mehta is holding her child.

When asked to explain the difference between groping, searching and seeking, Dr. Mehta said that when one is groping for answers, one has no clue and is going around in circles. When one searches, one is pointed in the general direction of what is right but has not yet found a path. One becomes a seeker when one is on the path.

Out of millions of gropers, a few thousand become searchers. Out of thousands of searchers, a few hundred become seekers. Out of thousands of seekers, a few embark on the Spiritual journey. Out of these fortunate and courageous few, a handful walks steadfastly on the path. Of the few that walk steadfastly on the path, a few hardy souls complete the journey. Only those who complete the journey reach the farther shore and realize the goal of life.

Many people like to hear the truths revealed by the Masters but get discouraged when they are told that the Spiritual journey is a hard one. Many give up without starting on the path. Still others fall prey to charlatans who promise them easy salvation for a sum of money.

After many years of seeking, I have reached a stage where I can speak with authority on the Spiritual Principles I have embraced and lived by. The following chapters are an attempt to share my experiences and these Spiritual Principles with the reader. I hope that this effort will be beneficial to those who read about and live by the Principles shared in this book.

I recommend that the reader should not accept what has been written. Rather the reader should observe himself/herself as explained in subsequent chapters. Test the Principles that are being shared. If the reader observes that what is written is accurate, then I would encourage the reader to take courage and start on the Spiritual journey without worrying about the final success. No effort is lost. Over time, one receives a cumulative benefit from one's struggle.

The next chapter explains how our own opinions come in the way of experiencing the Real.

Bahram R. Shahmardaan while working and studying in San Francisco, California, USA.

Circa 1969

CHAPTER 3
VALUE OF OPINIONS

At the risk of sounding coarse, I would like to again remind the reader not to accept what is written. Observe yourself and if you find that what is written applies to you then accept it, take heart, and try to live by it.

Life offers us choices and we make our choices based upon our opinions. It is important to understand how opinions are formed and whether or not they have any value. When discussions center on the esoteric aspects of life and the mystical world, quite often some of the participants make statements such, as: "I am a very practical person. I only believe what I can see, hear, touch, smell and taste;" or they may say, "I am a practical person. I like to have my feet planted solidly on the ground and not have my head in the clouds."

People who make such statements have not taken the time to really think clearly. First off, if we accept the way the universe appears to function as perceived by our senses, then we should believe that the sun goes around the earth and that the earth is flat. Clearly, our understanding and knowledge of the physical universe has grown beyond this naïve view of the physical world. And what is it that has helped us achieve this knowledge? Not just our physical senses but also our physical senses combined with a disciplined and discerning mind.

Further, I would like to point out to those practical persons who insist on having their feet planted firmly on the ground that the earth itself is not planted solidly on anything but is in fact spinning through space supported by unseen forces—forces that are so powerful that they support the weight of the earth in orbit around the sun and yet they are so fine that our satellites can travel through them and orbit the earth without any measurable resistance. It is therefore a very good practice to recognize that one's point of view is generally just that—one's point of view and not the truth.

To be sure, we all have opinions. We cannot help but form them. But rather than recognize their limitations, many of us insist on justifying our opinions without analyzing how we acquire them or form them. Before we defend our opinions and argue with those who disagree with us, it is important to examine the basis of opinions. Just how do we form opinions?

We generally form opinions based upon the *interpretations* we give to certain experiences. Invariably, the interpretations we give to our experiences and the opinions we derive there from are those that satisfy our mind and reflect our sense of values. We do not hold onto opinions that do not satisfy our mind. Our mind in turn is preconditioned by the circumstances of our birth. It is generally accepted that we have no control over the circumstances of our birth. No one asks a child whether it wants to be born a boy or a girl, nor does it have any choice over any of the other circumstances surrounding its birth. Yet we know that males have a view of life that is very different from females.

Similarly the other circumstances of our birth have a very profound effect upon shaping our attitudes and minds. The family we are born into, the race, country, religion, *et cetera,* all influence and shape our minds very strongly. Besides having no control over the circumstances of our birth, we also do not have any control over the school we are sent to and the conditions under which we grow up. All of these factors shape our minds and influence our attitude. As children we have very little resistance to and no control over the forces that condition our mind and attitudes.

Even as adults, most of us do not have any control over our respective minds and have little control over the forces that assail our minds and senses and try to influence them. Our mind is literally out of control. It is in constant turmoil and jumps from one thought to another.

What then is the basis of our opinions? Can they be relied upon if they are formed by a mind that is out of control? Are they real? Yes, they are, but they only represent a personal reality. They are not absolute, nor are they permanent. Our opinions on the same subjects change as we grow and change. How reliable can they be in the context of realizing the Truth about creation and the Source of all Sources?

A cat, a rat, a dog, a monkey, an earthworm, a fish, a bird and a man all experience this earth. Each will have a different experience and therefore a different opinion of the earth based upon their individual capacities. Whose experience of the earth is real?

We look with our eyes but we see with our minds. We hear with our words but we listen with our minds. What we listen to and see are influenced by two things:

- Our attitude at the time. Attitude which itself is shaped by the circumstances of our birth and our previous experiences.
- The knowledge we have accumulated based upon previous experience which is, itself, also shaped by our past attitudes.

We can see from this that our opinions are illusory. They are merely reflections of our own mind and the prejudices formed from previous experiences and attitudes, both of which can also change over time. These then bind us in a vicious cycle of our own making. This is one reason why history keeps repeating itself and we repeat mistakes.

Because of this conditioning, we do not see the world the way it is, but we create in our minds our own world based upon our own attitudes and experiences. We all share the same earth, but each of us lives in a different universe created by our own opinions. We are really trapped within this cycle of attitude and experience. Our attitudes shape our experience and our experience shapes our attitude and together they create the illusory world each of us lives in and continues to alter as we develop different attitudes and experience new situations.

That is why the Hindus have an ancient prayer, which when translated reads:

- From untruth lead me to Truth
- From darkness lead me to Light
- From death lead me to Immortality

If you examine yourself as you are reading this, you will observe that you are forming an opinion about this article and me, its author? Each one of my readers will have an opinion about me. I, too, have an opinion about myself.

The question then is, "Whose opinion *am* I?" The answer, obviously, is that I am nobody's opinion. I am not even my own opinion. What I am is beyond opinion.

Opinions are formed within the human mind, and what I am is beyond the human mind. To know the truth about who I am, and the ultimate "I Am that I Am," one has to go beyond the human mind.

So long as we live a life based upon our opinions we remain trapped within our consciousness and cannot grow beyond it to higher planes of consciousness and awareness. So, what to do?

To begin with, we need to have an open mind and align ourselves with the Creative Source commonly called God. In my view, the most perfect name for God is the Iranian word "Khudaa." "Khud" in Persian means Self and "aa" means to come. So "Khudaa" literally translated means, "Self to come," which is to say, to allow and assist the Real Self buried under layers of the sub-conscious and unconscious mind to rise to the level of the conscious mind. If we can achieve such a state of Being, we can then live a life that is consciously in tune with the Divine within us and through that be in touch with the Real Universe. How does one do that?

To achieve that, one has to live a life based upon Higher Principles and Values. Principles and Values that have been given to us by the High Beings who have descended to show us the way, and upon whose teachings the great religions of the world have been founded. But religions themselves have become bogged down in rituals and ceremonies that tend to bind the followers to superstitious dogmas rather than liberate them from the trap created by the human mind.

To get out of this dilemma, there are definite Universal Principles one can live by which will be revealed in subsequent chapters of this book.

In order to gain knowledge and experience life, many of us have a natural tendency to go out. But we have to first recognize that *attitude* is everything. Quite often, our decision to follow a particular set of teachings or a particular teacher is also based upon our opinion of the teacher and/or his teachings, even though we may know nothing about the basis of the teachings of that teacher or the teacher. In fact our belief systems are also based upon and sustained by our opinions. The world has been and is currently experiencing war because of the different belief systems all of which are based upon opinions. Opinions, which, as we have explored above, are illusory.

What is the solution? How can we protect ourselves from our own opinions and beliefs?

To do that, we need to learn to live by Principles. Principles that will help to filter out our prejudices and fears and thereby protect us from our illusory opinions which are the foundation of our beliefs.

But How does one do that? To begin with we have to first examine where we really live and experience life.

In order to gain knowledge and experience life, many of us have a natural tendency to go outside ourselves. Obviously we are a part of the Universe and the rest of the Universe is outside ourselves, so it makes sense that to experience the Universe, to understand it and to get to know it, we must necessarily look outside ourselves for the purpose of gaining knowledge. This is supported by the fact that our eyes face outwards, as do our other extremities.

The reality of where we experience life is very different.

If you will observe yourself, you will realize soon enough that there is no such thing as an external experience. To be sure, apparently—and the word "apparently" is deliberately used here—there are external *stimuli;* but in truth, there is no external *experience.* You can prove it to yourself by examining what happens when you experience with your senses. For instance: When you hear, what happens? When you hear, the sound travels from its source through the air into your ears, and from there it travels to your brain and you experience the sound within your consciousness. Unless the sound can travel *within* your being, you cannot experience it; and if you cannot experience it within your consciousness, then for you the sound does not exist. Deaf persons cannot experience sound, because they cannot experience it within their consciousness. Even though deaf persons may be surrounded by sound, because they cannot experience it within their consciousness, for them the sound does not exist.

Similarly when we see color, the image of the color gets transferred into our brain through our eyes and we experience the color within our consciousness. A blind person is incapable of internalizing the image and so cannot experience it. A blind person may be completely surrounded by color but cannot experience it because he/she cannot internalize color. We cannot distinguish color by the other senses, *i.e.,* touch, taste, smell and hearing.

So a person who is blind from birth has no concept of color because there is no way they can internalize color. Nor can you explain to them what color is because there is no way they can relate to it. Color can only be seen.

From the above we can conclude that unless we can *internalize* something, we cannot experience it. There is no such thing as an external experience. All experience is internal because all life is internal.

Proof that life is internal can be obtained by observing our daily activities.

For instance:

- When we breathe, where does our breath go? Within.
- When we drink, where does the liquid go? Within.
- When we eat, where does the food go? Within.
- When we think, where do our thoughts occur? Within.
- When we speak, where does the sound originate? Within.
- When we listen, where does the sound register? Within. *Et cetera, et cetera.*

All life is experienced *within* our beings. Even those stimuli that are external to us originate within some other being, and all of these experiences including ourselves are contained within the Universe, the source of our physical bodies. Thus if all life is experienced internally and originates within, it makes sense that all knowledge is also internal and not external. Perhaps this is the reason why the Lord Christ is reported to have said words to the effect, "The Kingdom of God lies within you."

All of us are connected to each other and to the entire Universe both externally as well as internally. Therefore, to see the world, by all means travel to different parts of the globe; but to experience the Universe, we have to go within ourselves. But how does one go within?

We are not taught to do that in our schools and universities, which are sometimes referred to as Centers of Higher Learning. In our public schools, there is a separation of Schools and Church mandated by law. Our public schools and colleges are focused on teaching students about the physical universe and how we can earn a living through it. We are so consumed with earning a living and paying bills that if we have any extra energy, we expend it to satisfy our desires. And why not? After all in the very Declaration of Independence of the United States of America, it is stated that we all have the right to "Life, Liberty and the Pursuit of Happiness."

Is there no connection between the Physical Universe and our Inner Beings?

Are we merely physical bodies with intelligence, separate from one another?

You can draw your own conclusions from your life experiences. In order to gain the maximum results from your efforts, it may help if we gained an understanding of how the cognitive human mind and ego get formed.

HOW THE COGNITIVE HUMAN MIND AND EGO ARE FORMED

Only that which is Limitless can be Formless. From Its Limitless State, It can create and descend into any form. All forms are contained within the Limitless and Formless Source of all forms. Anything that has a form, no matter how large it may be, is limited and its form defines its limits. Though very immense, because they have a form, the Physical Universe and Space are not Limitless.

Therefore no form can contain the Limitless Source of Creation that is commonly called God or Allah or Brahma. This is one reason why in some religions, *e.g.*, Judaism and Islam, there is the injunction that you cannot give any form to God who is Limitless and therefore Formless.

Some people may say that a liquid such as water is formless, and that it will assume the form of the vessel in which it is poured. From the Spiritual point of view, every atom has a form. Still, the example of a liquid assuming any shape may help some people understand why it is possible for the Limitless, Formless Source of all Sources to assume any form.

All of creation exists within the Limitless, which is commonly called God.

The Limitless has a Mind that is Limitless and which contains all possibilities.

Being Limitless it is not threatened by any possibilities and remains open to and supports all possibilities. This Limitless Mind can be called the Mind of God, or just God. All of Creation in its multitude forms arises and plays out its existence within this Limitless state of the Mind Divine. Since the Mind of God created everything that exists, it permeates everything and influences and ultimately controls and directs everything in all of Creation. It accomplishes this by setting up limits within which its creations may express themselves through a free will which is limited just as their forms are limited.

This is one reason why religious people assert: "God knows everything." God knows everything potentially but not consciously. This, too, is reflected in all of Creation but this phenomenon will be dealt with in a separate book.

An aspect of the Limitless Mind directs the activities and reactions of individual atoms and molecules. In this context one may say, that individual atoms and molecules have a mind of their own. But this mind is very conditioned and is the basis of the Instinctive Mind.

All atoms that have been identified exhibit certain known characteristics. Species of insects, birds and animals also exhibit certain known behavioral patterns governed by their instinctive mind which is nothing more than a more elaborate form of a chemical mind, *i.e.*, the mind locked up within an atom. It is because of the constrained mind that is present in all atoms that reacts in a predictable manner, that genetic engineering is possible. The instinctive mind should not be confused with the conscious mind that is linked to the free will.

From a Spiritual point of view, wherever there is movement, there is life. Based on this interpretation, life is locked up in the atomic and subatomic particles. However this is not biological life. It is chemical life and it has no free will. As the atoms combine to form molecules and as the molecules combine to form organic molecular chains, biological life begins as a result of the association of spirit with matter. Biological life is not known to exist in inorganic compounds. When biological life becomes complex, then higher spirit creations become linked with the material creations and such creations have a limited free will. The level of the spirit associated with the biological life determines the limit of the free will. The higher the spirit, the greater the free will. The physical plane becomes a filter through which Spiritual creations have to grow through before they can merge with the Divine.

When conception occurs, an embryo receives the basic imprint that will be the basis of its human mind (we could call it the cognitive mind), its instinctive mind, and the mind of its body, which will regulate the bodily functions. This basic imprint is imparted through the genes that are part of the chemical /biological makeup of the parents and fore-parents. However as the embryo continues to grow, all the three minds that are being formed, *i.e.,* the cognitive mind, the instinctive mind and the mind of the body, are very strongly influenced by the emotions, thoughts and activities of the mother.

That is why the ancients used to advise pregnant mothers to think happy thoughts, loving thoughts, courageous thoughts, Spiritual thoughts, *et cetera.* While the embryo is still within the mother, although its human mind is being formed, the ego is non-existent. The embryo is not even conscious of the mother's existence because it is not separate in any way from the mother. Within the womb, the embryo is in a stress-free environment, receiving all its nourishment automatically through the mother. However, once birth takes place, the embryo is separated from the mother. For the first time in its short existence, the embryo, now a newborn child, experiences separation and has to gasp for breath in order to live. Its comfortable existence within the womb comes to a sudden end through the process of birth. By its very nature, the process of birth and the separation that occurs must be traumatic and frightening to the embryo. Imagine the feeling one experiences being squeezed out head first through the birth canal and then at the end being slapped in order to be stimulated to breathe.

It is like having the earth removed from beneath your feet. This sudden separation that occurs at birth and the gasping for life sustaining air in a radically new environment forms a nucleus of fear and instability within the cognitive mind of the newborn child. This nucleus of fear becomes the basis of the consciousness of the child and is the basis of the consciousness of all human beings. The conscious mind of all human beings and indeed all creatures, are built around this nucleus of fear.

Outside the mother, the child's cognitive mind begins to develop. As part of the development process, the child begins to identify itself by what it is not. Within the womb, there was no conscious separate identity between the mother and the child. The child did not have to do anything to receive its needs. Everything flowed naturally and easily from the mother to the developing embryo. Outside the mother, the child begins to recognize its mother as separate from itself and also recognizes that it has to make its needs known. This awareness that it is separate from its mother causes the cognitive mind of the child to create its ego, its own separate identity. Outside the mother, the growing child receives its needs and things that gratify it through the process of crying. This causes the ego to become self-centered, *i.e.,* it learns from experience, which is continuously reinforced: whenever I need something, I should cry to draw attention to my needs and myself—then I am given what I want, otherwise I am ignored. Later on the child identifies with forms other than the mother.

As my older brother Bohman explains it, "The mind creates the ego by associating itself with everything it is not." The child is not the mother but identifies with it. It similarly identifies with the father and the outside environment, all of which are the not-self. Thus the ego begins to develop an identity and takes shape within the conscious human (cognitive) mind. The ego is a creation of the conscious mind, and like all creations, it exists within its source, *i.e.,* the conscious human mind. Therefore the mind and ego are linked inseparably, and the mind identifies with the ego it has created and *vice-versa*. All associations of the conscious mind and ego are with the not-self and are built around the basis of ignorance and fear that was created at the time of the physical separation from the mother at birth. This fear and self-centeredness become the very nucleus around which the cognitive mind and ego develop. Further, because of their associations with the not-self, the mind and ego are empty and unreal ... like a shadow that depends upon a physical object and light for its existence.

Being unreal, they create illusory relationships and live in a world of illusion created by their own consciousness. Being illusory, they can never be permanently satisfied since an illusion by definition is un-Real.

It is like trying to catch a rainbow. You just cannot do it and if you attempt to catch a rainbow, you will only experience frustration. Similarly you cannot satisfy the human mind and ego.

The human mind is formed first within the mother. However it recognizes its separate existence outside the mother and as a point of reference to its environment, the mind creates its ego/personality as it continues to develop outside the mother as follows:

- A sudden separation occurs between the mother and child at birth.
- This sudden separation and the gasping for air in a radically new environment sets up a nucleus of fear in the conscious mind of the child.
- This nucleus of fear is deepened by the lack of personal identity.
- This lack of personal identity causes the developing human mind to create an awareness arising from associations with forms that are other than it. This self-identity based on everything outside itself is the nucleus around which the ego gets formed.
- The child realizes that it is dependent on things and persons outside itself for its needs and survival. The child realizes over time that it receives physical gratification through crying and drawing attention to itself. This association of crying and subsequent gratification develops a selfish trait, which is a basic characteristic of the human ego.
- Thus the human mind operates from a basis of fear and strives to satisfy the selfish ego. The mind/ego combination becomes the center around which the mind creates its own universe, which is initially based upon the opinions and values that are thrust upon it by its parents and the education it receives. These may be changed later on according to its preferences.

The ego gets formed as the human mind associates itself with that which it is not, and also from recognizing that it has needs, which it cannot fulfill and must rely on others to do so.

The child learns to manipulate others to get its own needs fulfilled. This inability to fill its own needs and dependence on others, further feeds the nucleus of fear, which gets implanted in the human mind at the time of separation from the mother at birth and adds to the basic insecurity of the human mind.

The human mind and ego are interdependent and inseparable, and share a common basis of fear and negative associations. This negative basis and identity through separation are the reasons why human minds:

- Respond much more readily to negative impulses of fear rather than positive impulses of love. Fear of loss is a greater motivation than opportunity for gain: *e.g.*, people stop smoking for fear of cancer and not to gain good health.
- Cannot see the Unity in Diversity of Manifestation. The human mind and ego knows what it is *not*, but does not know what it *is*, and is conscious of its separate existence and individual needs for its survival.

This not knowing itself is the very basis of its insecurity and also of its quest for security and the need to find out "Who or what am I?" It is also the basis of the ancient Hindu prayer mentioned above, which is worth repeating here and which in the original Sanskrit is:

> *Asato ma sadgamaya*
> *Tamaso ma jyotir gamaya*
> *Mrityor ma amritam gamaya*

When translated this means:

> From untruth lead me to Truth.
> From darkness lead me to Light.
> From death lead me to Immortality.

Some people correctly point out that we cannot call this world un-Real because we can perceive it with our senses. When we get hurt, the pain is real. When we are dehydrated the thirst is real. How can we call these experiences un-Real?

The Source of all sources is all-pervading and is omnipresent. It is also present in the relative reality, which is what our earth experience is.

Compared to the Ultimate Reality, which is permanent and unchanging, the relative reality is temporary and changes continuously. Every moment the entire physical universe changes. Although individual changes may be miniscule and hardly noticeable, the collective change is immense. This relative and changing nature of the relative reality is what makes it un-Real, and exacerbates our basic insecurity and makes us desire security and peace.

It is this quest for security and identity that, if pursued to its ultimate solution, will lead the human mind to its Source, which is the Divine. That will happen when one breaks through the mind and kills the ego. To do this it is recorded that the Lord Christ said words to the effect, "You must hunger and thirst after

God and His Righteousness."

In order to live and work as a constructive member of society, we need our human minds and ego. However in order to grow to know the Divine, we have to break through and literally kill the ego that makes us consciously feel separate from the rest of creation.

Since the conscious human mind is the source of the ego, it can also destroy the ego. Though this can be done, it is almost impossible for most human beings. It is like asking a mother to kill her child. A much easier path is to replace the consciousness of the ego with the consciousness of God. However, the human mind is incapable of knowing God. How can it be conscious of that which it is incapable of knowing? That is where the need comes for a Spiritual Master who is in touch with the Divine. One needs to ignore the demands of one's own ego and serve the right type of Spiritual Master. Instead of serving a Spiritual Master, many of us prefer to strive to satisfy our own minds and ego which as explained above can never be satisfied and only leads to frustration.

Right Spiritual Masters are the very Presence of God in human form. A Spiritual Master is not God. As explained above, nothing that has a form can contain all of that which is the Limitless, Formless Source of all Sources commonly called God. However since the consciousness of a Spiritual Master is linked to God, we can surmise that when He focuses His attention on us, then we are in the consciousness of God and therefore in the presence of God. When we are serving a Spiritual Master then we are in the Presence of God through the consciousness of the Master. Through lack of attention and in the presence of the Divine, the ego will shrivel up and die.

One cannot consciously destroy one's ego. That is impossible, and it is wrong even to try, because much harm will result to the consciousness of the person who tries to do so. As mentioned above, if instead of being self-conscious we strive to remain conscious of the Divine, then as a result of inner spiritual growth the ego will be shed naturally and without harm. As naturally as when the shell of a seed bursts open due to the internal growth that occurs within when the seed surrenders to its source, the soil.

This internal growth will result naturally as one surrenders to the Divine.

How to practice the Presence of God and how to find the Right Spiritual Master?

One should never try to find a Spiritual Master. When one is ready to meet the Master, conditions get created for one to meet Him. The Right Spiritual Principles enable us to Practice the Presence of God and prepare us to receive the Master should He choose to come into our life.

To give some idea about how from the Limitless Formless State, the All Pervading Nothing commonly called God, created the universe, the following Divine Script received through Dr. Dinshah K. Mehta on October 24, 1957 is being reproduced here:

THOUGHT-SPACE

From that which is Me, Thought-Space I Be
In spaceless spaciousness of the Eternal See
The Thought is naught but that I Be
The Thought is the Light-Sound, the Space became Me.

Me that is Space is an End of that thought
But the Source of Matter the Light became
The Light filled Space and lights the Light
Each light a Sun that worlds begot.

Each one a mirror of My Eternal Word,
I Its Father, yet It fathers Me
That Word became men in end on this earth
The media of mine to make Me free.

When reading the rest of this book, it will be good if the reader remains aware of the illusory nature of his/her opinions and the importance of his/her attitude in shaping values and experiences all of which have a direct impact on how he/she chooses to live, deal with other people and Nature and the other creatures that cohabit this planet with us.

The next chapter discusses the difference between Natural Man, Technological Man and Civilized Man.

Chapter 4
Natural Man, Technological Man and Civilized Man

Most of us are aware of the expression, "Attitude is everything," and in the preceding chapter we discussed how our attitude determines and shapes our experience and *vice versa*.

Since prehistoric times, the attitudes of human beings towards nature have shaped their experiences. Based upon his attitude towards nature, man can be classified as:

- Natural man
- Technological man and
- Civilized man

NATURAL MAN

Natural man lived in the so-called primitive hunter/gatherer cultures and developed more fully into agrarian societies and those which herded animals.

Even today, there are primitive societies that live in keeping with nature.

Natural man's attitude towards nature is not adversarial. Natural man perceives himself as being an integral part of nature. The forces of nature are not perceived as being something man must conquer but something that man must live with. Nature with all her fury and diversity is perceived as a provider of livelihood, if not life itself. Natural man co-exists even today with Technological man. The natives who live in the forests of Brazil, the aborigines of Australia and natives everywhere that still cling to their natural habitat are examples of Natural man.

The attitude of Natural man towards nature is reflected beautifully in the famous speech recorded as given in the year 1854 by Chief Joseph Seattle of the Suquamish Tribe of Native Americans. In his speech, among other things, Chief Seattle stated:

> The Great Chief in Washington sends word that he wishes to buy our land.

The Great Chief also sends us words of friendship and good will. This is kind of him, since we know he has little need of our friendship in return.

But we will consider your offer. For we know that if we do not sell, the white man may come with guns and take the land.

How can you buy or sell the sky, the warmth of the land? The idea is strange to us. If we do not own the freshness of the air and the sparkle of the water, how can you buy them?

Chief Seattle continued,

This we know: The earth does not belong to man; man belongs to the earth.

This we know: Whatever befalls the earth befalls the sons of the earth.

Man did not weave the web of life; he is merely a strand in it. Whatever he does to the web he does to himself. Even the white man cannot be exempt from the common destiny. One thing we know, which the white man may one day discover—our God is the same God. You may think that you own Him as you wish to own the land but you cannot. This earth is precious to the Great Spirit, and to harm the earth is to heap contempt on its Creator. The whites too shall pass; perhaps sooner than all other tribes. Continue to contaminate your bed and one night you will suffocate in your own waste. ...

Chief Seattle's people still hold his views, as depicted in a story reported, circa 1999, by Mr. Tom Brokaw on *NBC Nightly News*. Members of the Suquamish Tribe still live near the city of Seattle in the State of Washington. Because of native rights they are allowed to fish for salmon using gill nets. Over the years, in the State of Washington, many dams have been built across the rivers. These dams disrupted the salmon runs and prevented the salmon from reaching their spawning grounds. To solve the problem and help the salmon swim upstream, the State of Washington and the Army Corps of Engineers constructed several steps that enabled the salmon to leap over the dams. These steps were so designed that it tended to group the salmon together in a sort of funnel that pointed them towards the steps, which they could negotiate to leap over the dams.

Nobody knows how it happened, but the California sea lion that lives more than 1,000 miles away from Seattle, learned that the salmon near Seattle were easy prey, because they all crowded together during their migration up the man-made steps. Many California sea lions swam to Washington and started hunting salmon. When the fishing season was upon them, the Native Americans would cast their gill nets, and the salmon would get caught in these nets. The California sea lion discovered that it was easier to steal the salmon from the fishing nets than to hunt them down. They proceeded to do just that.

The Native Americans had a dilemma. The sea lions were stealing their salmon. What should they do about it?

The Council of Tribe Elders held a meeting. At the meeting they concluded that there was not enough salmon to feed both the sea lion and the tribe.

They decided that since the sea lion was a creature of the water he had first right to the salmon. Rather than kill the sea lions, as most other people would do, the tribe stopped fishing and left the salmon for the sea lions.

Natural man lives in harmony with nature and recognizes that he is only part of the web of life. Because of his attitude towards nature, Natural man did not feel the need to war against and conquer nature, but rather strove to live in harmony with nature, derive his needs from her natural bounty and appreciate and enjoy her beauty. Nature was at times benevolent or violent, but was nonetheless beautiful and bountiful, and provided for his every need.

TECHNOLOGICAL MAN

Compared to Natural man, Technological man has by and large held an adversarial attitude towards nature, as can be deduced from statements made in the popular press.

When man finally learned to harness the power of the wind and was able to navigate the globe, it was announced, "Man conquered the sea." When man learned the principles of aerodynamics and achieved powered flight, it was declared, "Man conquered the air," and when man landed on the Moon, "Man conquered space."

Technological man has not *conquered* anything but merely discovered some of the laws of nature and how to work with them. That is a very great accomplishment. However rather than use this new-found knowledge to live in greater harmony with nature, because of his inherent adversarial attitude towards nature, Technological man tries to "manage" nature and "increase and improve" the bounty that he can extract from her to satisfy his own selfish ends. This is in contrast to Natural man who accepted the bounty Nature provided and yielded.

Instead of appreciating the fact that he is but a part of the web of life and therefore should work in harmony with it, Technological man seems to exploit Nature. In doing so, Technological man is literally at war with Nature. Technological man dams rivers and thus disrupts the flow of water; he paves over the best soil to build his cities and thus disrupts the cleansing and nurturing function of rain. He pollutes the air and water, which cause all sorts of health problems. Rather than living in tune with the natural rhythms of the sun, moon and earth according to the seasons, Technological man lives by the clock and works in artificially contrived shifts of 8 or 10-hours. The work shifts can even be 24 hours or longer in some professions. Shift work causes the circadian rhythms of the body to get disrupted and leads to additional health problems.

The actions of Technological man have led, among others, to serious problems such as Global warming, Urban Sprawl, habitat destruction of fish and other wild life. Each of these in turn has resulted in undesirable consequences. The new science of genetic engineering poses fresh challenges. For the interested reader, these issues have been discussed in the *Addendum.*

VALUE SYSTEMS: CLASH BETWEEN EARNING MONEY AND PRESERVING THE ENVIRONMENT

In large measure, societies manifest their value systems. What is the basic reason why Technological man seeks to make nature yield more than what she chooses to provide naturally? There are hosts of reasons for Technological man's attitude towards nature, but the basic reason seems to be money. Whereas

Natural man lived by harvesting the bounty of nature, Techno-logical man strives to accumulate wealth in the form of money by exploiting all the resources he can commandeer which in the past included enslaving his fellow man. Enslavement of man by man still continues in the form of economic enslavement.

By and large, technological societies have been built upon an economic foundation in which money has been given the most important value. For any project to be approved, it must be shown to be financially viable and politically/socially conven-ient.

Many of us have accepted the idea that we need money to live. After all without money we cannot pay our bills, buy food, pay our mortgage, buy our cars, the fuel to drive them and so forth. We have accepted the idea that we cannot live without money. Many of us give the very first value, above all else, to money.

I submit that we do not need money to live. In order to live, we need sunshine, clean air, pure water, good soil and space. *The Hindu Scriptures refer to Space, Fire (i.e., Sun or heat from any source), Air, Water and Earth as the Five Great Spirits, or the Five Elementals.* Life begins wherever they meet. In fact space is so important that our bodies need space even after we die.

If anyone doubts that we need food, water, air, heat and space to stay alive, let them take all the money they have and live in the desert without water for a week. If they have not taken leave of their senses, they will gladly part with all their money for a glass of water.

Yet, in the pursuit of money we are destroying the very envi-ronment that sustains life on earth. We are as it were threatening the web of life. Why is that?

It all boils down to the value we give to money above all else. In order to sustain and expand the economy, society has to constantly produce more goods and services. Without a constant and ever-increasing demand for goods and services, the economy will slow down and we will not have the money, which we think we need to live. Further since the United States of America is the superpower, it is the model that many societies are emulating, including societies where such a model is not only unnecessary but also counter-productive. To expand the economy new prod-ucts are constantly being introduced. The best minds are engaged in developing new hitherto unheard-of products and services to create new jobs and help the economy expand. *Importance is given to developing things for man rather than developing man.* We have a phenomenon in modern societies in which the homemaker works 40 hours a week to pay for all the labor saving devices we use at home. The hours spent working to pay for the labor saving devices may be used more effectively if homemakers used the time to care of their children and help them build good character and a balanced sense of values, all of which will make them feel more secure than a home full of gadgets many of which soon become obsolete. One cannot help but feel that well-adjusted, secure children will be able to contribute immensely to our national good and that of the world. They are indeed the best assets any nation can have. Instead of focusing on providing a secure and nurturing environment for our kids to grow up in, we seem to be developing generations of latch-key children many of whom grow up to be maladjusted adults.

The absurdity of pursuing profits at the expense of the quality of life, is very nicely described in the following hypothetical exchange between an American with a degree in business from an Ivy League University and a Mexican fisherman:

A boat docked in a tiny Mexican village. An American tourist complimented the Mexican fisherman on the quality of his fish and asked how long it took him to catch them.

"Not very long," answered the Mexican.

"But then, why didn't you stay out longer and catch more?" asked the American.

The Mexican explained that his small catch was sufficient to meet his needs and those of his family.

The American asked "But what do you do with the rest of your time?"

"I sleep late, fish a little, play with my children, and take a siesta with my wife. In the evenings, I go into the village to see my friends, have a few drinks, play the guitar, and sing a few songs ... I have a full life."

The American interrupted, "I have an MBA from Harvard and I can help you!

"You should start by fishing longer every day. You can then sell the extra fish you catch. With the extra revenue, you can buy a bigger boat. With the extra money the larger boat will bring, you can buy a second one, and a third one and so on until you have an entire fleet of trawlers. Instead of selling your fish to a middleman, you can negotiate directly with the processing plants and maybe even open your own plant. You can then leave this little village and move to Mexico City, Los Angeles, or even New York City! From there you can direct your huge enterprise."

"How long would that take?" asked the Mexican.

"Twenty, perhaps twenty-five years," replied the American.

"And after that?"

"Afterwards? That's when it gets really interesting," answered the American, laughing. "When your business gets really big, you can start selling stocks and make millions!"

"Millions? Really? And after that?"

"After that you'll be able to retire, live in a tiny village near the coast, sleep late, play with your children, catch a few fish, take a siesta, and spend your evenings drinking and enjoying your friends!"

The Mexican smiled at the good-natured and well-meaning American tourist and went on his way.

To satisfy Technological man's need for minerals and raw materials, primitive cultures that live in idyllic natural settings such as the Micronesian island nations in the Pacific, the island of Madagascar off the east coast of Africa and others in Africa and Asia are given money for the rights to mine their natural resources. And what do these people do with their money? Buy television sets, cars, trucks and gasoline to fuel them. The programs they watch through their TV do not help educate those who watch them. More often than not, conflicting values are introduced through the TV programs. What happens to these societies once their mineral deposits and other natural wealth are exhausted? The harvesting of their natural resources, for which they received money, destroyed their beautiful island, the money they received is used up, and they are left with television sets and vehicles which break down and which they cannot repair.

All of this exploitation has been done and still continues in the name of civilization and progress. These issues beg the questions: What constitutes progress? Who can be called civilized and what is "civilization?"

CIVILIZED MAN

The essence of civilization is harmony and balance. Balance between the internal and the external and harmony between man and his surroundings based upon a value system of mutual respect and one that allows all members of society to achieve their optimum potential. To be civilized man must strive to strike a balance between his needs, as opposed to his greeds, and nature's ability to supply those needs and build a society that reflects these values.

I submit that Technological man has not achieved nor experienced such a society.

By using technological progress as a benchmark for the progress of civilization, Technological man purports to think of himself as civilized. But is he really? A very strong case can be made that throughout history, Technological man has exploited Natural man. In the 19th and 20th centuries, the pace at which Technological man, particularly of European descent, decimated Natural man increased dramatically. In fact it can be said that *modern Technological man is the savage who has ravaged the earth*. Documentary evidence exists that in his ignorance and arrogance, modern Technological man has used all the means available to him, including trickery and treachery, to wreak havoc on Natural man and the other creatures that cohabit this planet and who together comprise the web of life and all that is natural, beautiful and wonderful.

And yet, all the perceived wrongs perpetrated by Technological man have to be balanced by the many astounding technological breakthroughs that have been achieved through his efforts. This book could not have been written but for the contribution of Technological man.

The aim of this book is not to catalog and analyze the negative and positive contributions made by Technological man. That will not accomplish much, if any, good. *We cannot change the past. We should learn from the past and move on.* However those who have any doubt or those who are interested in learning about the atrocities committed by modern Technological man against Natural man should research what was done, with the best of intentions, by European settlers against the natives of North and South America and their culture and justified in the name of Manifest Destiny, Christianity and other movements.

They can also read about the actions of the Colonial Masters in Asia, which are also well documented.

Similarly they can read about what was done to the aborigines of Australia under, among other things, an obnoxious policy that was adopted around 1910. As mentioned in the September 11, 2000 issue of *Time Magazine*, "This odious experiment was not abandoned until 1970 and did not become general public knowledge until 1997, when a report on it, 'Bringing them Home,' by Sir Ronald Wilson, caused a national outrage." Likewise the atrocities committed against the Africans by native Africans, Arabs and Europeans during the slave trade and those perpetrated in South Africa under apartheid and in the United States during segregation are all too well documented. The atrocities committed by the Japanese against China and Korea and other less-developed nations of Asia are also well documented.

In India, the atrocities committed against the untouchables, who are Hindus, by the other Hindu castes, which consider themselves spiritually superior, is also well documented. Similarly the wrongs perpetrated by the former Soviet Union, Communist China and other nations against their own citizens are quite well known. Indeed throughout history, conquerors have wreaked havoc on the conquered and rulers on the ruled.

But the web of life itself was never threatened. Now, because of the scale of modern technology and its tendency to create unforeseen problems, the very web of life itself is threatened.

Having said the above, to their credit, a small but increasing percentage of the technologically able recognizes the fact that in our zeal to understand and control nature we have caused a lot of damage. We are all looking for workable solutions. But solutions that help us get out of the big mess we are in necessarily call for a large sacrifice and a change in lifestyle.

Alas, Technological man still suffers from all the weaknesses of older civilizations. We still harbor hate, envy, greed, gluttony, anger, slothfulness and covetousness. We are more motivated by fear of our fellow man than out of love for him. In essence we are still savages, but because of our technological prowess, we can do much more damage to those who oppose us and from a greater distance than could less technologically developed cultures of the past.

Technology has advanced. Man has not.

87

In a very real sense we have remained savages that have become much more dangerous than our less technologically able predecessors. But because we can do things faster, build larger structures and travel to the moon and back we think of ourselves as being civilized. It has been generally accepted that the greatness of a society should be judged not by the size of its cities, the height of its buildings and the width of its streets but by the kind of people it produces.

And what kind of people are we producing today? What values do we cherish?

ARE OUR VALUE SYSTEMS AND LIFESTYLE VALID? ARE THEY SUSTAINABLE OVER THE LONG HAUL?

With our present lifestyle and the pressures that people are experiencing, road rage is an increasing traffic phenomenon. Rather than forgive those who trespass us, we prefer to sue to the fullest extent of the law.

Technological society seems to have been built upon the law of the jungle, which is what Darwin used to explain the principle of natural selection, *i.e.,* "The law of the survival of the fittest." In his book, *The Hidden Side of Things*, Bishop C.W. Leadbeater, a Theosophist, states: "The law of the survival of the fittest is the law for the evolution of the brute, but the law of sacrifice is the law for the evolution of man."

If we accept the law of sacrifice as the law for the evolution of man, then we have to ask ourselves, "Can a society that focuses its economic might on instant gratification enable its members to practice the law of sacrifice?"

How difficult would it be to practice this law of sacrifice? I submit that with a little practice it could become a way of life. It is, of course, a matter of priorities.

To become civilized we have to recognize that our priorities are upside down as one can deduce from the discussion that follows.

Generally speaking a normal healthy adult can live without food for about 40 to 50 days. That same adult may be able to live without water for about a week to ten days. How long can that person live without air? Perhaps ten minutes or at best half an hour? How long can we survive without the heat of the sun? If the heat of the sun were to be shut off instantly (as opposed to gradually because of the heat that has already been absorbed by earth), we would freeze instantly. Thus we need food, water, air, warmth and space. And because they are recycled our bodies need space even after we are dead.

Yet if we look at our value systems, we tend to give more importance to the quality of the food we eat than to the quality of the water we drink. We give more importance to the quality of the water we drink than to the quality of the air we breathe. When it is too hot or too cold, we complain; but do we really dwell on the sun and how it affects the earth and us? And how many of us even think about the importance of space as part of our life supporting systems? Without internal and external space our physical bodies, and physical life as we know it, would not be possible.

Based on the above, we can see that Technological man has his priorities backwards. Indeed as a technological society, we are spewing automobile and other industrial exhausts into the atmosphere. Many of us also smoke, thereby damaging our health as well as of those around us, and further pollute the atmosphere. We are also paving with concrete, acres and acres of pristine agricultural land and cutting down irreplaceable rain forests. We have polluted and continue to pollute the underground water tables and the rivers and oceans. By causing conditions that created a hole in the ozone layer, which continues to expand, we have in effect altered the way the sun affects us. Large portions of the earth are now exposed to the harmful radiations from the sun that were once blocked off by the atmosphere and now reach the earth through the opening in the ozone layer. And we have already begun to clutter space with our debris. With our current way of life, we have greatly affected all the five great spirits as identified by the Hindu Scriptures, *i.e.,* Earth, Water, Air, Sun and Space.

Just why do we continue to do this?

I suggest we did this and continue to do so because we have all bought into the concept that we need money to live. But do we really? If we had all the money in the world but did not have space, sunshine, fresh air, clean water and good food, it is obvious that we would not survive. Money is only a medium of exchange, and yet in the pursuit of money we are destroying the very fabric of life-sustaining nature of which we are but a part. At best we are damaging the web of life and at worst we are irreparably destroying it.

Can a society that damages the web of life be called civilized?

So, what to do? Is there any hope for us? There is always hope, but unless some immediate—and what may seem like drastic—measures are implemented, there is only a very small probability that we will be able to continue to live the way we do and not suffer the dire consequences of our own actions.

We have to remind ourselves, that regardless of how some people may interpret Scriptures, we are a part of the earth and it really does not belong to us. There are no passengers on spaceship earth. We are all crew. To cherish what remains of Earth and to foster its renewal is our only legitimate hope of survival. We are only passing through and are part of the natural order. If we tinker around with nature outside the natural boundaries, then we are literally biting the hand that feeds us. We are treading on dangerous ground. *When dealing with nature, if we must err, then it is better to err on the side of caution.* To preserve the web of life, it is essential to live with, act in harmony with the natural environment, and adopt policies that will not change it fundamentally. We should use technology to help us understand the mysteries of nature and use that knowledge to work more effectively with nature rather than upset the delicate balance of life.

We can only live in harmony with nature if our business and political leaders, and indeed our religious leaders, too, embrace the importance of preserving the natural relationships between the ecosystem and ourselves. Our leaders need to take a stand against giving money or mammon the primary place in our value system. As a people we should be willing to accept the changes needed to restore the natural balance.

Business and industry should focus on providing goods and services that improve the quality of life and not focus on making profits at all costs. An intelligent fool can make things bigger, more complex and more violent. It takes wisdom and a lot of courage to move in the opposite direction.

It is hard to understand how the quality of life can improve if the quality of the environment that supports life is degraded. When will we get serious about ensuring that we do not destroy the web of life? How can we talk about the quality of life when we are living in such a toxic environment?

When a society's primary value is the creation of money as opposed to wealth, then it can lead to extremes that manifest itself in scenarios such as the recent string of corporate disasters such as Enron, WorldCom, Adelphia, Tyco, ImClone. The investment bankers and banks, too, have settled with the Attorneys General for their misdeeds without admitting any wrongdoing.

Scriptures have always riled against the worship of mammon. Many people erroneously equate money with wealth. There is a big difference between money and wealth. Basic economic courses teach that *money is a medium of exchange* and a store of value or wealth. I submit to the reader that *money is not a store of many forms of wealth.*

Money is indeed a medium of exchange and purchasing power, but it can be so only for those goods and services it can purchase. *There are many forms of wealth that money just cannot buy, and so it is neither a medium of exchange nor a store of purchasing power and wealth in so far as the things it cannot buy.* If you value things, then indeed money is a store of value. But if you value other than things, then money is not a store of value.

The Hindus worship Laxmi, the Goddess of wealth. There are many forms of wealth that money cannot buy and for which it therefore cannot be a store of value or a medium of exchange. For instance, money can:

- Buy entertainment but not happiness
- Buy books but not knowledge
- Buy companionship but not love
- Buy a bed but not sleep
- Buy fineries like jewelry, clothes, *et cetera,* but not beauty
- Buy food but not appetite
- Buy medicine but not health
- Buy a house but not a home
- Buy memberships to clubs but not culture
  You get the idea.

Fresh air and an atmosphere that insulates and protects us from the harmful radiations of the Sun, good soil, pure water, a healthy environment, peace of mind, *et cetera*, are forms of wealth that money cannot buy. Yet in the pursuit of money Technological man is destroying these pillars of the web of life and states of being that most everyone will agree are worth having and represent true wealth.

Civilized man would not do that.

For Technological man to evolve into Civilized man, he has to learn to live in harmony with the natural environment. Man must approach nature with love, appreciation and understanding. We should deal with nature and respect her for what she is and not view her as an adversary or as a resource to be exploited to satisfy our whims and fancies. Let us use technology to understand the laws of nature and use this knowledge to work in harmony with nature rather than upset the delicate balance of what Chief Joseph Seattle referred to as "The web of life." If we do this then we will be in harmony with nature and experience peace. But to be in harmony with nature and his fellow man, man must first be at peace with himself. How does one do that?

To experience peace within ourselves, each of us must strive to transform himself/herself by employing the Universal Principle of Love. This will give us the wisdom and strength needed to make a paradigm shift which will transform us and enable us to get out of the mess we have created.

Let us learn to love people and use things and not love things and use people.

The next chapter explores the Journey of Creation and the purpose of life.

Chapter 5
The Journey

At the start of this chapter, I would like to once again stress the importance of having an open mind. The reader should examine what is written and if it makes sense have the courage to accept it and begin the journey.

From the Source unto the Source in keeping with the Principles emanating from the Source is the Journey of Life Eternal. All else is lifeless existence in Life Eternal.

The above quotation is from a Discourse given by Revered Dr. Dinshah K. Mehta in the year 1967 in Bombay (now Mumbai), India. Although one can understand the meaning of the individual words, it is difficult to comprehend the meaning of the statement. It took me about eighteen years to understand an aspect of the quotation mentioned above.

To get a better grasp of the meaning of the statement, it would help if one were familiar with the difference between a Principle and a Law. One hears about the Principle of Gravity and the Law of Gravity, the Principle of Safety and the Laws of Safety. Very often we use the term Principle and Law interchangeably when in fact they do have different meanings and characteristics.

Principles are universal whereas laws are not. Laws are limited to very specific situations. For instance, it is important to remain within the envelope of the Principle of Safety whether one is flying a plane, driving a car, sailing a boat, crossing the road, handling firearms or working in the kitchen with a knife or fire. In each case the Principle of Safety is the same. However the laws of safety that emanate from the universal Principle of Safety are different in each situation. If we were to apply the laws of safety as they relate to using a knife, when working with firearms, we would be violating the Principle of Safety and thus expose ourselves to danger.

Why? Because the laws of safety for using firearms are very different from the laws of safety for using a knife even though both sets of laws emanate from the same Principle of Safety. In fact laws of Safety are so specific that when it comes to working with fire, they change depending upon the kind of fuel one is working with. We have one set of laws if the fuel is wood and different laws if the fuel is gasoline, cooking gas or electricity.

It is very important to bear in mind this fundamental difference between Principles and Laws. Principles are Universal but Laws are not. As circumstances change, the Laws that emanate from the underlying Principle may change but the Principle never changes. In view of the above, let us once again examine the quotation.

"From the Source unto the Source in keeping with the Principles emanating from the Source is the journey of Life Eternal. All else is lifeless existence in Life Eternal."

The above Principle applies to all of creation no matter what the immediate source of the creation is. To observe the manifestation of this Principle, we must remember that the Journey of any creation is always from its source back to its source. This is reflected in the Biblical quotation, "Dust thou art and to dust thou shalt return. It can also be witnessed in the following phenomena:

- The source of all water on earth is the ocean. All forms of water begin their journey from the ocean and then meander back to the ocean.
- All vegetation emerges from the earth (or in some cases water) and then seeks to root itself in the earth or water and finally gets reabsorbed in the earth or water as the case may be.
- The source of the air we breathe is the atmosphere. And our breath returns to the atmosphere.
- The source of business may be identified as finance or capital. The goal of business is more finance/capital.

Any creation that violates the Principles emanating from the Source that creates and sustains it will not be able to complete the cycle of creation envisioned by its Source. For instance, let us say that a seed germinated in the soil then grew into a plant but after a certain stage of development stopped following the Principles of the of the environment that sustains its life.

What would happen to such a plant? It would be unable to complete its life cycle. It would just die. In order to realize its full potential, at every stage of its life, the plant must remain rooted in the soil and follow the Principles that emanate from its Source, the soil and stay connected to the environment that created it. Take a fish out of water and it will die.

Similarly when man goes into space he must take with him matter from his physical Source in order to live. Astronauts have to take air, water and food with them when they venture into space. Since sunlight and space permeate everywhere in our solar system, they do not have to take these two of what the Hindus call the Five Elementals of Life.

This essential need to conduct one's life in keeping with the Principle emanating from one's creator is universal, and permeates all activity and is applicable even in business. When growing a business proper Principles for sustaining and growing a business must be followed. If a business violates the Principles of sound business and financial management, it will fail. In order to complete its business cycle successfully, a business must at all times follow the laws of finance and capital appreciation. Many Dotcoms that flouted the principles of prudent business management, because their management and others touted themselves as being part of the New Economy, have been rudely awakened to the consequences of violating the Principles emanating from the Source of business. By following the Principles emanating from their respective Source, all life forms and economic enterprises will grow and fulfill their life cycles and thereby contribute to the enrichment of their respective Sources.

From the above, we can see that the basic Principle for creating and sustaining creation is the Principle of Circulation. Whenever the Principle of Circulation is violated then the activity that is being sustained by the circulation dies. For instance:

- Communication is a circulation of ideas. If one of the parties involved stops the circulation of ideas by refusing to speak or listen, then the communication stops.
- Breathing is a circulation of air between the lungs and the atmosphere. Stop the circulation of air and life ends.
- The circulation of goods and services sourced by capital creates an economy. Stop the circulation of capital and/or goods and services and the economy will die. Consumer spending

and capital spending are vital to keep the economy moving, because they keep the money circulating.

From within Itself the Source begins the process of creation. The Source also continues to sustain its creations. This is reflected in all of creation. All life on earth started from within planet earth, which includes the atmosphere and water. From within themselves, plants produce flowers and fruits. From within themselves, all creatures produce their offspring.

By definition, a Source has to provide for the needs of the re-Source. Similarly by definition the re-Source has to align itself with and further the interests of the Source. If a Source fails to provide the needs of the resource, then it is not a Source; and if a resource does not align itself with and further the interests of the Source then it is not a resource but in fact becomes anti-Source.

All creations have the potential of becoming a re-Source of the Source. But all creations do not become resources. In fact some creations become anti-Source.

For instance an employer creates a job for an employee. The employer is the source of the job. He must provide his employees with a suitable work place and a livelihood as well. If the employer fails to do that and does not pay the employee then he is not an employer (source) but a thief. Similarly if an employee accepts wages but does not perform the work needed, then the employee is not a resource but a parasite that drains the employer.

From the above we can see that it is in the interest of the Source to support its resource, and it is in the interest of the resource to align itself with the Source and further the interest of the Source. Such a relationship will be mutually beneficial and create an upward spiral of growth. The reverse would create a downward spiral of destruction.

Now let us examine the first part of the Principle:

From the Source unto the Source in keeping with the principles emanating from the Source is the journey of Life Eternal.

From the above we can see that:

- The basic Principle of Creation and sustaining creation is the Principle of Circulation.
- The Source of any creation is also the Goal of the Creation.
- The Source sustains its creations. Those creations that follow the Principles emanating from the Source realize their full potential and in the process strengthen the Source in a mutually beneficial upward spiral.

Those creations that do not follow the Principles emanating from the Source are detrimental, both to themselves and to the Source.

We can also make the following observation: "Whatever exists lives within its Source."

Examples abound.

Fish live in water, the source of fish. Plants are rooted within their source the soil. The source of all things on earth is the earth itself and all things live within the environment that is the earth. The source of our solar system may be the galaxy within which it exists. The source of all matter is the empty nothingness we call space and all matter lives within this empty nothingness that is called Space. Space is all around us and within us. In fact space is so vital to the existence of matter that we need space even after we are dead.

We can now make another observation: That which is nothing is the Source of everything.

Examples abound.

Space, which is no matter, is the source and end of all matter. All matter exists, lives within and is supported by Space.

Silence, which can be called no sound, is the source of all sound. Sound emerges from silence, is sustained by silence, then merges back into silence, and is totally surrounded by silence. In fact were it not for silence, we would be unable to hear sound. To hear sound, we have to become silent, *i.e.,* no sound.

Likewise, light is supposed to be colorless. Yet when we refract colorless light through a prism, we see the seven colors of the rainbow out of which all the colors of the world have emerged. When we merge the seven colors of the rainbow, we once again get colorless light. That which has no color is the source of all color.

Think on that. Is it any wonder then that the mystics call this world of matter, this world of forms, a world of illusion?

Along the same line of thinking one can reason that zero is greater than infinity. Infinity emerges from zero, is supported by zero and merges back into zero. Nothing is the Source of everything. Everything emerges from nothing, is sustained by nothing and merges back into nothing. This cycle repeats itself endlessly throughout creation. Civilizations rise from nothing, grow, decay, die and merge into nothingness.

So the Source creates, fosters and recreates its creations. It is in the interest of the creations to become a resource for and of the Source.

But what happens to those creations that choose not to become resources and in fact become anti-Sources? Does the Source destroy them?

No. They destroy themselves. How? Because the Source cannot sustain those creations that are not aligned with it, any creation that does not follow the Principles that created it and keep it alive will naturally perish. The Source does not actively destroy its creations. The Source continues to support all its creations because that is the nature of Source.

Perhaps the following may clarify this concept further.

For every manifestation there is an immediate cause, a remote cause and an ultimate cause. For instance the immediate cause for a tree could be the seed from which it sprouted, or another tree. The remote cause may be the soil or earth or even space, depending upon how profoundly one wants to think.

But what are the source of space and the Source of the source of space? That is what would be the ultimate Cause of any manifestation. Dr. Mehta called this the Source of all sources.

One can get some idea of how the Source of all sources nurtures Its creations by observing how nature supports her creations. Nature does not destroy. Nature always plays a supporting role and surrenders her bounty to her creations. Even though we pollute our own bodies through smoking or ingesting wrong kinds of foods and drink, Nature does not punish us. Through the various systems within our bodies, she strives to clean up the toxins we may ingest or which may arise from the metabolic processes. If we pollute the soil, water and air with toxic chemicals, again we are not struck down. Nature will strive to clean up after us. No matter how much we go against Nature, she still supports us.

Even when we finally reach a point when our ability to pollute the environment exceeds Nature's capacity to clean up, then too Nature does not kill us. She continues her clean up effort. It is only when we succeed in polluting the environment at a rate, which is faster than that which the natural processes can deal with, that we begin to suffer because our bodies can no longer live in the pollution caused by us. This happens not because Nature has decided to punish us but because our bodies cannot adapt to the unbalanced state caused by our own pollution.

Paraphrasing the words of Chief Joseph Seattle, if we continue to contaminate our bed, one night we will suffocate in our own waste. Similarly when creations do not align themselves with the Source, they continue to be supported by the Source until such time as they can survive. They will exist within the Source but will eventually die and are reabsorbed by the Source. Bodies of plants and animals get reabsorbed into the soil and bodies of fish and other creatures of the sea dissolve within the ocean or are washed ashore where other natural processes disperse and/or absorb them. The breath that we exhale and indeed all gases also merge into the atmosphere, which is the Source.

Let us examine the second part of the quotation:

All else is lifeless existence in Life Eternal.

The following analogy may clarify this statement.

A seed or a spore is *alive* but it does not *live*. It merely *exists* and lies dormant until it lands in the proper environment. A plant is alive *and* lives: it grows and reproduces itself. It is only when the seed surrenders itself to its Source the soil, that, given the right conditions, the Source will nurture it and the seed will begin to grow. Once it is in contact with its Source, as a natural consequence of the contact, there will be internal change and growth within the seed. As a result of the growth that occurs within the seed, the shell breaks open and out come the root and the shoot.

No external force is necessary for the growth to occur. Only continuous contact with and surrender to the Source are needed for the seed to begin its life and sustain itself as a tree. By surrendering to its Source, the right environment gets created, and a chain of natural events gets started for the seed to grow to its full potential and fulfill the purpose of its being.

If the seed did not come in contact with (and surrender to) its source what would happen to it? What would happen to its Source? The seed that does not surrender to its Source would continue to remain dormant for years, decades and perhaps centuries—but not forever. Ultimately after a sufficient period of time, the seed will lose its vitality and die. The matter that formed the seed would decompose and be reabsorbed by its Source, the soil.

Nothing happens to the Source. It continues to remain as Source and creates other potential resources.

The Source of all sources is limitless. This is reflected in all.

For instance, *something* has a limit, but *nothing* is limitless. Silence, which is no-sound, is limitless. Sound has a limit. Sound is limited by silence, resonates within silence and is totally surrounded by silence.

Space as we think of it is limitless as far as we are concerned. The galaxies, however large, are not. The point here is that all resources have a limit, are contained by, and exist within their respective Source.

Therefore it is in the interest of a resource to surrender to the larger interest of the Source and align itself with the Source.

For a time, one may *exist* in one's Source. But in order to *live* and grow to realize one's full potential, one has to *surrender* to one's Source and remain in continuous contact with it through the Principle of Circulation.

And as already been pointed out several times, if we ponder on the subject, we will realize that in reality all creations are only channels of their respective Sources, and are sustained by the Source that continuously pours itself into them and absorbs their excretions. Just as an embryo within the womb of the mother is continuously carried and nourished by the mother, all creations are continuously carried and nourished by their respective Sources, within which they are created and live out their existence. Fish live within the waters of the earth and are nourished by them. The earth continuously feeds plants, and mammals are continuously supported by the air, water, food, sunlight and space that flow through them. By themselves, creations have no power to sustain themselves. Creations derive their sustenance *only* by remaining in contact with and being channels of the Source. If this contact is broken they will die, unless they can find an alternative Source.

This same relationship also exists in the world of business: for example, between an employee and employer. Employees are after all only channels through which the employer conducts business, and so long as the relationship between the employee and employer endures, the employer will continue to sustain the employee. If the relationship ends, the employee has to find another source of livelihood.

The question arises: Where is one's Source? The Source of our physical body is the earth. But the Source of our Life, the Spirit that lives through this body, is beyond the physical realm. And unless the body is in touch with that Source, it cannot remain alive. Once the spirit leaves the body, then matter cannot keep the body alive. Where is the Spirit that keeps our body alive, and where is the Source of the Spirit?

The answer: It is within oneself, and all around as well. But as discussed in the chapter entitled *Value of Opinions,* because we experience everything within our consciousness, the only place we can hope to experience our Source is also within ourselves.

As mentioned earlier, even superficially one can observe that when:

- One speaks; the sound arises *within* one's body.
- One thinks, the thoughts arise *in* one's mind.
- One hears, the sound *enters* one's consciousness through one's ears.
- One breathes; the breath *enters* one's lungs.

In fact everything one perceives moves *within* one's consciousness.

The very first verse of the Dhammapâda, which contains some of the sayings of the Lord Buddha, states:

> All things arise in the mind, are sustained by the mind
> and are illusions generated by the mind.

All experiences are *internal*, and all life and all growth also occur *internally*. The manifestation may be external, but the life experiences and growth are internal.

Therefore to get in touch with one's Source it is very important to learn to go *within* one's consciousness. Instead, all our lives many of us have been going *outward*, away from the center. We have not been taught to go *within*, and much less has it been explained to us why it is fundamentally important and beneficial to do so.

It is interesting to note that the further a phenomenon travels from its source, the more it takes on characteristics that tend to be the exact opposite of the Source. For instance, if we shine a flashlight, we can observe that up front, close to the light bulb, the rays of light that make up the beam emitted by the bulb are bright. As the beam travels farther away from the bulb, the rays of light become fainter and fainter until they are no longer light but have become dark. Similarly the farther rays of heat travel away from their source, they too become weaker, until they no longer provide any heat. The same is true of sound.

Also the human mind has traveled so far away from its Source; whatever satisfies the human mind is generally the exact *opposite* of what is good for itself and its Source.

Because most of us cannot control our respective minds; our lives are chaotic. An example of the similarity and difference between chaos and progress may help clarify the assertions being made here.

Chaos and progress are similar because they are both dynamic situations. They are also different, however, because in chaos one has no control over the dynamic forces that impact the situation whereas in progress one can control the dynamic forces that influence the situation. In any dynamic situation there are only two possibilities:

- We *cannot* control it and so it will be chaotic.
- We *can* control it and so we can direct it and it can be progressive.

There is no third possibility. (The only third possibility is that it can become static in which case it is no longer dynamic. Hence this is not a possibility applicable to a dynamic condition.)

Life is dynamic. Therefore there are only two possibilities. Either one is in control and can direct one's life, or one is out of control and life is chaotic. Most of us live chaotic lives. Why? Because we have no control over the vehicle through which we are traveling in this life. That vehicle is none other than the human mind and body. The only medium through which we are communicating with the universe is the medium of our mind and body. If we have no control over the medium through which we are communicating, is it any wonder that the message gets distorted? To bring order into our lives, we must strive to gain control of our mind and senses.

More than 2,500 years ago the Lord Gautama Buddha said words to the effect:

> "Like an archer an arrow, a wise man steadies his trembling mind, a fickle and restless weapon. Flapping like a fish thrown on dry ground, it trembles all day, struggling to escape the snares of Mara the temptress. The mind is restless; to control it is good. A disciplined mind is the road to Nirvana.
>
> Look to your mind, wise man, look to it well—it is subtle, invisible, and treacherous. Clear thinking leads to Nirvana, a confused mind is a place of death. Clear thinkers do not die. The confused ones have never lived."

The chapter entitled *Value of Opinions* explains why we all live in a world of illusion. We are incapable of seeing the world as it is. We look with our eyes but we see with our mind. We hear with our ears but we listen with our mind. But most of us have no control over our mind. Therefore if our mind is out of control, the message we receive/transmit will get distorted. As a result, although the world we live in is real, the world we experience is an illusion created by our mind. Since we have to function through the mind, the mind that is out of control becomes the greatest barrier that prevents us from knowing the truth and experiencing the real.

The human mind has a natural tendency to create and live in a world of self-created illusion. It lives in a world of relative reality, and is therefore incapable of knowing the Ultimate Reality. It strives only to satisfy itself and justify its every desire. The mind jumps from thought to thought all day. Before it can be put to any worthwhile use, it has to be brought under control like a bucking bronco that has to be controlled before we can ride him.

To begin with we have to make the mind steady. A mind out of control is a tyrant that enslaves us and we become victims of our own thoughts. Some people may feel that the reason we can think is because our minds are full of thoughts. That is as unrealistic as believing that the reason we can hold things in our hands is because our hands are full of things that we happen to be grasping at the time. In fact if our hands are full with things that we are holding, then before we can grasp any additional thing, we have to first *empty* our hands by laying down the things we are holding in them or grasping with them. It is only when our hands are empty that they are free to grasp and hold onto new things. Similarly one cannot think clearly when one's mind is full of thoughts. The thoughts that occupy one's mind prevent one from thinking, hearing and/or listening clearly and seeing one's environment the way it is. The thoughts come in the way; impart their bias on everything one experiences and prevent one from experiencing the situation the way it is.

In order to sustain Its creations, the Source creates and fosters the will of Its creations and then surrenders Its Will to the will of the creations.

In order to live and grow, the creations too have to surrender their small will and align it to the omnipotent Will of the Source. This mutual surrender of wills creates an upward spiral of evolution through which the resource will live within the Source and the Source will live in and grow through the resource.

Examples of this relationship of mutually beneficial surrender abound.

For instance, in order to sustain our bodies, the atmosphere (or the earth), which is the Source of the air we breathe, surrenders itself to our lungs and we inhale. However for the process of life to continue, we have to surrender the air in our lungs back to the source that is the atmosphere.

Thus the atmosphere supports us and we too influence the atmosphere. The earth yields its resources to our bodies and the body processes those resources, be they air, water, food, *et cetera*. Our droppings in turn nourish the earth. Without this process of mutual surrender, life as we know it would not be possible. Here again we see the Principle of Circulation sustaining creation. Without mutual surrender, the circulation gets blocked and the Source cannot sustain the resources it has created and grow through them.

The Principle of Circulation makes it possible for the creations (resources) to remain in continuous contact with the Source and receive the wherewithals for their survival.

The Ultimate Reality lies beyond the human mind. Anything that has a form is not real in the sense that it is constantly changing and has a temporary existence. It is a passing phase. Further, anything that has a form can be experienced by the human mind within the limits of its ability to perceive.

Through its ability to perceive, the mind creates an illusion that satisfies it. The human mind is incapable of perceiving the Infinite Limitless Formless Source of all sources, which is the Source of all forms. This Source of All Sources alone is permanent and real. In order to know the Truth, the Real, one has to go beyond the human mind.

How does one do that?

In order to go beyond the human mind, one has to first empty the mind. As long as the mind is filled with human thoughts, it cannot receive subtle thoughts from higher planes of consciousness. When it is empty, these thoughts will descend into it and they will experience the Reality that lies beyond the human mind. This is perhaps what Revered Dr. Mehta, quoting the Lord Christ, meant when he said words to the effect, "The empty alone shall be filled." When one is able to completely steady one's mind, empty it and yet remain conscious, it is said that the mind of one's soul descends into one's human mind. This particular state of consciousness is referred to as meditation.

This brings up another problem posed by a characteristic of the human mind. Before it will commit to do anything, the human mind generally wants to first *understand* the results it will experience prior to embarking upon any new activity. Why? Because it is insecure, and through the understanding it hopes to achieve both a sense of security and satisfaction. Also by seeking to understand first the human mind seeks to escape possible discomfort and asserts itself.

What the human mind does not want to accept is that it is incapable of understanding a new phenomenon unless it first *experiences* it.

Further, even if it does succeed in understanding that is not the same as knowing. Perhaps the following experience will help clarify the point.

Try understanding the taste of salt or sugar without ever tasting anything like salt or sugar. That is not possible. Having tasted salt or sugar, try to describe the taste to someone who has never tasted anything remotely close to either salt or sugar. Again that is not possible. The only way to *know* something new is to take the risk of *experiencing* it.

Similarly one may try to understand how to ride a bicycle by reading a book on the subject. But the only way one can learn to ride a bicycle is by actually mounting a bicycle and attempt to ride it. No matter how many books one may read on how to ride a bicycle, one will never *know* how to ride a bicycle until one actually attempts to ride one. On the other hand if one has a bicycle one can learn to ride it without ever reading a single book on the subject, by having a go at it.

The point being made here is that you can only gain knowledge by direct *familiarity*, and seeking to *understand* has very little value and in most cases has anti-value. We have to strive to *do*, and through the doing we will gain knowledge; and then understanding will not be necessary. In the business world this is called "on the job training."

We already have the vehicle with which to journey through life: it is our human mind and body. We have to learn to use them. When learning how to ride a bicycle, we expend a lot of energy as we struggle to achieve a state of balance. Until we achieve balance, we cannot really enjoy riding the bicycle nor use it effectively. Yet once we achieve balance, then we are free to use our energies to propel the bike and direct it, and are ourselves free to look around. So, before we can really use a bicycle and enjoy it, we must achieve the ease of balance.

The same is true when it comes to using the human mind and body. The human mind is out of balance. It is very unsteady and constantly jumps from thought to thought, and generally it jumps between the past and the future thereby escaping the present. Since the human mind controls the human body, one can imagine the impact the unsteady mind has upon the body.

Once we manage to balance the mind, then towards what end should we direct it?

Many of us are brought up to think that the object of life is to satisfy the human mind and the senses. One can't fault society for feeling this way. All that most of us know about ourselves is what we perceive with the mind, and having created the ego, the mind deceives us into identifying with it. We thus feel that when we satisfy our mind and ego, we have satisfied ourselves. Other than striving to satisfy their respective minds and egos with whom they have identified, most people don't have a goal *in* life, and hardly anyone has identified the goal *of* life.

It is important to distinguish between the goal *in* life and the goal *of* life.

The goal *in* life may be to travel the world, become financially independent, prominent in any field of endeavor, or it may be simply to satisfy oneself with the least amount of effort. The goal *in* life ends with life. The goal *of* life transcends human existence, and by its very nature transcends the goal *in* life. In order to lead an integrated life, the goal *in* life must fit hand in glove with the goal *of* life and must be subservient to the goal *of* life.

If in order to live and grow, we need to be in constant touch and aligned with the Source, then from the foregoing discussion, we can conclude that there is only one Right goal of life, namely to return to the Source. All else is lifeless existence in Life Eternal. Therefore the goal *in* life should be to live in keeping with the Principles that emanate from the Source.

But how can one do that with a mind that is out of control?

We must remember that the human mind is constantly seeking to satisfy itself, and in doing so creates illusions with which it is comfortable. If we can appreciate this fact and constantly remind ourselves of it, we will recognize that we really do not know anyone. All that one is capable of knowing are one's *opinions* about another individual or object. As we have discussed earlier, our opinions are unreal because they are shaped by our attitude and experiences and the impressions that get created as a result of the process that started with our childhood conditioning.

Indeed, if one is prepared to examine the human mind honestly, one will realize that the human mind is incapable of love. Why? Because love and fear cannot coexist any more than ignorance and knowledge can or light and darkness can coexist. In the presence of knowledge, ignorance disappears and in the presence of light, darkness is dispelled. Also, in the presence of love, fear disappears. As long as one is fearful, one has not experienced Pristine Love that is the Ultimate Source of All. Because the human mind and ego are built around a nucleus of fear, they are incapable of experiencing Love until the nucleus of fear is eliminated.

When one falls in love, one does not fall in love with someone else. Instead one only falls in love with one's own *opinions* about the other person.

Further, the thoughts and opinions one falls in love with are always those that satisfy one's mind. One does not fall in love with someone about whom one harbors unpleasant thoughts and feelings. And even if one falls in love with positive thoughts about a person, one falls out of love with the same person when one's opinions and feelings about the person no longer satisfy one's mind. Even if the other person may have improved for the better, if that individual no longer satisfies one's mind then one tends to fall out of love with that individual.

If the human mind is incapable of love, why is it then that we all are driven to love. Further, why is it that most of us yearn for love, long to *fall* in love but do not *grow* in love?

The reason we all need to love is because the seed of the Divine, commonly called the soul, is present within each one of us. We are created by the Light of Divine Love, and in reality are linked to the Divine and are totally surrounded by this Love. All Great Spiritual Masters and Sages through the ages have taught that the Source of all Sources, commonly called God, is Love and Light. From within Itself, the Source creates the universe with Love, sustains it and totally envelopes it with Love. Being a product of Love and enveloped by Love, the Universe cannot help but be influenced and moved by Love. Indeed Love is the basis of all creation and emotion, including hate.

Lest we forget, we have to continuously remind ourselves that all creations live within their Source. Let us go over it again. Vegetation emerges from its source, the soil, derives its nutrition from and through the soil, remains rooted in the soil and finally is reabsorbed by the soil. Fish emerge within the water and live therein. They draw their sustenance from and through the water and when they die, they become nourishment for the other creatures that live in it. The bodies of mammals emerge from and through their parents. The bodies of the parents are the source of the child through its fetal stage. During that stage the fetus is totally surrounded by and lives within the body of the mother. The body of the mother lives within its source, which is the earth. As far as the fetus is concerned, the mother is its immediate source whereas planet earth is its remote source.

The moment the fetus emerges from the body of the mother into its remote source, the earth, the mother nurtures it until it is able to live independent of the mother. Its true source, the earth or the Universe, surrounds the body of the infant from the time it leaves the mother's womb.

The severing of the umbilical cord is a reflection of the fact that the mother is not the ultimate source of the child. The mother is an intermediate source of the child and is merely a medium through which the child was delivered from the unseen (source) side of the Universe to the seen (resource) side. She can continue to nourish the child until such time as the child can fend for itself. But once the child is born, the natural mother is not indispensable. Wet nurses or other sources of nourishment can replace the mother. The physical Universe that is the Source of the body totally surrounds the body, sustains it and reabsorbs the body. In order to live, the creations have to be in continuous contact with their Source.

This can be seen all around us. In order to survive, plants must remain rooted in the soil, fish must remain in water and even when man goes into space, he must take with him life sustaining air, water and food from the earth. Space and heat (light) are present throughout the universe so man does not have to carry them with him in his space ships.

Based on the foregoing discussion, we can make the following observation:

"Before a creation comes into existence, the Source has already provided for its every need."

For instance, the atmosphere was already there waiting for the emerging child to draw its first breath. The soil already contains the nourishment for the seeds that may enter within it. The ocean already contains the sustenance for the life that emerges within it and the womb of a mammal has the resources to nourish the fertilized egg/fetus that attaches itself to the wall of the womb.

The Source of all sources has provided for our every need. The Source of all sources is Love and therefore all that emerges from it is also in essence Love. This is true even about those creations that oppose the Source. At their core is love. Those who love to hate, cannot do so without the Love that enables them to hate. From within Itself the Source creates, sustains and totally surrounds its creations with Its Infinite Love. However because our minds are filled with our own thoughts we are unable to experience the Infinite Love even though we are totally surrounded by it.

Our thoughts make up the barrier that separates us from the consciousness linked to the Spirit within us. It is only when the human mind is emptied of all its thoughts that a part of the Infinite Love descends into the human mind and the mind realizes an aspect of the Infinite Love to the extent of which it is capable. Once the human mind *experiences* the Light of Divine Love, it becomes enlightened. Fear cannot exist in a mind that is enlightened by Divine Love.

In order to receive this enlightenment, we have to open ourselves. To do so we have to open our minds: first to empty it, and then to receive. This is perhaps the basis for the statement attributed to the Lord Christ, namely, "Ask and ye shall receive." It is only when the creations align themselves with their Source, *i.e.,* are open to their Source and surrender to their Source, that they will realize and reflect their true nature, which is Love. This is true even about those creations that are at present the anti-Source including what is generally called Satan, the Devil, Ahriman, Shaitan, and Mara, *et cetera.*

Left to its own devices, the human mind seeks only to satisfy itself. In the name of love, the human mind seeks satisfaction. Instead of surrendering to its Source that is Love, the human mind seeks to use Love to satisfy itself.

It does not *grow* in Love. Instead it *falls* in Love. The human mind soils Love with its selfish point of view and Love is reduced to mere attachment.

However this very attachment can be used to *grow* in Love. By transferring the attachment from the thoughts, things and people to that by which one is attached to the Source, one can slowly but surely empty one's mind of the self and thus grow in Love. To grow in Love one has to surrender oneself to the

Source, and if not the Source then to begin with to one's Spiritual beloved, who is linked to the Source. In Love there is no self-satisfaction; only self-surrender and joy in service.

The very process of Creation begins with an act of surrender by the Source in the role of Creator. Since in the beginning, there are no creations, and only the Limitless, Formless, Source exists, only the Source can yield. The Source starts the process of creation by yielding some of Its Power to create. It is this power, which the Source willingly yields, that creates and sustains the creations. This yielding of power by the Source also starts the Process of Circulation. The creations have the freedom to use the Power in keeping with their own will. If they do that, however, it will be detrimental to their well-being and it will not help the Source. However if the creations choose to *surrender* the power they have received back to the Source then they will complete the Process of Circulation that will then sustain the cycle of creation, sustenance and recreation—thus will begin an upward spiral of Growth rather than a stagnant cycle of lifeless existence. The Creation will grow and the Source will also experience Itself through Its creation and grow.

The world would not be able to exist, let alone evolve, without the Principle of mutual surrender between the Source and the resource.

Throughout our daily lives in every field of activity we are constantly engaged in mutual surrender. We do have a choice as to whom or to what we surrender. We have a choice: do we surrender to our physical desires and exist in this physical world and then ultimately die within the Source, or do we choose to surrender to and become aligned with the Spiritual Source within us and around us and live and grow through It and with It even after we shed this physical body.

If we surrender to our physical desires over which we have no control, our lives are bound to be full of chaos and suffering. If we surrender to our Spiritual Source, then the Source will help us to slowly untangle our lives and enable us to grow to know our full potential. The process of disentangling our lives is also rife with suffering, but it is suffering that will liberate rather than further bind us.

But how do we surrender to our Source? Since the Source is within us and we are also totally surrounded by it, surrendering to the Source should be easy. But it is not. Why? What is it that makes it difficult? The Lord Gautama Buddha alluded to the problem centuries ago when He said words to the effect:

> Look at the fool. He runs to the mountain, he runs to the forest, he runs to the beaches, he runs to the temples. He does not realize that there is no escape. No matter where he goes, he has to take himself along.

Self-conscious human nature coupled with an insecure human mind is the problem. The result of this combination is described very nicely in one of the letters that the Apostle Paul wrote to the Galatians. The original has probably been paraphrased but it gets the message across.

THE SPIRIT AND HUMAN NATURE

As for you, my brothers, you were called to be free. But do not let this freedom become an excuse for letting your physical desires rule you. Instead, let love make you serve one another. For the whole Law is summed up in one commandment: 'Love the Lord thy God with all thy heart and all thy mind and all thy soul and love thy neighbor as thyself.' But if you act like animals, hurting and harming each other, then watch out, or you will completely destroy one another.

What I say is this: Let the Spirit direct your lives, and do not satisfy the desires of the human nature. For what our human nature wants is opposed to what the Spirit wants, and what the Spirit wants is opposed to what human nature wants. The two are enemies, and this means that you cannot do what you want to do. If the Spirit leads you, then you are not subject to the Law.

What human nature does is quite plain. It shows itself in immoral, filthy, and indecent actions; in worship of idols and witchcraft. People become enemies, they fight, become jealous, angry and ambitious. They separate into parties and groups; they are envious, get drunk, have orgies and do other things like these. I warn you now as I have before: Those who do these things will not receive the Kingdom of God.

But the Spirit produces love, joy, peace, patience, kindness, goodness, faithfulness, humility, and self-control. There is no law against such things as these. And those who belong to Christ Jesus have put to death their human nature, with all its passions and desires. The Spirit has given us life; he must also control our lives. We must not be proud, or irritate one another, or be jealous of one another.

Galatians 5.12-26

Life is not a playground where one plays and dies. Life is a battlefield in which one fights and survives. But who fights whom? Who dies and who survives?

As the Apostle Paul and others before him and since have tried to explain, your own small ego and individual human mind are the barriers that prevent you from experiencing your soul, your Real Self, which, according to various Scriptures of World religions, is a spark of the Divine. You have to do battle with your mind, ego and body and gain control over them. You have to achieve balance and totally empty your mind of all attachments to thoughts, things and people, all of which are temporary. Once this is accomplished, you will be able to surrender wholly to your Spiritual Source, which alone is permanent.

But how can a mind that is finite and incapable of comprehending the Infinite surrender to the Source of all Sources, which is Formless and yet is the Source of and contains all forms?

There are definite Principles that you have to study and live by in order to surrender to the Divine. There are seven such Principles, and these are discussed at length in the next chapter. Do read them with an open mind and with courage.

CHAPTER 6
SEVEN PRINCIPLES OF RIGHT SURRENDER

THE NEED TO SURRENDER

The need to surrender our human will to the Divine Will has been emphasized in one way or another by the High Beings through whom the religions of the world have been founded and who are considered by the followers of the various religions to be intermediaries between the relative or human plane of consciousness and the Absolute or Divine plane of consciousness. For instance, it is recorded that the Lord Christ said words to the effect, "I am the door and I am the way. Those who will come unto me will be saved." It is also stated in the Srimad Bhagavad Gîtâ that Sri Krishna said words to the effect, "Surrender the situation, surrender the action, surrender the result unto me and I will take care of the rest." The Buddha inspired His disciples to surrender to and seek refuge in the Buddha, the Dharma and the Sangha of the Buddha. And the very word *Islam* literally means "Complete and utter surrender to the Will of Allah."

However, many human beings are not aware of the need to surrender our will to the Divine, and of those who are aware, quite a few are not conscious that they do need to surrender on a daily basis; and of those who are conscious of the need to surrender daily, if not every moment, hardly anyone knows how to surrender the situation and one's will to the Divine. The complete step-by-step process of surrendering one's will to the Divine Will was not fully revealed in any scripture until the Divine Mind did so through Rev. Dr. Dinshah K. Mehta. Some of the individual principles have been revealed in past Scriptures, but all of them have not been codified as they have been through Dr. Mehta and as presented in this chapter.

This chapter tries to explain how to surrender your human mind and will to the Divine Mind and Will. The chapter also discusses in fair detail each of the steps involved and explains the basis for each of them.

Like most exercises, in order for self-surrender to be effective, it must be done in the right way. That is why the words "Right Surrender" are used when discussing the Spiritual Principles that will enable you to surrender your will to the Divine Will.

There are seven Principles of Right Surrender.

These Seven Principles of Right Surrender are a gift from God to humanity and have been delivered by God through Rev. Dr. Dinshah Kaikhushroo Mehta from the Higher planes of Consciousness from which scriptures of all the world religions have descended. As mentioned earlier, Revered Dr. Mehta is the Founder Chairman of the Society of Servants of God, and has over the past decades given many discourses explaining, among other things, the basis of the Seven Principles of Right Surrender as well as how God Himself came into Being.

SURRENDER IS NOT SUBMISSION

The question may arise: Why surrender at all? The word "surrender" seems to imply a sense of weakness. This implication of weakness does not appeal to some of us who think of ourselves as strong-willed, independent individuals who can influence, if not control, our own destiny. Similarly people in the armed forces, and civilians with a militant attitude, find the word "surrender" distasteful. The author also did not initially like the word "surrender" because of the usual connotation associated with it. Conquering heroes do not surrender; only losers surrender. And who wants to be a loser?

Rev. Dr. Mehta explains that in the Spiritual context, surrender does not indicate weakness. Rather it is the *inability* to surrender that is a result of weakness and ignorance. Spiritual surrender requires disciplined self-restraint and is an act of wisdom and strength associated with love. In the usual way of life, when there is a clash of wills, the weaker submits to the stronger. One submits to the oppressor against one's will. But the Good Lord never oppresses: if He did, how could He be called "Good"? Even though His Will is omnipotent, if we have the slightest resistance to what He Wills, He lets us go our own way, until such time as our will clashes with the manifestations of His Will and threatens to upset the balance in creation. Only then does He assert, and that too, only in the interest of the greater good. But we can voluntarily surrender to the Lord long before things come to such a drastic pass. In a Spiritual context, one surrenders to one's Spiritual Beloved voluntarily and with joy, realizing that it is mutually beneficial to do so. This is reflected in earthly relationships in which lovers voluntarily surrender to each other's will and gladly endure hardships to satisfy the will of the beloved.

UNIVERSALITY OF THE PRINCIPLE OF SURRENDER

The Principle of Surrender is universal. You can only live and grow through surrender. As explained in the chapter entitled *The Journey*, the process of life and creation itself would not be possible without the Principle of Surrender.

An analogy from the physical world may help to refresh the reader's memory. Even though an analogy may not be perfect in every respect, all the same it may give an idea of how important the principle of surrender is for all life.

Let us take the situation of a newborn child. When a child is born it immediately gasps for breath. As soon as it gasps for breath, the atmosphere—which is the source of all air on earth—surrenders itself to the child's gasp, and fills the child's lungs with itself. After the atmosphere surrenders to the child's gasp for air, the child then surrenders the air back to the atmosphere. Because of this mutual surrender of air between the child and the atmosphere, the cycle of breath is completed, and the child begins to live. Without this mutual surrender of breath between the atmosphere and the child, life for the newborn infant could not even begin; and life continues only so long as this mutual surrender continues. Life begins when the atmosphere, the source of air, first surrenders to the child; and life ends when the child or adult—which are the creations—surrenders the last breath back to the atmosphere: or more correctly can no longer continue the process of mutual surrender because the link between the life form and the spirit associated with it ended. Thus life for the created begins with the Principle of surrender, with the source surrendering first to the demands made by it; life is sustained by continuous mutual surrender between the source and its creations; and life ends when the mutual surrender ends. All life thus gets started with and is sustained by the principle of circulation which is effectuated by mutual surrender.

THE FIVE GREAT ELEMENTALS OF NATURE

The Hindu Scriptures explain that life on earth depends upon the five main elementals known as the *panch mahá bhootas* or Five Great Elementals. These are the earth, water, air, heat and space or âkâsh (or what may be referred to in modern terminology as the all-pervading ether, and is often erroneously called the "space-time continuum"—erroneously because if time and space are combined into one, there can be no such thing as movement. Without movement there can be no change. By definition movement means a change in the location of something over a period of time; and there can, of course, be no experience without movement and change). The Principle of surrender also manifests itself in our relationship with these other elementals. We receive food from the earth, and after it passes through our bodies, whatever remains is surrendered back to the earth. The same thing happens with water, heat and space. And just as we are not consciously aware of the blood that flows through our vascular system—although we know that it does—similarly we are not consciously aware of the mutual surrender that occurs between our bodies and space, even though it is occurring all the while.

Biological creations have to surrender to the source of their biological bodies, which are the five elementals as explained above. This Principle of surrender is universal and cuts through all national, geographical and religious boundaries. All human beings, if they want to live, regardless of the circumstances of their birth be they paupers, millionaires, ministers or kings, or whether they believe in God or not, must engage in mutual surrender or exchange—if you prefer the word exchange to the term surrender—with the earth, water, air, heat and space. Life for all biological creations ends when the mutual surrender ends with respect to any one of the five elementals. Thus we can suffocate to death due to lack of air; die of thirst or dehydration; die of hunger and cold; and our bodies would collapse into a solid point having no dimensions were it not for the space between the various cells and organs of the body. Indeed our bodies need space even after we are dead.

One can see that this Principle of surrender is universal in its manifestation. Yet how many of us are cognizant of this universal Principle of surrender?

NATURE OF SURRENDER

In the discussion thus far we have observed five things about the Principle of surrender:

1. Willful surrender to one's Source is not a sign of weakness, nor is it submission. Love gives us the wisdom, strength and discipline needed to consciously surrender to and cooperate with our Source.

2. Surrendering is a natural process—as natural as breathing—and our physical life depends upon surrendering to the natural source of our bodies.

3. The material Source that sustains our bodies is both outside and inside us. We are totally surrounded by the atmosphere, and it also fills our lungs. Likewise the earth, water, sun and space are all around and within us.

4. The Source of any creation surrenders first to its creations. Thus the atmosphere surrenders first to the gasp of the child. The mother feeds the first milk to the child, *et cetera*.

The Source does not stop surrendering to its creations. Life ends when, for any reason, an individual life form can no longer continue to surrender to Its Source and the cycle of circulation is broken thus preventing the transfer of life-sustaining materials from the Source to the life form and so it dies.

These points are being repeated because it is so very important to grasp and be conscious of this phenomenon of the Source surrendering a portion of it to begin life for Its creations, and the need for mutual surrender between the creation and Its source to sustain life. We should never forget that physical life begins when the Source surrenders the first breath of air to the child; life is sustained by continuous mutual surrender between the atmosphere, which is the source, and the child; and life ends when the mutual surrender ends, only because the life form—and not the source—can no longer continue the process of surrendering. Even a dead creature's lungs and stomach are filled with air.

Just as the physical body needs to enter into a relationship of mutual surrender with the Five Elementals, which is its source so that it may live, similarly we need to enter into a relationship of mutual surrender with our Spiritual Source so that we may take a Spiritual birth and actuate our Spiritual lives.

It is necessary to point out at this juncture that we have given physical examples to illustrate the principle of surrender in manifestation. However, some readers may get the idea that what is physically true is also true Spiritually. The author wishes to emphasize that is not the case always. As it is said in the Bible: "God made man in His Image;" God did not make Himself in man's image. Whatever is true Spiritually is reflected in the material, but the reverse is not necessarily true. The Principle of surrender is Spiritual, and is reflected throughout not only the physical creation but also all of creation, physical or otherwise.

TO WHOM AND THROUGH WHOM SHOULD ONE SURRENDER?

Most of us surrender to our desires and the source of our desires, namely the human mind and ego. This only leads to further desires with all their accompanying problems.

Just as you had to be physically conceived to take a physical birth, and then surrender to your physical source in order to live physically, similarly you have to be conceived spiritually in order to take a Spiritual birth, and then surrender to your Spiritual Source in order to live spiritually.

But how to be conceived spiritually, and where is your Spiritual Source?

Just as the five elementals, which are the source of the physical body, are all around and within the body, similarly your Spiritual Source is all around and within you. Also, just as you need a medium or an intermediary, your parents, to be conceived physically and through whom you took a physical birth, similarly you need a medium or an intermediary to be conceived spiritually and take a Spiritual birth.

That medium or intermediary through whom you can be conceived Spiritually and take a Spiritual birth is none other than a High Spiritual Master such as Buddha, Ram, Krishna, Christ, Zarathushtra, Mohammed, the Jain Tîrthankars, the Prophets of Israel, the Gurus of the Sikhs, The Bab or Baha'ullah of the Baha'i faith—all of whom have taken birth on earth—or they can be High Beings who have never descended in human form but have been given human and other forms in various religions.

These Divine Beings are known in the Hindu religion as Brahmâ, Vishnu and Mahesh, also called Shiva.

They form the Triad or Holy Trinity, and are mentioned in all religions by different names.

Revered Dr. Mehta has taught that in the Old Testament, the members of the Triad are called by the names Rapha'el, Gabri'el and Micha'el, and in the New Testament, they have been given the names The Father, The Son and The Holy Ghost. Zarathushtra called them Asha, Vohu-Mana and Kshathra Vairya. Other religions have given them other names, but virtually all religions acknowledge the Holy Triad or Trinity. Even those religions, which do not acknowledge the Holy Triad in their exoteric or orthodox teachings, do so in their esoteric teachings.

You may surrender to the Spiritual Masters who have taken birth on earth, or members of the Holy Triad whom the Hindus have named, Brahmâ, Vishnu and Shiva, or their shaktis (feminine counterparts or wills), namely Saraswati, Lakshmi and Pârvati. As Revered Dr. Mehta has taught, all six are represented in the Shield of David (which is sometimes erroneously called the "Star of David").

Ultimately one surrenders only to God who is accepted as the Source of all creation. However since most of us cannot even conceive of God let alone know God in His Limitless, Formless State, we need to surrender through some High Beings who have a form that we can recognize and identify with. Hence the need to surrender to and through one of the High Beings and their forms mentioned above.

However, some people may argue these forms are not God. And they are right!

SOME CHARACTERISTICS OF THE HUMAN MIND

In order to grow to know the Divine, we have no choice but to work with and grow through the conscious human mind because that is the medium through which we communicate with the universe. Therefore, it will help us if we are familiar with some of the characteristics and tendencies of the human mind.

Just as water from all sources has certain common characteristics, all human minds share certain common characteristics. We can agree that water, whether it is from a spring, well, pond, river, lake or sea and whether it is fresh water or salt water, and whether it is dirty or clean, all water is wet and will wet us. Similarly we know that we need water to drink, cook, clean, *et cetera*. Water helps us live but it can also kill us. Try as we might, we cannot change the characteristics of water. For instance we cannot make water dry. It remains wet because that is its basic characteristic. But once we understand its characteristics, we can learn how to work with it, and use it to our advantage. It is also the case with the human mind. The human mind has certain characteristics.

Once we understand what those are, we are in a better position to use it and work with it. Kindly observe your own mind and see whether it has at least some if not all of the characteristics mentioned below.

1. It should be clear that the human mind is limited.

Being limited, the human mind is incapable of comprehending Absolute States of Being. It can only understand relative states of being. For instance it cannot comprehend a condition of being nowhere and everywhere. Nowhere and everywhere are absolute conditions. The human mind can understand the condition of being somewhere because somewhere is a relative position between the absolute states of nowhere and everywhere. Somewhere being a relative condition has a form in the limitless states of nowhere and everywhere. Indeed when we are told something has no value, we give it the symbol of zero or 0 to indicate that it is nothing. Now we all know that 0 has a form. It is not formless nothing.

(Hopefully the author is expressing himself clearly enough for the reader to comprehend.)

The human mind cannot visualize the condition of formlessness because the very words "vision," "concept" and "idea" conjure up thought forms. Only that which is Limitless can be Formless and contain all forms. Thus all of Creation lives and moves within the Pristine, Infinite, Limitless and Formless Source of all Sources. The formless material space within which all material forms exist is a reflection of this.

2. In the chapter entitled *Value of Opinions* we have explained how, during the process of birth, the cognitive human mind acquires a nucleus of fear. After birth, the human mind develops its own self-identity by creating an ego. The human mind creates the ego based on associations with everything out-side itself. Thus the basic fear of the mind is exacerbated, be-cause the ego that it has created is not rooted in self-knowledge. This fear causes the human mind to seek to escape. Over millen-nia, it has developed a tendency to escape the situation it faces in the present by jumping from thought to thought. Generally the human mind jumps between the past and the future. It tries to escape the present by living either in the past, which is dead and thus cannot hurt it, or the future, which has not yet arrived, and thus cannot hurt it either.

If you will observe your own mind, you will notice that it is in a state of constant agitation. This state of constant turmoil has made the human mind unstable. The constant agitation has de-veloped its own inertia. As a result, the natural condition of the human mind is to remain unstable and reactive. This instability deepens the mind's sense of basic confusion and adds to the feel-ing of insecurity.

This sense of insecurity further stabilizes the nucleus of fear that is formed during the process of birth. Thus fear has become the basis of the subconscious human mind. The sub-conscious human mind strongly influences the conscious human mind and very often is responsible for our unwilling reactions to situations over which we have no control: reactions that we cannot explain and frequently regret. This basic fearful tendency of the human mind has now become inherent and instinctive, and is passed on from generation to generation through the genes of the parents and fore-parents.

This further strengthens the basis of fear and increases our propensity to be motivated by it.

3. Further, because of its nucleus of fear the human mind seeks to satisfy itself to gain a sense of peace, achievement and purpose. To satisfy itself the human mind creates and lives in states of illusion, which it forms with the help of opinions, which have no real basis other than the point of view held at the time, which in turn is influenced by the prevailing attitude, circum-stances of birth and past experiences. However, as each of us has experienced, the human mind cannot be permanently satisfied, and sooner or later it becomes disillusioned. We have all experi-enced states of satisfaction that are then followed by states of dissatisfaction. After repeated cycles of satisfaction and dissatisfaction, pleasure followed by pain, the human mind experiences a condition of frustration if not despair. But rather than tackle the fundamental problem, most people will continue to try to seek fresh states of satisfaction by creating new illusions.

4. The human mind cannot remain unattached. Because of its inherent fear and instability, the human mind has developed a tendency to grasp. In an attempt to stabilize itself and gain a sense of security, the human mind grasps at thoughts, things and people and attaches itself to them much like a frightened child will cling to its mother. It in effect seeks to be part of a group and join a club. Because the basis of the human mind is fear, it has been maintained by some psychologists that fear of loss is a greater motivator than the opportunity for gain.

5. Because the human mind is generally in a state of agitation, it is out of control and tends to react to the situation it experiences. This reaction increases its turmoil and adds to its instability.

6. The limited human mind cannot understand the Limitless; it cannot comprehend the Unity in the Diversity of Manifestation. In an attempt to understand the Limitless Universe, the human mind needs to separate the Infinite Unity of manifestation into smaller parts that are within its ability to comprehend. Thus to overcome its own insecurity and limitations, the human mind has no choice other than to divide the Unity in manifestation. Instead of surrendering to the Unity in the Diversity of manifestation, the human mind divides the Infinite Unity into many parts in its futile attempt to understand the Limitless Infinite Whole. In order to have a sense of security and control, this need to comprehend the infinite Unity by dividing it reinforces the need the human mind has to cling to its separate identity. Rather than viewing the perception of separation as part of the problem, it sees it as necessary for its survival and therefore views it as part of the solution. It therefore resists discipline and domination.

Do you find that your mind shares some of the above characteristics? If yes, continue to read. If not, you might as well discard the book.

These characteristics of the finite conscious human mind—its basic insecurity, and its tendency to grasp at thoughts, things and people in order to gain a sense of security and satisfy itself—is what binds the mind and therefore the person to the objects which it desires, *i.e.,* the thoughts, things and persons all of which are made up of matter. Thus the person becomes matter-bound, and is tied to cycles of pleasure followed by pain, ecstasy followed by despair: cycles which the human mind itself creates by its attachments to illusions which also it creates in order to satisfy its craving for security which it hopes to gain through satisfaction. These cycles eventually lead to frustration and agony, which is repeated throughout an individual's life and binds it to cycles of birth, life and death. Through many incarnations over eons of time, the suffering soul finally cries out in anguish for mercy and begins its long journey inward towards its Source commonly called God. This journey of the soul seeking to satisfy its desires by going away from its Father in Heaven and then falling into despair and returning back to the Father's Kingdom is reflected in the Biblical parable of the prodigal son.

How does one become free from this matter-bound state and cycles of birth, life and death?

We have no choice but to work with and utilize the very tendencies and limitations of the mind to help it grow through them. The Seven Principles of Right Surrender have taken into consideration the characteristics of the human mind, and have utilized these very characteristics to first steady the mind, then unify it, and purify it and ultimately to empty it. The human mind has to be emptied of all the material thoughts and attachments before it can receive the Divine. Indeed, as mentioned earlier, Revered Dr. Mehta has often quoted the Lord Christ as saying words to the effect: "The empty alone shall be filled."

With this introduction to the characteristics of the human mind, we can now begin to expound and explain the Seven Principles of Right Surrender.

FIRST PRINCIPLE: THE ENTITY

The very first principle of right surrender says: "Select one and only one Entity to whom and through whom one wishes to surrender to the Divine." As explained above, the Spiritual Entity can be any one of the Descending Masters through whom the world religions have been founded, or those who are considered in the various religions to be intermediaries between the relative or human plane of consciousness and the Absolute or Divine plane of consciousness. These can be Zarathushtra; the Prophets of Israel; Jesus the Christ; Hazrat Muhammad; Bhagwân Buddha; the Avatâras of Hinduism; the Gurus of the Sikhs; the Tîrthankars of Jainism; the founders of the Baha'i religion, the Bab or Baha'ullah; or the Vedic Divine Beings Brahmâ, Vishnu or Shiva, or their female counterparts or shaktis: Saraswati, Lakshmi and Pârvati.

Here, selecting one and only one Entity is very essential. The question arises, "Why only one? If all these great High Beings can help one grow, why not solicit help from all of them by surrendering to all of them?" Also, some people who claim to have an open mind and practice religious tolerance assert that they respect all the High Beings equally, and feel that if they select only one Entity it will be a sign of religious intolerance if not bigotry on their part, and lack of respect for the High Beings.

To clarify the need to select only one Entity we can again give a few analogies from everyday, so-called practical life. For instance, although there are millions of women in this world most of whom are capable of conceiving and giving birth to a child, no child can be conceived by or be born through more than one woman simultaneously. Similarly, even if a room has more than one door, from a practical point of view you can enter or leave the room through only one door at a time. And likewise, even if many roads could lead you to a destination, you cannot travel on more than one road at the same time, or sit in more than one vehicle at the same time, *et cetera*.

You can grow unto the Divine through only one Entity.

This does not mean that you should not respect the other Masters. By all means respect them, their teachings and those who follow them; but surrender to and through only one Master or Entity. Therefore select one and only one Entity.

There are five aspects to the First Principle. The first aspect says: "Select one and only one Entity to Whom and through Whom to surrender all that you have and all that you are, body, mind and soul."

The second aspect says: "Give the Entity a form."

Now some people in certain cultures have a real problem with this aspect of the First Principle. This is particularly true of our Jewish and Muslim brothers and sisters. Why? Because in one of the Ten Commandments received by Moses and accepted as sacred by both religions it is recorded that God said words to the effect, "Thou shalt make no engraving of me nor depict me in any other image or form."

Fair enough. This is a genuine concern. However what we wish to point out to people who have this concern is, that this aspect of the First Principle is not suggesting that you make an image of God. This aspect of the First Principle requires that you should give a form to the *Entity*, who is not necessarily God but rather, a Servant of God; an *intermediary* between man and God. The Entity is the door and the way through whom you wish to grow towards God. Please be very clear about this. The Entity is *not* necessarily God.

The word "necessarily" is used here deliberately. It is reported that the Lord Christ has said words to the effect, "He who has seen me has seen My Father, but My Father is greater than I." Similarly, the Hindus believe that the Master in human form is God on earth. The Lord Christ did not say that He is the Father, and the Hindus do not say that the Master is God in His Limitless State.

In the chapter entitled *Value of Opinions* it has been pointed out "Only the Limitless can be Formless." From His Limitless State an aspect of God can descend into any form. These forms are represented by the Spiritual Masters such as Zarathushtra, Râm, Moses, Krishna, Jesus Christ, Buddha, Rasul Mohammed, Guru Nanak and others.

Obviously *all* of God's Limitless Being cannot descend into a single human being. But because the consciousness of these great Masters is linked to and is merged with the Divine, it can be said that the Master is God in human form *to the extent* the Limitless, Formless God can descend into and be contained in a form whose consciousness/mind is linked to the Consciousness and Mind of God.

An example may help clarify the point. It might legitimately be claimed that whoever has seen my finger has seen me, because my finger and I are one. Nevertheless I am greater than my finger.

Another question arises: Why give the Entity any form at all? We need to give the Entity a form because as mentioned earlier, the human mind cannot conceptualize a condition of being formless. All human thoughts have a form.

Here, in order to avoid misunderstanding, we should point out that we are using the words "form" and "formless," in the sense of being equivalent to *any* thought or concept. *Anything* that can be conceptualized has a form, because in this sense anything that has a limit has a form. We use the word "form" in this way because in the present case, we are trying to speak of the Absolute—which cannot be conceptualized, since it is limitless and therefore formless—in opposition to the relative, which is limited and therefore has a form and can be conceptualized.

Indeed, if one uses the word "form" in this sense, it is clear that the human mind cannot *avoid* giving the Entity a form. If the human mind thinks even about God, it will perforce conjure up a form for Him, because when we discussed some of the characteristics of the human mind, we concluded that the limited human mind cannot truly conceptualize a Limitless or a Formless state.

Therefore in order to grow unto the Absolute, the human mind needs to start by focusing on a finite form, which appeals to it and with which it can identify. The human mind can surrender through this finite form to grow to know the Infinite Formless, which is both Nowhere and Everywhere. Hence the need to give the Entity a form.

For the benefit of the readers, some of the popularly accepted forms of various religions that can be used to give a form to one's chosen Entity are printed beginning on Page 253 of this book. Readers are encouraged to select and accept a form of their liking for a Master of their choosing.

The third aspect of the First Principle says: "Let the form be fixed and not changing."

Here again those with a questioning attitude may ask why does the form need to be *fixed*. The fixed form makes it easier for the wandering human mind to focus. It is easier to focus on the same form repeatedly rather than focus on a new form each time. Further because of the nature and characteristics of thought forms, there are other benefits also.

The fourth aspect of the First Principle says: "Study the teachings of the Entity but let only one teacher interpret the teachings of the Entity." Indeed, as Revered Dr. Mehta once told the author, the teacher can be either a person or books written by the person. However if no teacher can he found then let your conscience interpret the teachings of the Entity. But not your *static* conscience. You must use your *growing* conscience to interpret the teachings of the Entity.

This bit about the conscience needs some explaining.

In religious class some of us are taught that one's conscience is the voice of one's soul if not the voice of a Guardian Angel or even God Himself. This is not true. At best one's conscience is the voice of one's experience, and therefore is not constant. One's conscience goes on changing with one's consciousness. Why? Because conscience is subservient to consciousness. The higher an individual's consciousness, the finer will be his/her conscience. The conscience of a saint will not permit him to do what the conscience of a sinner will allow.

Conscience is linked to the level of consciousness. The conscience of an individual can change if the consciousness of the individual is altered.

When the individual is calm and alert the conscience will function at one level. But, if the same individual is disturbed, or under the influence of alcohol or other consciousness-altering drugs, the person's conscience will sink with the consciousness. When a person is drunk he may do things that his conscience may prevent him from doing when he is not under the influence.

If you choose to use your conscience to interpret the teachings of the Entity, you should use your *growing* conscience. As your consciousness grows, you may develop new insights into the teachings of the Entity, and you should follow the latest insights of which you become aware.

The fifth aspect of the First Principle says: "Raise the level of your consciousness to as high a level as you can, so that you are more alert than normal and your mind is nearer the super-wakeful level."

Normally most of us are not wakeful at all. We appear to be awake, but we tend to daydream. In order to achieve surrender we have to be what is called super-wakeful.

Now, how to become super-wakeful? To begin with you have to will yourself to do so, and at the same time transfer one's attachment from sleep to becoming super-wakeful, and gradually over a period of time you will become more alert and aware.

But how can you will yourself to become super-wakeful? Just imagine what would happen if, all of a sudden, a snake or another intruder were to enter the room you are in. You would immediately become alert and watchful and watch every move of the snake or intruding tiger. Of course some people may run if they see the snake. Thus, it is something like that.

A word of advice is in order here. Imagination is more powerful than will power. If you imagine that you are feeling sleepy, and then try to will yourself to become awake, that will not work, because your imagination will weaken, if not overpower, your will.

Instead you should imagine yourself to be awake, and also will yourself to be so. This way your will and imagination will support each other to make you wakeful. This is one reason why you should transfer your attachment from sleepiness to wakefulness. This in itself will go a long way towards making you super-wakeful.

At this stage, after you have followed all the aspects of the First Principle and have become super-wakeful, *do nothing*. Just remain at the super wakeful level and watch your thoughts come and go.

This is important to understand. Your mind is full of thoughts and they are constantly agitating the mind, and these thoughts have to be emptied from the mind. Why? Because they prevent you from hearing and experiencing your soul. Therefore, continue to remain in the super-wakeful state and watch your thoughts. Don't get involved with the thoughts that arise in your mind. Also don't push away any thought no matter how painful or vile it may be. Nor should you try to recall a particular thought or hold on to a pleasant thought. If a thought enters your mind, let it come. If it remains in the mind, watch it without getting involved. If it wishes to leave, let it go.

For some people it is simple to watch their thoughts; but for most it is very difficult to do so without getting *involved* with the thoughts that arise in the mind. Watching your thoughts is similar to watching people come and go at a street corner, in an airport, train station, bus depot or supermarket. You do not stop the people passing by on the street corner, airport or supermarket, nor do you get *involved* with them or attached to them. You just *watch* them. Similarly you should just watch your thoughts at the super-wakeful level.

Now why is it important to watch your thoughts? What happens to the thoughts when you watch them? When you watch your thoughts, you are really watching some of the movements within yourself and are beginning to take charge of your life. The Buddhist sacred text *Dhammapâda* in its very first verse expresses an idea to the following effect: "All things originate in the mind, are sustained by the mind and are created by the mind." When you watch your thoughts you are really watching and focusing on the source of all your words and actions; indeed it is the source of all the things you are and do. The teachings of Zarathushtra have also been crystallized on the three pillars of "Good Thoughts, Good Words and Good Deeds." But Good from the Divine point of view and not the relevant human point of view. The first thing that happens when you watch your thoughts is that you are literally taking hold of yourself.

When you watch your thoughts, they begin to become weak and they break up and disappear. Why? This happens due to the nature of mind and thought.

Thoughts that rise to your conscious mind are like bubbles of air that rise to the surface from the bottom of a pond. When the bubbles at the surface are exposed to the intensity of the rays of the Sun, they burst and thus lose their form. Similarly when you focus the intensity of your mind on your thoughts they become weak, dissipate and no longer disturb the mind. By merely watching your thoughts over a period of time, your mind will become unified, purified and ultimately empty.

This First Principle of Right Surrender is very important. If you practice just this one Principle every day it will calm you down quite a bit and take you a long way on the Spiritual Path.

SECOND PRINCIPLE: HUMILITY

The second principle says that we should develop *humility*. Why? You need humility to receive. Like water, everything else flows from the top down. A great Chinese Sage used to counsel his disciples along the following lines:

> Look at the ocean, the rivers, the streams and the springs. Which of these is the largest and which is the smallest? The spring having the highest abode remains the smallest. It is only when it descends down that it combines

with and receives water from other springs and becomes a stream.

The streams empty into the rivers, which are lower still. The mighty ocean places itself in the lowest position and thus compels the springs, streams and rivers to empty everything they are capable of carrying into it. Thus to receive the wisdom of the world, you should strive to be humble like the mighty ocean.

Humility is very important. You may wonder, "Is God Humble?" "Are the Great Masters Humble?" We have already discussed that the Source of any creation surrenders first to the creation. Thus we pointed out that the atmosphere surrenders itself to the first gasp of the newborn child. The mother, representing the earth, surrenders herself and the nourishment her body provides to the child.

Surrender is an act of strength born of love, humility and service. Unless the source Surrenders first, creation cannot even begin, let alone exist.

Thus, only the strong have self-control, humility and love to give of themselves and joyfully *surrender* with love, to love and for love. The weak *submit* with resentment.

Further it is important to remember that the Source has prepared for every need of its creation. The earth does not rush to manufacture air for a newborn child after it gasps for its first breath. The atmosphere is awaiting the child's gasp. Similarly the earth or soil has prepared for all the needs of the seed before the seed enters and surrenders to it. Just as the air for the child's first gasp exists before the child is born, similarly the soil is ready to receive and nurture the seed in the anticipation that it will surrender. The Surrender, Love and Humility of the Source are so complete that it anticipates and provides for every need of the creations. A mother who anticipates every need of the child and prepares for it is but a reflection of the Source. In order to receive the sustenance from the Source, the creations only need to surrender to the Source.

God has prepared for every need of ours and has already surrendered His Omnipotent Will to our limited human will, and sustains it. But just as the atmosphere cannot help the child unless it gasps for its first breath of air, and the soil cannot nurture the seed unless it first surrenders itself to the soil, so also the Lord of all creation cannot help us further until we surrender our puny will to His Omnipotent Will. That is why the Lord Christ said words to the effect, "Ask and you shall receive. Seek and you shall find. Knock and the door will be opened unto you."

Now although it is difficult for people to understand this, try and imagine from this the Humility and Love of God. However humble we may try to be with our limited human mind, we can never equal the Limitless Humility of God, and of the Great Masters who are revered in many religions as intermediaries between our human or relative plane of consciousness and the Absolute plane of consciousness called the Mind of God. Therefore, try to develop as much humility as possible.

As the author has discovered independently, in order to succeed in any field of endeavor you must practice three very important principles. These three principles are like the three legs of a three-legged stool. A three-legged stool cannot stand on two legs. It needs all three otherwise it will fall.

Similarly to succeed in any field of endeavor you need the following three principles.

- The first of these principles is Humility. You need humility to receive.
- The second principle is Discipline. You need discipline to achieve.
- The third principle is Commitment. You need commitment to fulfill.

It is the author's conviction that unless one implements all three principles one cannot succeed. And although all the three principles are important, of the three, humility is most important. Without humility one cannot receive anything. The qualities of commitment and discipline will grow out of humility.

The next in importance is commitment. If you lack the discipline or knowledge to do anything, but have the quality of commitment, then you can develop the necessary discipline. The great American scientist Thomas Alva Edison is reported to have said, "Genius is 99 percent perspiration and one percent inspiration." If you have the necessary humility and commitment then you may fail repeatedly but you will refuse to give up until ultimately you develop the necessary discipline to succeed. When Edison was working to develop the incandescent light bulb, it is reported that he tried and rejected about 1,500 filaments before he found the right one. When he rejected what was about the 1,489th filament, one of his assistants suggested that he give up because he had tried 1,489 filaments and failed.

Edison continued working and told his assistant words to the effect that it only means there were 1,489 less filaments to worry about. Such was the quality of commitment, and tenacity of this great American genius.

The quality of commitment is very necessary—more so than discipline. If you have the discipline but lack the necessary commitment, you may unnecessarily give up too soon, and will not be able to overcome the obstacles that are bound to arise. The world is full of disciplined people who have failed due to lack of commitment. On the other hand there are many instances in which deeply committed people have succeeded against overwhelming odds.

To succeed in the Spiritual way of life the attitude should not be to do *or* die, but the commitment should be nearer to do *and* die. What must die and needs to be killed is not your physical body but your small ego self. Your small mind with its limited point of view and ego consciousness linked to it. After humility the quality of commitment is most necessary. With humility and commitment, discipline is bound to follow.

Thus the Second principle of Right Surrender is to develop humility.

Some people dislike the term "humility," imagining that in order to be humble, they have to lower themselves in their own or others' eyes. This is most emphatically *not* so. Humility, in this context, is *recognition of the greatness and majesty of God*, and that of one's Entity—the Door and the Way unto God.

Any sensitive person feels humble when becoming conscious of something very great: say, when standing at the foot or base of a very tall mountain, or before a great work of art, or when contemplating the size and grandeur of the entire cosmos. Just imagine, in comparison, how much greater and more majestic God is—God Who is the Source of all things in the cosmos, and indeed of the cosmos itself. When one contemplates, even to a tiny extent, the greatness and majesty of the Lord of all creation, true humility results naturally.

THIRD PRINCIPLE: ATTACHMENT

The Third Principle of Right Surrender has to do with *attachment*. The Principle says, "Transfer all your attachment from the thoughts, things and persons to which you are attached gradually, in increasing proportion to your Entity, until eventually all your attachment is transferred to your Entity and through your Entity to the Divine."

It will help if you can understand how this principle of attachment works.

For this you have to consider the nature of the human mind and use its inherent characteristics and tendencies to control it and make it work for you rather than become enslaved by it.

You will recall from our discussion of some of the characteristics of the human mind that the human mind is insecure and is in a constant state of agitation. Just as a little child clings to its mother to get a sense of security the human mind has developed a natural tendency to grasp at thoughts, things, people and situations which it likes in an attempt to become stable and feel secure.

Nothing wrong with this. This is a natural tendency of the mind and we have to recognize and accept it. This very tendency of the mind to grasp at thoughts and objects, and of getting attached to them, can be used to liberate the mind, provided we follow the Right Spiritual Principles.

Without following the Right Spiritual Principles, this grasping tendency of the mind will bind it to the material world. Why?

Attachment by definition binds the mind to the objects to which it is attached, which almost always are material thoughts, things and persons. Herein lays the cause of karma and the bondage to cycles of birth, life and death and the concurrent suffering within the rounds and between the rounds. It is said that when Bhagwân Buddha achieved Nirvâna He said words to the following effect:

"How many births have I known without knowing thee, O builder of this body? How many births have I looked for thee? It is painful to be born again and again. But now I have seen thee, O builder of this body. The raf-

135

ters have crumbled. The ridgepole has been smashed. Thou
wilt not build them again.
   All desire is extinct. Nirvâna has been attained."

It took the author about 45 years to finally understand what
Bhagwân Buddha said in the above verse. Who is the "builder of
the body," and how does it build the body? In the final analysis,
the builder of the body is none other than the human mind.
   And it builds the body through this principle of *attachment.*
By getting attached to matter in various forms that are invariably
thoughts, things, people and situations, the mind remains bound
to them and causes the soul, the Divine Spark within each of us,
to be born again and again to experience the objects of its attachments and learn the lessons it needs to from the relationships
forged through the attachments, until finally it recognizes the
reality that attachment to these objects is the cause of its suffering and rebirth. It then strives to become free from attachment to
all material objects, and thus become free from matter-bound
states and the cycles of birth, life and death.
   That is why many well-meaning Spiritual teachers call to our
attention the fact that one should *detach* oneself from everyone
and everything with whom one comes in contact. But that is not
possible *by itself.* Spiritual teachers who preach detachment have
not taken into consideration the nature of the human mind. Revered Dr. Mehta explained that because of the natural tendency
of the human mind to grasp and to get attached, it is not possible
for the human mind to detach itself from one object without getting attached to some *other* object. The mind continuously
grasps for something, just as the lungs continuously gasp for air.
How does one liberate the mind that wants to remain attached?
   This is where the Third Principle of Attachment helps us. It
allows us to use this very grasping tendency of the mind to liberate it from the matter-bound states. This can be achieved by
transferring your attachment from the material thoughts, things
and persons to which your mind clings, to the very instrument of
Spiritual liberation, *i.e.*, the Spiritual Beloved or Entity you have
chosen to surrender to and grow through to know your soul, and
through your soul to ultimately know the Divine.
   It is like climbing the rungs of a ladder. You can only do so
by letting go of the rung you are on and grasping the next rung

up the ladder. The same is true when you are descending the ladder. But you cannot climb the ladder if you are not attached to it. You can only climb the ladder if you *are* attached to it but continuously transfer your attachment to higher rungs of the ladder. This Principle of attachment is most important for Spiritual Growth.

You should start gradually by transferring the attachment to your Spiritual Beloved in increasing proportion. By doing this, gradually you create an opening for your Spiritual Beloved to enter your life, and the more rapidly and readily you surrender to your Spiritual Entity, the more readily He can enter your life and help you grow towards the goal of Spiritual liberation and achieve the sense of stability and feeling of security you seek.

As long as you remain attached to material thoughts, things and persons, you can never achieve the stability and security you yearn for. Why? Because the mind, which is itself unstable and full of turmoil, can never achieve stability and security by attaching itself to another object that is *also* unstable and temporary. It is only when the mind is anchored to an object, which is permanent, stable and secure, that it can achieve a sense of stability and security.

Such an object is one of the Spiritual Masters/Entities mentioned above whose consciousness is one with the Divine.

Because the consciousness of the Master is linked to the Divine, the form of the Master/Entity represents the Form of the Divine in matter.

Revered Dr. Mehta explains that attachment is a *positive* force and should not be viewed negatively. Attachment is a result of *Love*. The Spiritual Love that radiates through the Divine Spark, the soul, within each and every one of us is the source of and sustains the Principle of Attachment. When the human mind tries to use the Spiritual Love that radiates from the soul to satisfy itself, the Spiritual Love gets soiled, and is reduced to mere attachment.

By removing the self-satisfaction from the attachment, we can purify it to reflect Spiritual Love. That is why to manifest Love you have to sacrifice your small self—your human mind and ego—to serve the Spiritual Beloved. As you sacrifice your ego and empty your mind of thoughts most of which have their origins in desire, the mind begins to get steady and unified around your Spiritual Beloved. Through this process your mind also gets purified and becomes a worthy receptacle to receive Spiritual thoughts and Divine Love. The usual situation though is that most of us fill our minds with desires that feed the self. The process of satisfying the mind and ego binds us to the object of desire. When the object of desire no longer exists, the desire lingers and so we suffer.

How does one purify this attachment?

To purify attachment you must surrender yourself as well as the object of your attachment, and also the attachment itself, to your Spiritual Beloved, who is the door and the way to the Source of all sources and is Love. When you do this, then your mind gets purified to the extent that your thoughts associated with the object of your attachment and the object itself are surrendered to the Entity. Then the Entity will deal with the objects of attachment in keeping with what is good for you as well as for the objects you are attached to, be they things, situations or people.

It is good to recount here why people fall in love. Why do we *fall* in love and not *grow* in love? We usually fall in love with someone who satisfies our mind. When the mind uses love to satisfy itself, the love falls and becomes attachment. As long as the object of attachment satisfies the mind, they continue to remain in so-called love. But the mind cannot be permanently satisfied; and when the dissatisfaction experienced with the object of love becomes greater than the satisfaction received, they fall out of love.

By contrast, to grow in Love, each person involved in the relationship has to sacrifice the mind in the service of Love that is God that is manifesting through the Beloved. This is best done when each one surrenders one's attachment to the Spiritual Entity and receives the purified Love of one's partner from and through one's Entity.

It is like breathing air through the atmosphere. Although we breathe each other's emissions, we do not breathe directly into each other. Each of us surrenders our breath and other emissions to the atmosphere. The atmosphere purifies it and we then receive it. The same principle applies to love and indeed everything else.

We must realize that we really do not know anyone or anything. All we really know are our own *opinions* or *points of view* about the persons or objects with whom we come in contact. When we fall in love with someone, all we are really doing is falling in love with our own thoughts, and the reverse is true when we fall out of love. Similarly when we are attached to things, we are again attached to the thoughts associated with the things to which we are attached. In the final analysis when we say that we are attached to thoughts, things and persons we are really attached to our thoughts associated with the things and persons: *i.e.*, our point of view.

We can see from this that if this Principle of Attachment is used wrongly we remain attached to our own thoughts. In other words we are attached to our own opinions, which are necessarily imperfect and illusory—at least to some extent—since they are created by our own imperfect and finite minds with our limited points of view.

And as long as we remain attached to our own thoughts, we remain trapped in our own minds with all our limitations. We are held hostage by our own thoughts and remain imprisoned in our mind. And the sad part is that the thoughts are not clinging to us so much as we are clinging to them!

When we transfer our attachments from our thoughts to our Entity, what are we really doing? We are really giving up our attachment to our illusions, our own *false* opinions and insecurities. Now, should that be hard to do? Surely not. Yet because of the inertia of the mind, the habit mind and its basic insecurity, most people cling to their opinions. Why? Because through their opinions they derive a sense of identity, satisfaction and security: all of which, however, are illusory.

It is only when we surrender our limited opinions and points of view to the Higher Mind of the Entity that we can create an opening for the Higher Mind to descend into our consciousness; and through the descent of the Higher Mind we can begin to experience Reality as it truly is. As we empty our human mind by surrendering to the Divine, then to the extent we do so, our consciousness will open up to the Divine and the Divine will enter into our consciousness, as certainly as the air from our lungs flows into the atmosphere when we breathe out, and fresh atmospheric air flows into our lungs when we breathe in.

The more you surrender to the Divine, the greater will be this mutual exchange of consciousness between yourself and the Divine, until finally when you surrender completely to the Divine through your Entity, then you will experience what Lord Christ referred to when He said words to the following effect: "I am the Truth and the Life. Those who will come unto me will know the Truth, and the Truth will make them free; and I will live in them and they in me just as I live in My Father in Heaven and My Father in Heaven lives in Me." Other Masters have said similar things though phrased differently.

This Third Principle of Attachment should be properly understood and practiced. When you attach yourself to the Higher consciousness, your mind will gradually get detached from the lower consciousness. But so long as you cling to experiences and attachments of the lower mind, you can never experience the Higher Mind. You cannot remain earth-bound and also soar like an eagle.

FOURTH PRINCIPLE: SURRENDER

This then brings us to the Fourth Principle of Right Surrender. The Fourth Principle says, "While remaining in tune with the first three Principles one should *surrender* one's entire being at the Feet of one's chosen Entity."

As you begin to practice the first three Principles of Right Surrender, the superficial thoughts in your conscious mind will be easily eliminated. In time, deeper thoughts from the subconscious and unconscious mind will begin to surface. As thoughts from the subconscious and unconscious mind get eliminated, then thoughts from the past of this life, as well as of your previous lives, will come to the surface. These thoughts can be very disturbing, and they may not go away by mere watching. Also, as you begin the Spiritual practice of Right Surrender, your near and dear ones may protest strongly. Family members and friends may get upset and request you to give up this foolish attempt to surrender your life to your Chosen Entity. Even if they do not object, subjective fears about their well-being—and your own may enter your mind.

This Fourth Principle of Right Surrender will help you deal with all such objections and disturbing thoughts. The anti-Divine, commonly called Satan, has three weapons. The author asserts that Satan does not need a fourth weapon, because these three work so well! The three weapons are temptations, fears and doubts. Now what is a temptation? It is *attachment* to a thought of some manifestation through which you can derive mental, emotional and/or sensual pleasure. Similarly fears and doubts are also *attachment* to thoughts of a different nature. Temptations, fears and doubts all operate from and through the mind and ego. You can deal with most of the temptations, fears and doubts by merely watching them. But mere watching may not shake the deeper attachments and deeper temptations, fears and doubts, particularly the fears and temptations linked with the instincts of self-preservation and procreation.

You should realize that temptations, fears and doubts couldn't torment you unless you are attached to them. To get relief from and conquer the temptations, fears and doubts all you have to do is *surrender* your attachment to and fear of them to your Spiritual Entity. Similarly you should surrender your attachment to your near and dear ones, your family, children, *et cetera,* to your Spiritual Entity and let Him take up the load and deal with the problematic situations and do what is spiritually right for you as well as for your near and dear ones.

Unless you surrender to the Spiritual Beloved, He cannot help you any more than the atmosphere can help you if you refuse to surrender your breath to it.

Right surrender does not occur at the level of the usual wakeful conscious mind. Right surrender happens at nearer the super-wakeful state and beyond.

As you raise your consciousness to nearer the super-wakeful level, you reach a level in the wakeful conscious mind where the rational (thinking) faculty, the emotional (feeling) faculty and the ability to perceive with your senses coalesce. At that level, as Revered Dr. Mehta has explained, even though you are conscious and awake, you are unable to distinguish whether you are thinking with your mind or feeling with your emotion or perceiving with the five senses.

Remaining at that level where the thinking, feeling and sense perception faculties coalesce, surrender all the disturbing thoughts pertaining to any situation or relationships including your near and dear ones at the Feet of your Spiritual Beloved and let Him deal with the situation the way He wants to. With daily practice you will be able to achieve this state of consciousness.

Now from time to time you may wish that a problem you are surrendering should be resolved in a certain way. You are always free to suggest to your Spiritual Entity how you would like the problem resolved, but after making the suggestion you should always qualify it with the thought that your Entity should only accept your suggestion if it is in keeping with His Will.

Qualifying your request by leaving the final decision to your Spiritual Master will create the opening for the Entity to accept your suggestion if it is in keeping with the Spiritual Point of View, or not accept your suggestion and deal with the problem in some other way that will be more beneficial. If you do not give the Entity the freedom to act according to His Will, then the Entity will not intervene, but will support your suggestion even if it is not in keeping with His Will, and may even be ultimately detrimental to your well-being.

The Lord Christ in the garden of Gethsemane reflected this attitude of ultimate surrender. It is said that in the garden of Gethsemane, the Lord Christ prayed to God to the following effect: "Father let this bitter cup pass," and then added, "but only if it is Thy Will my Father and not mine."

Such was the total surrender of the Lord Christ to the Will of His Father that He left an opening for His Father to work out His Plan through Christ. God did not let the bitter cup pass and Jesus the Christ had to go through the subsequent suffering according to the Will of God.

Therefore, you are free to suggest any resolution to the problem you are surrendering, but you must be careful to allow your Entity the freedom to decide and intervene according to His Will and Plan for you; otherwise you are going to unnecessarily create problems for yourself, since the Entity will not impose His Will.

After you have completed your sâdhanâ or Spiritual practice wherein you have watched your thoughts, and before you are ready to end the exercise, you may mentally offer to the Entity a leaf or flower or any physical object such as a pin or a piece of stick. This is a symbolic way to mentally affirm your complete and utter surrender. Mentally attach all of your thoughts and feelings to the object. Then you may symbolically place that object at the Feet or picture or statue of the Form you have given to your Entity. When placing the object, with all of your thoughts linked to it, at the feet of the Entity you should make the appeal, "I am surrendering these thoughts and situations at Thy Divine Feet for Thee to deal with them according to Thy Will." You may use the same object repeatedly if you wish to, but need not do so.

Now as you practice the above Four Principles of Right Surrender you can be certain that you will encounter suffering. This suffering and tension is due to nothing more than your continued attachment to your point of view regarding the persons or situations in your life. Nevertheless the mental and emotional anguish is real. How do you deal with it?

You should deal with the suffering, which is sure to arise by following the Fifth, Sixth, and Seventh Principles of Right Surrender, which are: Silence, Fortitude and Faith.

FIFTH PRINCIPLE: SILENCE

The Fifth Principle says, "Do not give expression in words or action to the disturbing thoughts and emotions that arise. Live in the experience and thoughts in Living Silence."

Some people equate pain with suffering. Although they are associated in many instances, in many other instances they are not associated. Pain is physical whereas suffering is mental. An athlete endures pain when exercising his/her body but does not experience suffering. A mountain climber endures pain, bitter cold and danger but does not experience suffering. You get the idea.

Suffering arises in the mind—and we have to realize that the suffering is *always* in the mind. We may experience pain in the body, but it is the mind that suffers. Why? Because the mind causes you to identify with the pain, and is the source of the ego and it attaches itself to the pain and the pleasure the body is experiencing. It is this attachment to pain either negatively or positively that causes the mind to suffer, and because most of us identify with our mind, we think we are suffering. When you experience suffering you should not become expressive. Discussing the pain with others will not in any way reduce your suffering. Instead you should remain *silent* and live in the suffering in keeping with what is termed "Living Silence."

You should try and understand this concept of Living Silence.

When a hunter is waiting for his quarry, it may appear that the hunter is not doing anything. Actually, the hunter is doing a lot. He is deliberately sitting still and intently watching the surroundings for any sign of the quarry. It is very difficult to sit perfectly still and intently observe what is happening. It is very different from day dreaming which takes no effort. Living Silence is something like that. Watching with intent, without being emotionally attached to the pain and creating additional negative or positive thoughts about the experience.

To achieve the state of Living Silence you should try to not *escape* the suffering, but watch the thoughts that arise within your mind while you are going through the suffering. When you try to escape suffering, your actions are still controlled by suffering because you are reacting to it. When you confront suffering, it no longer can control you because you are now dealing with it in a proactive manner. By merely watching the thoughts, the suffering will diminish. You should surrender to your Entity those thoughts, which are unbearable. While you are thus living in the state of Living Silence, you should remain conscious of your Spiritual Beloved, and keep transferring your attachment from the suffering to the Spiritual Beloved, until slowly but surely all of the suffering passes on to the Spiritual Beloved, who will take up the load Himself and deal with it in the right way.

The best way *out* of any situation is *through* it, and the best way *through* it is to practice Living Silence while you are dealing with the problem, and simultaneously to surrender the problem, your attachment to the problem, and yourself to your Spiritual Beloved. You should never try to run away from a painful experience that cannot be avoided. Instead you should try and learn the lesson the experience is trying to teach. If you do not learn from your mistakes, you are doomed to repeat them.

The same principle applies to all experiences. It seems reasonable to believe that under normal conditions, if your soul did not require a particular experience, your body and mind would not need to go through it. But because the soul needs to learn the lesson of the experience, no matter how painful it may be, you should go through the experience cheerfully, and grow through it by practicing Living Silence and Right Surrender.

Instead of teaching suffering people how to deal with the painful experiences by helping them cope with the pain psychologically and with pain killing drugs, there is a growing trend in Europe and America to embrace euthanasia or mercy killing. Some countries in Europe have already legalized euthanasia, as has the State of Oregon within the USA. As Revered Dr. Mehta has taught, if the people who select euthanasia or commit suicide as a means of escaping their suffering only knew the reality of their situation, they would gladly endure the pain. By killing themselves they do not escape the suffering. At best they postpone it for some lives. They will have to go through the same suffering in some future life.

Why? Because, according to Revered Dr. Mehta, the soul needs to go through the suffering to cleanse itself. By committing suicide they do not escape the suffering but instead they increase it, because now they have to go through the added karma brought upon by their suicide or euthanasia as the case may be.

As Revered Dr. Mehta has suggested, if instead of being encouraged to opt for euthanasia or suicide, the people who are suffering are taught how to deal with their suffering, and empty their minds and souls through the suffering they have to endure, then the suffering will not be in vain, but will have served a useful purpose as intended by the Mind Divine and the individual's soul. During periods of intense physical suffering, if the suffering person's human mind is managed in the right way by following the Right Spiritual Principles, then the person's mind and soul get cleansed very rapidly, and can be liberated much sooner from the attachment to material things and thoughts.

The mere fact that one is trying to escape the suffering means that one is attached to it. Negatively attached, to be sure, but attached all the same; and all attachment, whether negative or positive, binds one to the object of attachment, which in this case is the suffering one is trying to escape. One should not try to escape from the suffering but use it to cleanse one's soul by practicing Living Silence.

One of the Four-fold Truths revealed by Bhagwân Buddha is that "Suffering is." It just is. Like Space is, the Sun is, Life is, Death is. Similarly suffering just is. The Lord Buddha said words to the effect: "Whatever consists of component parts must perish. Whatever consists of components parts is full of grief. Whatever consists of component parts is not the real self. It is wisdom to know this."

145

The very process of birth is so painful to both the mother and child that to expect life to be painless is unrealistic. In the process of natural birth the child is forced through the birth canal headfirst. That must surely cause a minor headache. Then as is the usual practice, immediately after a child is delivered, it is held upside down and slapped on the buttocks to stimulate breathing. What a way to start life.

Having been born, one has to breathe air, live in space, and experience death. Similarly one has to experience suffering. One should accept the fact that suffering is. One should strive to deal with suffering, and learn to grow through it regardless of the pain associated with it.

This is not to say that if the physical pain associated with the suffering is very intense, one should not take pain-killing medications to cope with the pain. But one should take advantage of the intense pain one is experiencing as a great opportunity to empty one's mind and soul.

Why? Because, as mentioned above, Revered Dr. Mehta has explained, during periods of intense suffering the process of purifying and emptying one's mind and soul is very rapid, provided one goes about it in the right way.

When viewed from this angle, suffering can be seen in a positive light as achieving a useful purpose. If however instead of focusing on the process of emptying one's mind and soul, one indulges in self-pity and tries to escape the suffering by attaching oneself to thoughts, things and persons other than one's Entity—such as thoughts of death, suicide or euthanasia—one increases the burden of the soul by adding significantly to the karma that one has to work out.

Instead of encouraging the people who are suffering from terminal illnesses to seek death as an escape from suffering, they should be encouraged to purify and empty their minds and souls by experiencing the pain in Living Silence, and surrendering the experience, their negative attachment to it as well as their entire being to their Entity in keeping with the Seven Principles of Right Surrender.

Getting back to the Principle of Living Silence: when practicing Living Silence, if for psychological reasons, you need to discuss the problem with someone, then you should discuss it with your Spiritual teacher. In the absence of a Spiritual teacher you may discuss the problem with one or two individuals who are preferably seekers on a Spiritual path, failing which they could be well-wishers or professionals who are in a position to help. It is the author's conviction however, that unfortunately nowadays the so-called professionals cause more problems than they cure, particularly in the field of psychology. You should positively avoid discussing your problems with others in order to gain sympathy in an attempt to satisfy your mind.

This now brings us to the Sixth Principle of Right Surrender.

SIXTH PRINCIPLE: FORTITUDE

The Sixth Principle is *Fortitude*. When you are dealing with the pain you are bound to experience as you begin to transfer your attachments through these principles of Right Surrender, the Sixth Principle stipulates, "Bear the pain with Fortitude."

In this context, "Fortitude" means enduring courage born of conviction and not bravado. When you are practicing Living Silence you should not try to talk your way out of the disturbances and difficulties because that will not help. However if you genuinely need help you should seek it out and not refuse it, thinking that seeking or accepting help would be a violation of the Principle of Living Silence. Bear the pain in Living Silence with Fortitude and not bravado, otherwise you could break down physically, emotionally and mentally.

SEVENTH PRINCIPLE: FAITH

The Seventh Principle is *Faith*. You should have full faith that as you practice the above Six Principles of Right Surrender in your life on a daily basis that your problems will and must disappear—gradually to begin with, and at a much faster pace later on.

This Principle of Faith is very important. Even the Lord Christ rebuked his disciples with the words "O ye of little faith." According to the New Testament, Lord Christ told His disciples that they could perform all the miracles He did if they had faith in His Father as He did. But instead of having Faith in God and His Principles we seem to have faith in our wealth, in other people and in other things.

Some of us think if God or the Master will provide us with

economic security by giving us sufficient money to take care of all our needs of life, if not our greeds of life, or some other form of wealth that satisfies our mind, then our faith will increase. That is our mind playing tricks on us. We think like that because we have more faith in mammon, which is the god of wealth, than we do in God, Who is the Source of all things *including* wealth. Money is the least important form of wealth.

Our faith in God will not increase no matter how much money we have. If possessing money were to increase our faith in God then all the wealthy people should have a lot of faith in God; but they do not. In any event what could one do with all the wealth in the world if one could not have the next five hundred breaths? Therefore, having economic security will not increase one's faith.

How does one develop faith if one lacks it?

We have to start by recognizing that faith is required in any endeavor or field of life. For instance, our economic system would collapse if we did not have faith in the value of our currency. Our banking system is also based upon the faith that our money is secure in the banks.

Likewise, in embarking upon a voyage of discovery, one takes it on faith that one will discover something of value; for if one did not do so; it would make little sense to embark upon the voyage in the first place. Those who claim to need to be convinced about the authenticity of something before they can have faith in it are always going to remain bound to their past experiences and will be unable to forge ahead into new dimensions.

In science, one begins the process of discovery by formulating a hypothesis, and then, having faith that the hypothesis is correct, one tests it. If one did not have faith that the hypothesis is correct, even before it was proved correct, one would not be bothered to test it, and consequently it would never be proved.

The same thing applies to the Seven Principles of Right Surrender. If you do not have faith to begin with, then you should assume as a hypothesis that the Principles are correct, and practice them in the right way as explained above; and as you practice the Principles, your faith will automatically develop and increase, because you will see the Principles in action, and their results; and thus, with time, the faith will be tested and justified, and the truth of the Principles proved.

RIGHT MINDFULNESS

As you practice the Seven Principles of Right Surrender, slowly but surely you will develop the quality of what the Buddha called Mindfulness. As you continue in your practice you will grow into Right Mindfulness. Mindfulness is the capacity of being aware of everything that is happening around you and within your consciousness.

As Bhagwân Buddha has Himself explained in His Discourse on Right Mindfulness, which is called *Satipatthâna*, Right Mindfulness is the ability to know what is right from the Spiritual point of view of the Truth in all the situations one experiences. You will automatically develop the capacity of Mindfulness and Right Mindfulness as you practice these Seven Principles of Right Surrender. You do not have to force the issue. You cannot force growth. It happens naturally from the inside out as you practice the Principles. The seed that surrenders to the soil grows naturally from inside. This natural internal growth of the seed breaks the shell open to begin life as a shoot and a root. Similarly as you live these Principles of Right Surrender the growth will naturally occur.

THE COMING OF THE MASTER

Then—as Revered Dr. Mehta has explained—at some point the Right Spiritual Master or Sat Guru will come into your life. You should heed a note of caution here. Never, never, never go in search of a guru. Do not seek out a guru. All you have to do is to follow the Principles of Right Surrender, and when you are ready to receive the Teachings and Guidance from the Right Spiritual Master, He will create the conditions whereby you will meet Him. The Master may be either incarnated in human form or discarnate, but He will appear in your life at the right time. Just as the atmosphere is waiting for the first gasp of breath from the new born child and the soil is awaiting the arrival of the seed, so also the Right Spiritual Masters are ever alert and are waiting and watching for the potential disciple to develop to the right pitch before they make themselves known.

An analogy may help to clarify the point. If a child is born very prematurely due to a miscarriage or some other reason, the child needs special care until such time as its lungs and other organs develop to the point that it can interact on its own directly with the atmosphere and other elementals. If the needed special care is unavailable to such a premature child, then the child will die. Similarly, before one can interact directly with a Spiritual Master, one needs to develop the right Spiritual attitude reflecting the qualities of Humility, Obedience, Discipline, Commitment and Faith. Without these qualities one is not ready to receive Spiritual Guidance from the Master or Sat Guru. (Although the Principles of Obedience, Discipline, and Commitment are not part of the Seven Principles of Right Surrender as such, they are nevertheless also a paraphrase of what Revered Dr. Mehta taught in different words: namely, as the Three Principles for following Spiritual Assignments, *viz.* [1] First Value, [2] Strict Obedience and [3] Unto the Last).

The right Spiritual teachers or upagurus can help you develop the attributes necessary to meet the Master. By living the Seven Principles of Right Surrender in your daily life, and living according to the instructions of the right teacher or upaguru, you will automatically develop the necessary characteristics; and as said earlier, when you have developed them to the right pitch, the Master will create the conditions whereby you as potential disciple will meet Him.

Remember, the disciple does not select the Master; the Master selects the disciple. This is reflected in the life of Jesus Christ as well when He selected Peter and his brother and pronounced words to the effect that he would raise them from being fishermen to being fishers of men. The Master does not need the disciple any more than the soil needs the seed or the atmosphere our lungs.

Some disciples erroneously think that the disciple serves the Master. It is the author's own experience that the reverse is true. Followers do not serve a leader/Master. As long as it is in the interest of the followers to support the leader, they will. When they discover that it is no longer beneficial to them to support the leader, they will denounce him. This again is reflected in the life of Jesus Christ when, as it is has been recorded, Peter denounced him thrice before the cock crowed. Examples of the disciples/followers abandoning the leader/Master during times of crisis are in the lives of other leaders/Masters as well. Thus, it is the Master who always works for the disciple even when in outward manifestation it may appear that the disciple is working night and day for the Master. The Master does not *serve* the disciple—the Master serves only God—but by performing Spiritual therapy on the disciple, the Master helps the mind of the disciple to turn inwards and through Spiritual practices the disciple gradually comes to know his/her own soul. This is known generally as salvaging the soul of the disciple, which is in keeping with the Will Divine.

In the interest of the disciple, before a Right Spiritual Master or Sat Guru accepts any disciple, He will test the disciple hard. The tests will always be within the limits of the disciple's ability to pass the test, but at the highest level of that disciple's capability. The test is to see whether or not the disciple's mind is ready to receive Spiritual Guidance from the Master with due humility, obedience and surrender, and to make sure that the disciple is truly committed and is not just saying so. Even if you want to go on an adventure such as climbing a mountain, you need to test your skills. How much more important is it therefore to have your intentions and commitment tested when you are planning to go on the ultimate adventure, *i.e.*, the Spiritual Path. Hence the test is in the interest of the disciple to ensure that he/she has the humility, discipline and commitment necessary to complete the journey.

You should bear in mind that the word "disciple" is related to the word "discipline." You need *discipline* to become a disciple. If with discipline, the disciple surrenders to the Will of the Master then the Master will Grace the soul of the disciple. The Master is very gentle on the soul of the disciple, but is usually very hard on the disciple's mind. The Master is very gentle when the conscious mind of the disciple is attuned to the soul of the disciple. Usually the average human mind is turned away from the soul. The Right Spiritual Master appears to be very hard on the human mind of the disciple. This is generally found necessary in order to turn the mind of the disciple inwards towards the light of the soul. As the disciple changes in keeping with the instructions of the Master, his/her mind will become more and more in tune with his/her individual soul. At that point the disciple will find the instructions of the Master to be more acceptable than early on in the Spiritual training.

The Seven Principles of Right Surrender will guard the disciple against the unspiritual and anti-spiritual tendencies of his/her own mind and thoughts; they will guide the disciple and the Master will Grace the disciple. The human mind of the disciple will not know that the soul connected with it is being Graced. Why? Because, as Revered Dr. Mehta has explained, the human mind is full of thoughts, and until such time as it is emptied of all the thoughts within it, it will be unable to experience the light of the soul.

It is only when the human mind is unified, purified and emptied that the mind of the soul can descend into it, and the disciple can experience a state of Spiritual Meditation or samâdhi and will then know what is spiritually right at the level at which the disciple happens to be within the Spiritual hierarchy. There is a Spiritual hierarchy.

On this issue the Guru Granth Saheb of the Sikhs also advises us to scrub our mind clean. It says in Punjabi, *Tu apné man ko mânj lé* ("Scrub thy mind clean"). Before one can scrub a vessel clean, one has to first empty it of all its contents; then only can one scrub it clean. Only a clean vessel is fit for receiving clean material. The thoughts from the Divine are clean and pure. One can only experience them when one has a clean and pure mind that has been emptied of all human material thoughts, and thus made ready to perceive the Divine.

As has been emphasized again and again by Revered Dr. Mehta, when the Right Master appears in one's life: Never, never, never miss the chance. You should not allow your human mind and petty ego to come in the way and resist the Master's Mind and Will, but with due humility you should surrender to the Will of the Master. If you resist, even a little, the Master will not force His Will. Just as God does not force His Will upon His creations but lets them face the consequences of their own actions through the law of causation or karma, similarly His Masters do not force their Will upon the disciples. If a disciple resists the Master's Will, the Master will leave the disciple at the disciple's own level to work out his own karmas, and the disciple will have missed the chance of linking up with the Master who alone can show the way and lead one out of one's bondage to the kârmic cycles of birth, life and death unto Spiritual liberation.

Revered Dr. Mehta has repeatedly said that the chance of meeting the Spiritual Master comes once in hundreds of lives.

Therefore once the disciple misses the chance, the same chance may never come again. This is very important to understand. Many people foolishly think, "So what if I miss the chance. There are so many gurus." However, Revered Dr. Mehta has taught that there are very few Right Spiritual Masters, and if a disciple misses the chance given by a Right Spiritual Master, then an impress is left on the disciple's soul, and no other Right Master will take up the cause of such a disciple.

This is especially true, as Revered Dr. Mehta has explained, if the Master is a Descending High Being such as the Lord Christ or Bhagwân Buddha or Sri Krishna or any of the other Highest of the high Spiritual Masters: those who are capable of mediating between the relative or human plane of consciousness and the Absolute or Divine plane of consciousness. No other Master will touch such a disciple who has missed the chance. Only the Master who had given the original chance that the disciple missed can give the disciple another chance, and He may not do so for lives to come. Why? It is the author's view that this is because the Master has many candidates to choose from, and many other issues of creation occupy His energies. Thus, He concentrates only on the deserving candidates. (The author would like to say here, however, that this is only his own reasoning at the human level, and there may be quite a different reason at the Spiritual level).

If an undeserving candidate is given a chance, he/she could cause very serious, even catastrophic, harm to all the Master's efforts throughout creation. Therefore, never miss the chance. If a disciple misses the chance and the Master decides to give such a disciple another chance, such a chance will generally be given at a lower level.

Here again people ponder, why? An analogy may help put things in perspective.

Suppose one wishes to become a weight lifter and goes to a master trainer to be trained in the sport of weight lifting. The master may not select the aspirant if he considers that the aspirant lacks the potential of becoming a good weight lifter. If he does select the aspirant, then he may test the aspirant's strength with the highest load the aspirant is capable of lifting. If the aspirant cannot lift a given load, the master will suggest a lighter load, since the initial load was more than the aspirant could bear, and if the aspirant were forced to lift it regardless, the attempt could even hurt the aspirant physically. Also, if the aspirant is not willing or is incapable of following the rigorous training necessary to reach his maximum potential as a weight lifter, the Master may even refuse to train him. It is something like that. The Spiritual Master tests one at the highest-level one is capable of passing the test. If one fails the test and if the Master gives another chance, it will be given at a lower level to protect the disciple from harm, and also to safeguard the Master's own work.

Therefore, for one's own sake, one should not miss the chance given by the Right Spiritual Master, but one should conduct oneself with due humility, obedience and surrender. As Revered Dr. Mehta has often said, "Woe be unto the person who misses the chance." Other Masters and even teachers have said similar things: for example, Sri Aurobindo is reported as having said, "Thrice woe be unto such a person."

FUTILITY OF UNDERSTANDING

Wherever possible in this article the author has tried to explain the "Why" of things. Why the human mind is insecure; why it has developed a tendency to grasp, *et cetera*. This is because in the past the author's own mind demanded to know how and why things worked. The author can tell the listeners with authority born of experience that trying to understand the "why" of things in a Spiritual context is a *waste of time*. This applies even in the practical way of life, though not quite to the same extent. For instance, one need not know how a car or a computer works in order to use it, even though such knowledge may help in some instances. The engineers who design the machine need to know these things, but those who use them don't necessarily need to know. The driver only needs to know how to drive the car, and the one who uses a computer does need to know the necessary commands to make the programs run. But it is not an absolute requirement for such people to know how the machine is designed and made, and exactly how it works.

Now in a Spiritual context—as in the material—the human mind attempts to understand how and why the Principles work before it will begin to live them. But in the Spiritual context—as opposed to the material—this is futile. The human mind uses this need to understand as a pretext to avoid practicing the Principles until such time, as it understands them and by so doing also tries to gain ego-satisfaction from the understanding it may achieve. Revered Dr. Mehta has often said that so long as you understand, you are "standing under" the knowledge. This may be taken to mean that as long as you stand under the knowledge, you are not yet one with the knowledge.

It has also been the author's own experience over many years that Spiritual understanding cannot be acquired before undertaking the Spiritual practice. Spiritual knowledge comes only from direct *experience*, which in turn can come only from the right Spiritual *practices.*

Spiritual scriptures repeatedly advise us that this is a world of illusion, and that to *experience* the Real, the Truth, we have to silence our senses.

Spiritual experiences are beyond the realm of the material. This is a very fundamental reason why it is impossible to *understand* the Spiritual with our material mind and senses. To perceive Spiritual experiences we have to silence our human mind and senses, which are made of matter. Compared to the Spiritual, our mind and senses are limited and coarse. They are incapable of perceiving the finer Spiritual vibrations.

As we have mentioned earlier, we cannot even feel the blood that is flowing through our arteries and veins. How then can we depend upon our finite mind and senses to discern Absolute Spiritual Truths, and the Infinite, which are beyond the physical realm?

It is the author's own experience that no amount of reading really helps as much as a little *practice*. Instead of wasting time and energy trying to understand the "why" of Spiritual practices, you are much better off learning the "how" of Spiritual practices, and actually implementing what one has learned. Once you learn how to practice the Seven Principles of Right Surrender, you should *implement* them in your daily life. Through such daily practice of the Seven Principles of Right Surrender, you will automatically develop the mind necessary to receive the Spiritual Truths that descend from the Higher Planes of consciousness.

How does one practice the Seven Principles of Right Surrender?

PRACTICING THE SEVEN PRINCIPLES OF RIGHT SURRENDER

The First Principle says that you must select an Entity to whom and through whom you wish to surrender. Now, how does one do that? Herein comes the universal application of the Principles. Just as the atmosphere or the force of gravity is not restricted to any one country or continent so also these Principles are not limited to any religion. They are universal. Further, as explained earlier, because the Masters represent God in human form, their forms are also interchangeable and not limited to any one religion, or the religion started through them. All the major religions of the world have been founded on spiritual principles that have emanated from the same Source and lead back to It.

In other words, there is no competition between the Spiritual Masters. Nor can there be any, since all of them have descended from the Source of all sources, which in English is commonly called God (and which is called differently in different languages), to expressly fulfill the Will of the Almighty. Even though some religions, like Jainism and Buddhism, eschew the term "God," they too acknowledge the Ultimate Source of all sources. For instance, in Mahâyâna Buddhism the "Mother of all the Buddhas" is called by the term Antîm Shûnyatâ, "The Infinite Nothing-ness."

Now all true Spiritual Masters while on earth have served the Ultimate Source and are still serving the Divine in their discarnate state. All of them have preached that mankind should surrender its will to the Will of that Source, which in most religions of the world is known as the Will Divine as described in their language of choice.

There is no competition between the Masters. But those who only *claim* to follow the various Masters—not the *true* followers—compete and fight against each other, even in the name of the Master, to spread the teachings of the Master according to their own concepts. The true followers of different Masters do not fight against each other. They are focused on the battle within. They and their respective Masters always co-operate with all seekers to fulfill the Will Divine, since that Will emanates from the One Source which they all strive, with their heart of hearts, to worship and serve with love and devotion.

When it comes to selecting an Entity, you may select any of

the Avatâras of Hinduism, the Prophets or Archangels of Judaism, Christianity, and Islam, the Buddhas, Bodhisattvas and Arhants of Buddhism, the Gurus of Sikhism, the Tîrthankars of Jainism, the founders of the Mazdayasni Zarathushtri or Baha'i religion, or the Vedic Divine Beings Brahmâ, Vishnu, Shiva or their shaktis or feminine counterparts.

You should not feel that if you are born into a family practicing a particular religion you are restricted to selecting as an Entity the particular Prophet or High Being through whom the religion got started. Such thinking is not spiritual, and is more representative of religious thinking; indeed quite often it has an anti-spiritual basis. Being universal, Spiritual principles include all religious practices. Spiritual Principles are therefore by their very nature inclusive and not exclusive. Nothing and no one is excluded from practicing the Spiritual Principles. They can be reflected in all forms of worship, religious or otherwise.

Of course there is nothing wrong in selecting as an Entity the Prophet or Founder of the religion of the family into which you were born, if that is what appeals to you. But you are also free to select any other Entity if the Entity who started the religion practiced by the family into which you were born does not appeal to you. Thus if you are born into a Christian family, you could select Bhagwân Buddha as an Entity; one born into a Hindu family may select Zarathushtra as an Entity; a person born into a Zoroastrian family may select Krishna or Christ or Mohammed as an Entity; and so on.

What is the basis of selecting an Entity? One should base one's choice of an Entity upon one's emotional feeling of *love*. Select the one Entity that most *appeals to one's heart*, irrespective of the *religion* started through the Entity. As Revered Dr. Mehta has emphasized: "Be in *love* with your Entity." You should be so much in love with your Entity that nothing and no one can take the Entity's place in your heart of hearts.

Once you have selected an Entity, the first aspect of the First Principle says that you must give that Entity a form. Now what form should you give?

Suppose you have chosen Bhagwân Buddha as the Entity through whose teachings you wish to grow, but you prefer the picture used to depict the form of Zarathushtra or Christ. Fine. There is no problem or conflict. You can surrender to the form

157

generally associated with Zarathushtra or Christ, but follow the teachings of Buddha, and vice-versa. What is important to note here is that you are free to select any one form, but should stick to only the form you choose.

Also—as Revered Dr. Mehta has said personally to the author—select any one set of teachings, but only *one* set of teachings. Why? Because as explained earlier although any one of several roads may lead you to your destination, you can only get there by traveling one road at a time. Therefore, follow only one set of teachings and surrender through only one form.

Now as explained earlier our Muslim and Jewish brothers and sisters may have a problem here. What form should they give their chosen Entity in light of the prohibition in their respective religions regarding ascribing to the Divine the form of an image?

Well, although many of them may not realize it, the Jews and the Muslims do have numerous forms sanctified by their respective religions, through whom the Divine is and has been worshipped from ancient times. For instance, the Jewish people have the Shield of David (also called "The Star of David"), and also the form of the Torah, which is kept on the altar in every synagogue. Furthermore, they have the form of the two tablets on which Moses is said to have received the Ten Commandments. In ancient times they had the Ark of the Covenant and the Temple in Jerusalem where it was housed; and in more recent times they have the menorah and the Western Wall (which is a remnant of the Temple in Jerusalem). The tetragrammaton (which is what scholars call the four Hebrew letters *yod-hey-vav-hey*, representing the name of the LORD God) is also considered sacred by the Jewish religion, as also the Hebrew letter *shin*, and the combination of the Hebrew letters *yod* and *hey*. Then there is the mezuzah, which is nailed to the door of every Jewish home. These are all forms through which the Divine is, and has been, remembered; and thus they too are aids to communion with, and ultimately union with, God.

Similarly the Muslims have the Ka'aba. Every Muslim, no matter where he/she is in the world, is required while praying to turn towards the mosque in Mecca in which the Ka'aba is housed. Every Muslim who prays five times a day (as required by Islam) turns towards this form of the Ka'aba. Some of the other forms associated with Islam are: the Sword; the Dome of the Rock in Jerusalem; the Crescent Moon and Star; the word "Allah" and/or "Ali" written in Farsi or Arabic letters; and of course the Holy Koran. All Muslims accept—and have accepted through the centuries—these forms as holy, and with or without their knowledge have developed an attachment to these forms; and they all recognize the value of these forms as aids toward communion with the Divine. If these forms are not, for Muslims, symbols of the Most Holy, then no Muslim should get upset if anyone else desecrates them; but they do. They accept these as symbols of the Divine. No one says that these symbols *are* God. But they do *represent* the Divine, and can be used to grow towards the Divine.

It may also be kept in mind that the word "form" in this context applies to anything that can be conceptualized. In this sense, then, a form is not merely something that must be visualized. Under this definition, even a sound has a form, a touch has a form, and our concepts of "The Infinite" or "Nothing"—insofar as they *are* concepts and can be manifested in thought, word and/or deed—also have forms. The Jewish and Islamic scriptures often speak of "The Voice of the LORD" or the "presence" of God or of Allah. These, too—to the extent that they can be conceptualized by the human mind—are forms, since they are thought forms.

Also, through both these religions, many worthy people have grown to know the Divine by direct experience. They would not have been able to do so unless they, too, had been following the Principles, knowingly or without their knowledge. Thus it is clear that, despite the prohibition in these religions regarding the ascribing of an image to God, it is possible that their adherents also used forms to grow unto the formless.

Similarly the Hindus have the symbol for the Word of God, pronounced "Ohm."

Here again it should be emphasized that the Seven Principles of Right Surrender do not advocate giving a form to *God*, but to one's *Entity*. Now although it is true that in some religions—such as the Buddhist—the Entity may Himself be regarded as the Supreme Being, this is most emphatically not so in the Zarathusti religion or the Jewish religion or in Islam. In Zoroastrianism, Judaism and Islam, no Prophet of God or Messenger of

Allah, regardless of how exalted he was, can ever be considered as equal in Spiritual stature to God Himself. Thus for Jewish or Muslim worshippers wishing to follow the Seven Principles of Right Surrender, there would never arise a situation in which they have to ascribe a form to God or Allah.

Many people do not know that thousands of years before the birth of the Prophet Mohammed, the Prophet Zarathushtra had taught His followers to pray five times a day. Scholars have also recently established that the three wise men, the three Magi's who brought gifts for the baby Jesus were Zoroastrians.

Which form does one select? It is advisable to select any one of the historically accepted forms of the Masters of the various religions, or the historically established symbols of the religions. Thus the Christians may use the cross as a symbol for Christ, or any one of the accepted figures represented in the paintings and statues of the Master. The Hindus have a great many forms for Sri Krishna and Sri Râm and the Vedic Divine Beings and their shaktis. The Zoroastrians have their forms for Zarathushtra and other Zoroastrian symbols, such as the Sacred Fire or Atash, and the Farohars. The Sikhs have the Guru Granth Saheb as well as the paintings of their Gurus; the Buddhists have forms of the Buddha; and so on.

Start with a form that has already been historically accepted within the religion, and through whom other individuals have ascended unto Divine realization. It is not advisable to start one's own form. Why? By accepting a form that is historically established within a particular religion one gets the benefits of the various thought forms established by those who have grown to Divine realization through the same religion. These thought forms left behind by such persons are like the roads that have been built by the people who lived before us. We do not insist on traveling only on roads built by our generation. We take advantage of the roads and bridges built by others who preceded us. Similarly by accepting the forms already established within the religions, we get the benefit of the efforts of those who have grown through the same religion before us. Therefore one is better off selecting a historically established form of the Entity one wishes to surrender to and through, rather than starting a form of one's own.

Once one has selected the Entity and given the Entity a form, let the form be fixed and not changing, and then practice the Seven Principles of Right Surrender as explained hereunder.

THE MECHANICS OF SURRENDERING

The question may arise in the mind of the reader: How do I begin the practice of Right Surrender? Should I stand, sit, kneel down, bow down or assume some other posture?

The object of the Spiritual practice of Right Surrender is to totally silence one's mind while remaining fully conscious. From a Spiritual point of view, human thoughts represent noise, and our minds are full of thoughts.

When the mind is totally silent, *i.e.*, when it is devoid of all human thoughts, then the thoughts from one's soul will descend into one's human mind, and this is called Spiritual Meditation. As Revered Dr. Mehta, quoting the Lord Christ, has often said, "The empty alone shall be filled;" and it is also in keeping with the advice given by the Guru Granth Saheb of the Sikhs to scrub one's mind clean so as to be worthy to be filled with Divine Thoughts.

Now what follows is the author's own exposition of what is preferable, based on his own practice of more than 30 years.

In order to watch your thoughts in keeping with the First Principle of Right Surrender, the mind has to be freed from any demands of the body. For this reason the body should be kept healthy and supple. Before starting the practice of Right Surrender you may put yourself in any comfortable position so long as your back is straight. For those who can adopt it, the yogic posture of padmâsan is the ideal position because it maintains the body in total equilibrium and keeps the spine erect.

However most people from outside India, and even many people within India, are unable to assume the posture of padmâsan. There are many other yogic postures you could assume which are less demanding than padmâsan. Indeed, if you are uncomfortable squatting on the floor, then you may sit on a cushion or pillow like some Japanese monks who practice Zen Buddhism do. If even this is not possible, then you may sit on a chair or a recliner, or you can even lie on your back on the floor or on the bed, so long as your back is straight and not slouched. The problem with lying on the recliner or the bed or floor is that the horizontal position is usually associated with sleep, and the mind will, due to force of habit; sink down into sleep instead of becoming super-wakeful.

For the purpose of practicing the Seven Principles of Right Surrender it is best to assume any comfortable position that allows you to keep the spine upright and straight, and keep the mind wakeful.

Once you have assumed the posture in which you intend to start the practice of Right Surrender, you should remain perfectly still. To facilitate this, you may either clasp your hands together in your lap, or place the hands on your thighs or at your sides as it suits you.

The next thing is to close your eyes and steady them. You will find that even when the eyelids are closed, the eyes will tend to move. For this reason it is helpful to focus your closed eyes on some point. To start with, you may focus your eyes on the tip of your nose. After you are comfortable doing that, after several days or weeks, you should raise your gaze to the bridge of your nose, until eventually you are comfortable turning your eyes inward and focusing them between your eyebrows and about half an inch inward. The idea is to keep the eyes steady as part of the effort to keep the body perfectly still.

To start the practice of Right Surrender, assume a comfortable posture keeping the back straight; hold your hands steady; and keep your eyes focused on a point as explained above.

Now you are ready to begin practicing the First of the Seven Principles of Right Surrender. Raise the level of your consciousness to the super-wakeful level and do nothing. Just watch your thoughts come and go and then follow the remaining Seven Principles of Right Surrender.

One of the first things you are likely to observe when you begin watching your thoughts is that you become aware of all sorts of sensations on your body. Your skin may feel itchy and the urge to scratch may be very strong.

You may not have been aware of these sensations even though they were there before you began the practice of surrender. Why? Because your mind was diverted by thoughts within and situations outside yourself. However when you close your eyes and begin to watch your thoughts, you become aware of all sorts of thoughts and sensations. So, what to do? Resist the urge to scratch and watch the thought of the urge to scratch and the itch as well, and both will go away. But suppose as you are watching your thoughts an insect were to crawl on your body and begin to bite you as has happened to some seekers then you should do what is necessary to get rid of the insect, and after that is done once again resume the practice of Right surrender.

HOW EACH PRINCIPLE HELPS

The author has found that each of the Seven Principles of Right Surrender helps those who practice the Principles in a very specific way. They utilize the very nature of the human mind to help it become unified, purified and ultimately emptied.

The First Principle helps because through it you select a Spiritual Entity who becomes your Spiritual anchor, a veritable beacon of light and strength in which you can become centered. Further, by watching your thoughts as is required by the fifth aspect of the First Principle, slowly but surely a mind that is watchful begins to develop within your unsteady and reactive conscious mind. As this new mind watches the activities, *i.e.* the thoughts that rise and fall within your restless reactive mind, it begins to stabilize. We can call this new mind the watchful mind as contrasted with the reactive mind. This new watchful mind, when fully developed, will exercise a degree of control over the unstable reactive mind, which has a tendency to jump around and get attached. In essence, you will become the seer and the seen. To a certain extent many of us already have such a mind, but it is not very well developed and has not stabilized.

When this watchful mind is fully developed it will make you alert and aware of everything that is going around and within you. Eventually this watchful mind will grow unto what the Buddha called Right Mindfulness This state of Right Mindfulness will enable you to act in keeping with Spiritual Principles and Values rather than react to your desires and external stimuli. This new mind will enable you to gain control over your life and help you overcome your desires by eliminating them. You will then be able to act and control the circumstances in your environment rather than succumb to them and be controlled by them.

The First Principle helps you to become *centered* in a Spiritual Master, grow unto Right Mindfulness and gain control of your thoughts, words and deeds.

The Second Principle of Humility makes you *receptive*, thereby allowing you to receive instructions from your Spiritual teacher to begin with, and later on receive inspirations from the Higher levels and planes of consciousness within yourself as well as outside yourself.

The Third Principle, the Principle of Attachment, helps you to become *steady* and also helps to empty yourself. By transferring your attachment to your Entity who is very stable and will serve as the Spiritual anchor and beacon of Light on your Spiritual quest, you begin to slowly but surely empty your mind and become stable. Focusing your attachment on your Entity will help to *unify* your thoughts around your Entity, and this same action will also *purify* your thoughts.

The Third Principle helps you to unify and purify your thoughts and also helps your unsteady mind to become stable.

As you practice the above three Principles and then add the Fourth Principle of Right Surrender, then along with the first three Principles, the Fourth Principle of Surrender will help to *empty* your mind of all the unified and purified thoughts, and thus prepare your mind to receive the Master when He appears in your life.

As you go on practicing these first Four Principles of Right Surrender and your mind becomes fully emptied—as Revered Dr. Mehta has said—you will be able to receive thoughts from your soul, and through your soul of Higher Beings who are Guiding your soul and with whom your soul is connected. Once this has been achieved, you will know by direct knowledge how to live according to the will of your own soul, and ultimately, according to the Will Divine.

The Fifth Principle of Living Silence helps you to fully *experience* all the situations in your life including your suffering in all its intensity, and empty it out for good.

The Sixth Principle of Fortitude gives you the courage to *face* the adversities and suffering with a calm and cool disposition.

The Seventh Principle of Faith helps to develop the quality of *commitment*.

This will enable you to endure the suffering in Living Silence with Fortitude, no matter how great the pain may be and/or how long it lasts.

As you implement these Seven Principles of Right Surrender in your daily life, slowly but surely, a step at a time and a step *in* time, your mind will become unified, purified and ultimately empty. The empty alert mind will be a silent mind and will be ready to hear the voice of your soul or âtmâ, and through your soul, of the oversoul or what the Hindus refer to as the param-âtmâ.

Will everyone who reaches that state experience the same thing? The answer is: Most definitely not. Although the Ultimate Reality is Changeless, everyone's experience of their soul and the Ultimate Reality will be unique ... as unique as they are and their capacity to experience the Ultimate Reality.

THE NEED TO SILENCE ONE'S MIND

It is important to try and fully realize *why* it is so very necessary to silence your mind. Earlier we have noted that we cannot even feel the blood flowing through our arteries and veins. Compared to that the Voice of the soul is infinitely more silent and subtle. Try and imagine the degree of silence we must achieve in order to experience the Voice of Silence: and how much more subtle must be the Master's Voice and the Voice of God? The whole purpose of practicing the Seven Principles of Right Surrender is to fine-tune our minds and bodies to communicate in a very real sense with the Universe. The physical universe is merely the outward manifestation of the Unseen Universe that is the Source of the physical universe. To move around and communicate with the physical universe we need our physical senses; but to communicate with the Silent Universe, which is the Unseen, we have to *silence* our senses and go beyond the usual conscious human mind.

From this one can get some idea how important it is to practice these Seven Principles of Right Surrender to silence one's mind.

In this chapter the Seven Principles of Right Surrender have been explained in fair detail. We have also provided numerous examples to illustrate the universal application of the Principle of Surrender. To help the reader look at his/her mind, we have also pointed out some of the characteristics of the human mind and its tendencies. How the Principles utilize the very character-istics of the human mind to stabilize it and help us grow through it to experience the Divine within us has also been expounded. The specific way each Principle helps us has also been detailed. Finally, the mechanics of how to practice the Principles of Right Surrender have also been laid out.

For the sake of recapitulation, we will now summarize the Seven Principles of Right Surrender.

SUMMARY OF THE SEVEN PRINCIPLES OF RIGHT SURRENDER

The **First Principle** is, "*Select one and only one Entity* to whom and through whom to surrender."

There are five aspects to the First Principle.

1. Give the Entity a form.
2. Let the form be fixed and not changing.
3. Study the teachings of the Entity through only one teacher. In the absence of a teacher, let your conscience be your guide, but your growing conscience and not static con-science.
4. Raise the level of your consciousness so that you become as wakeful as possible, nearer if not actually at the super-wakeful level.
5. At that super-wakeful state just watch your thoughts come and go.

The **Second Principle** is, "Have utter *humility* before your Entity."

The **Third Principle** is, "*Transfer your attachment* from all things, thoughts and persons to your Entity in increasing propor-tion, until eventually all your attachment is transferred to your Entity."

The **Fourth Principle** is, "*Surrender* all your thoughts, de-sires, fears, *et cetera,* to your Entity."

The **Fifth Principle** is, "Do not give expression in words or action to the disturbing thoughts and emotions that arise. Live in the experience and thoughts in *Living Silence.*"

The **Sixth Principle** is, "Bear with *fortitude* the pain experi-enced in Living Silence."

The **Seventh Principle** is, "Cultivate belief amounting to conviction leading to *faith* that as you follow the first four principles, right surrender will and must become effective and your thoughts will get purified, unified and emptied ultimately raising your consciousness a step a time, each step leading towards the ultimate mukti or liberation."

These Seven Principles of Right Surrender if practiced daily will and must work for all those who implement them, as certainly as the principle of gravity influences everyone and everything that comes within its reach.

Furthermore, these Principles are universal and can be practiced by followers of any religion and/or any Master. There is no conflict between these Principles and the teachings of the Great Masters. After all, the very First Principle of Right Surrender tells us to select one and only one Master of our choice, and to follow the teachings of the Master. Therefore people who are following different religions are all practicing aspects of this First Principle when they select the Master and the teachings of the religion they choose to live by. In many instances, this is the religion of the family into which they were born. People of any race, religion, country, sex or race can practice these Principles.

It is important to emphasize that in order for Right Surrender to be effective, one must follow *all* the Seven Principles of Right Surrender as explained above. After all, if when driving a car, flying a plane or baking a cake, we have to follow *all* the steps necessary to achieve the desired result, we should not expect to achieve the desired Spiritual results by not following all the Principles needed to reach the Spiritual goal.

As you practice these Seven Principles of Right Surrender, you will automatically grow to realize the Unity in Diversity of Religions. As more and more individuals who follow different religions practice these Seven Principles of Right Surrender in their daily life, more and more people will grow to realize the Unity of God, and thus also the Unity of His message.

This realization in turn will reduce the conflicts that are occurring in the name of religion, in the minds of the people concerned to begin with, and later on in society in general, to the extent that members of society at large accept and adopt these Principles in their way of life.

Thus these Seven Principles of Right Surrender, if followed properly, have the potential of reducing conflicts in an individual's life, as well as contributing to world peace by making the Unity in Diversity of Religion a reality.

You are lucky to be counted among the fortunate who have been exposed to these Principles of Right Surrender. This may sound pompous and arrogant, but consider this: It is estimated that currently there are 6 billion people on Earth. Even if 20 million copies of this book are sold and a total of 60 million people read it, that is still only 1% of the estimated total population of the world. Based on the above figures, those who read the Principles explained in this book, would represent about 1% of the population of humanity. That in my judgment is quite a small percentage. Now how many of the people who read the Principles will actually begin to implement them and live by them? How many of those who decide to live by them will do so in the right way? How many of these latter individuals who live by the Principles in the right way, will go all the way?

Very often people who decide to embrace and live by the Principles do so, but not in the right way. Then instead of taking responsibility for their own lack of knowledge and seeking help, many of them blame the Principles as being ineffective and give up. In order for the Principles to work, they have to be implemented in the right way and all the way. That is why they are called the Seven Principles of Right Surrender.

You can see from the above that just because the Principles have been revealed by the Divine, this does not mean that the problems we have created through our ignorance and the resulting suffering are going to go disappear. Do not wait for others to practice the Principles before you decide to do so. Embrace the Principles and take charge of your life. Do not let your human mind get the better of you.

If you choose to ignore and/or reject these wonderful Universal Principles, which are a gift from God to humanity, then you run the risk of falling into the category of those reportedly described by the Lord Christ as, "None so blind as those who refuse to see."

For their own benefit and that of others, the author requests the readers not to merely read the Principles and set them aside, but strive to put them into *practice* and give them a chance to *prove* themselves in your own lives. Study these beautiful Seven Principles of Right Surrender and weave them into your life. Test them for yourself. When you see for yourself that they do work, continue to practice them.

The Principles will Guide you. They will Guard you and the Master will Grace you.

Some people ask: How long should we practice these Principles? I ask them, "How long do you intend to breathe?" They smile and say, "As long as I live" and with their answer to my question, realize that they have answered their own question about how long they should practice the Principles.

For the benefit of the reader, "The Story of Life" is printed on the following page. Hopefully this *Script* will motivate the reader to commence his/her Journey of Life Eternal.

The Story of Life

Seed is like Me, the beginning and the end
Of life on earth as in Heaven I meant.
A seed must die in order that it lives;
Thus one becomes many and its bounty gives.

Unless it dies, it shall abide alone
And die in wilderness without being known.
First is the death born of surrender to Love,
Second is the death born of selfish love.

When the seed surrenders with love to My earth,
She nurtures it with love and gives it a birth.
Before, during and after the birth of the tree,
Angels of water, sun and air give love free.

For the love seed gives, many more times it receives
On this food of love, it thrives and lives.
During its lifetime, it spreads its kind around;
Thus it spreads My bounty of Love unbound.

But seed that surrenders not, when planted in ground,
Lives alone a while in the midst of love all round.
Then it begins to rot and in the end dies,
For such a one, not even the mother sighs.

This is the story of life of plant and men
A reflection of Truth in the spiritual realm.

Script received at Mayfair House, Bombay
June 11, 1956 at 9:00 p.m.

Chapter 7
The Taliban Tragedy

That the Taliban were an oppressive lot was obvious to those who lived under their rule and all who followed their administration. However due to apathy, the world was not prepared to do much, if anything, about the situation in Afghanistan.

Not being satisfied with oppressing their own citizens, the Taliban were moved to assert their authority and thumb their noses at the world by blowing up the two Statues of the Buddha that were carved out of the cliffs in Bamiyan between the 2nd and 4th centuries A.D., *i.e.* before the advent of the Prophet Mohammed. As soon as this was reported on March 2, 2001, many people who are spiritually aware declared, in private conversations, that by desecrating the statutes of the Lord Buddha, the Taliban had struck their own death knell. Just as, during the time of the Lord Moses, the Pharaoh had decided his own fate and that of his subjects by issuing an edict that the army should kill the first-born of every household of the Children of Israel, similarly, by desecrating the statues of the Lord Buddha, the Taliban had decided their own fate. When later in the month of June 2001 the Taliban decided to force the Hindu citizens of Afghanistan to wear a yellow badge so that they could be identified easily, one could sense that the Taliban had taken leave of their senses and that the end of their rule was imminent.

It was not clear how the Taliban would be destroyed or by whom or by what means but there was no doubt that their days were numbered. A little more than six months after the Taliban blew up the statues of Lord Buddha the World Trade Center was destroyed on September 11, 2001. It was fascinating to watch and realize that the United States of America, the bastion of Freedom and Capitalism, had become the reluctant champion to root out the Taliban, to free Afghanistan from Taliban tyranny and to fight world terrorism. It is also noteworthy that the Taliban received the same treatment that they meted out to the statues of the Lord Buddha. The Taliban blasted the statues with explosives and they themselves were blasted out of the caves they were hiding in by explosives.

The war had begun with the Taliban and Al-Qaeda firing the

first shots. In the process of rooting out terrorism from the world, the United States of America will also have to deal with and root out the evil within Capitalism as it is being practiced hitherto. The fact that the Enron debacle began unraveling shortly after September 11th is not coincidental. As part of the battle against terrorism, we will also have to focus on rooting out the greed in our society that fosters the practices that led up to the collapse of Enron and the problems faced by WorldCom, ImClone, Tyco, Adelphia and others.

The Lord Shiva, known as Michael in the Old Testament, has begun to dance as the Natarâja ... performing his dance of destruction. Shiva is really part of the Holy Trinity of God and manifests the Re-Creator Principle.

When Shiva dances as the Natarâja then all that is not in keeping with the Will Divine first gets destroyed. When Shiva finishes his dance of destruction, good grows out of the ashes of evil as surely as new biological life emerges out of the ashes of the aftermath of a volcanic eruption or a forest fire. Thus the world has to be prepared to witness a lot of change in the next few years. Political leaders of the world may think that they are currently in charge of their respective governments and are shaping the events of the world. Whether they accept it or not, Shiva has taken over the charge. Natural and man-made events that no one had planned for will occur.

Most Muslims I know do not support the Taliban's point of view. Indeed, even most Muslims who supported—and many still do—the Taliban's right to practice their oppressive form of Islam, and tolerate the Taliban, would not themselves want to live under the conditions imposed by the Taliban. It is good to be tolerant of others. After all, Allah is known as Merciful, Benevolent and Kind. To tolerate the Taliban is good provided they keep their beliefs to themselves and do not force it upon others. But in the name of Allah, the Taliban was anything but tolerant. Even though they may claim to represent the truest form of Islam, their actions belied their claim. Those who are not tolerant towards others who disagree with them cannot represent Allah the Merciful, Benevolent and Kind.

After all, only those who have erred and/or disagree with us and/or cannot support themselves and are in need, require our mercy, tolerance and help.

172

One of the popular stories of Prophet Mohammed that was narrated to me showed how tolerant the Prophet was towards those who held him in contempt. The story was told to me by Hazrat Pathan, my Muslim Spiritual teacher and goes something like this:

"On his way to the Mosque to say his daily prayers, the Prophet walked through an alley. A rabbi occupied one of the houses in the alley.

The rabbi had heard about Prophet Mohammed and did not like the fact that he was preaching a new religion. Everyday, the rabbi's wife would sweep the house and instead of allowing her to discard the trash, the rabbi asked his wife to give the trash to him in a bag. When it was time for the noon prayer, on his way to the Mosque, the Prophet Mohammed would walk through the alley and pass by the rabbi's house. The rabbi lived in a house that had two floors. At the appointed time, the rabbi would wait by the window on the top floor with the day's trash. When the Prophet passed below his window, the rabbi would dump the trash on the Prophet. The Prophet would not bother to look up at the offender and/or rebuke him. He would merely brush the trash off his head and shoulders and continue on his way to the Mosque to say his prayers. This ritual went on every day for several months. Finally one day, the Prophet knocked on the rabbi's front door. The rabbi's wife opened it partly and saw that it was the Prophet. The rabbi was in the other room lying on his bed and was curious about who was at the front door. He called out to his wife and asked her who was at the door. She replied that it was the man upon whom he was throwing their household garbage. The rabbi got concerned and enquired, 'What does he want?' His wife replied, "He is asking if you are sick because for the past few days no one has been throwing garbage on him." The Prophet's concern for his offender's well-being made the rabbi feel so ashamed that he instructed his wife to invite the Prophet into their house for some refreshments. After spending time with the Prophet the rabbi then became his friend and eventually converted to Islam."

Some people who hear the above story may think that the Rabbi was a very bad person to do what he did to Prophet Mohammed. The reality is very different.

As explained in the last chapter, when a disciple is ready to

173

meet the Master, then the Master will create the conditions that will enable the disciple to meet the Master. A descending spiritual Master like Prophet Mohammed would not come into the life of an individual to personally teach him unless the individual was a soul worthy of such attention.

In the above story, in my opinion, the Rabbi was a very high soul. In all likelihood, Prophet Mohammed created the conditions that allowed him to come into the life of the Rabbi and thus help the Rabbi and his family to grow towards Allah or God.

Also, it is important to know that usually when a Master descends to do God's Work, he brings along his helpers with him. It is very possible that without his knowledge, the Rabbi was a participant in the play of Mohammed's plan to teach us to tolerate and forgive each other. Further, before we condemn all Rabbis, we should remind ourselves that we do not know whether the above story is true; after all we were not witness to the events described in the story. Even if the story is somewhat true, we do not know if the offender was indeed a rabbi. Even if he were, not all rabbis—or for that matter all people of any race, creed or nationality—are prejudiced. Besides, quite frequently stories change over time, and it is the author's experience that soothsayers and Spiritual teachers adapt stories to suit the occasion at hand and to ensure that the people they are addressing can relate to the characters in the story and get the message they are trying to deliver. Such stories should not be taken as factual but only as they are intended: *i.e.,* to deliver a certain point of view.

The above story is meant to illustrate the tolerance the Prophet had towards those who offended him. If the story is true, then it shows that the Prophet himself tolerated a prejudiced person who also happened to be a teacher. How then can the Taliban or anyone who is intolerant claim to represent Prophet Mohammed or for that matter any Prophet. To represent Allah or God is a much bigger claim.

It is also recorded that Jesus said words to the effect, "If someone were to strike you on one cheek, offer him the other cheek." Jesus is also recorded to have said words to the effect, "Anyone can love a friend or a relative and a well-wisher. But he who knows love, will love his enemy." It is recorded that the Lord Buddha told his monks words to the effect, "Monks, you should train yourself in such a way that if someone were to cut

174

off your arm with a sword, not a single thought should arise within you that will wish any harm to him."

There is another very good story that is worth mentioning. It is said that Guru Nanak, the founder of the Sikh religion, had gone to Mecca on a pilgrimage. When in Mecca, to show respect to the Ka'aba you are supposed to always face it, *i.e.,* not point your feet towards the mausoleum in which the Ka'aba is housed. Well, Guru Nanak slept with his feet pointing towards the Ka'aba. Naturally the other pilgrims objected vehemently. Then Guru Nanak asked them, "Brothers, kindly take hold of my feet and point them in the direction in which God is not." Naturally those who challenged Guru Nanak were dumbfounded and silently fell back. Guru Nanak then resumed his position with his feet pointing towards the Ka'aba. Guru Nanak did not show any disrespect to Prophet Mohammed. Being a great Spiritual Master Himself, the Guru was simply making a point to teach those who seemed to have a closed mind.

All Prophets have preached tolerance of the opinions and views of others, especially those who not only disagree with but also vehemently oppose our point of view. The fact remains that if we accept that God and/or Allah created the entire Universe, and that He is everywhere and in everything, then, if you love God and/or Allah, you have to love all His creations. This is an inescapable Truth.

What is interesting is that Hazrat Pathan, my first Spiritual teacher, was a devout Muslim. Yet he never asked me or even suggested that I should convert to Islam. Everyone who is on the Spiritual Path knows that it makes no difference what religion one is born into or practices. Why? Because religions tend to be exclusive whereas the Spiritual Path is inclusive. The ceremonies and rituals of one religion may not apply to another religion, but Spiritual principles are universal and are the basis of, and support, all religions. Goodness knows no boundaries. After all if we accept that God or Allah is good and that He is omnipresent, then He must include all and accept all. No one is excluded, but everyone is accepted at the level at which they are comfortable, so long as they do not cause discomfort to others. Goodness penetrates all barriers and permeates all cultures. Unfortunately, to a large extent, so does evil permeate almost all barriers below the material plane, on the material plane and a bit above it.

175

Many people are confused by the presence of evil. They think in human terms: *i.e.,* if God is all-powerful, he should be able to destroy evil. What we have to recognize is that because of His love for all His creations and the free will that he has given us, God *permits* even evil to express itself so long as evil does not threaten to destroy all of His creation by upsetting the balance in favor of evil. This need for balance in the cosmos is reflected in the struggle for balance of power between countries that is going on in the world. God does not wish to *destroy* evil; God chooses to *transform* evil into goodness. That can only be done with and by the power of love.

Love is the most powerful force in the Universe. It cannot get depleted or overwhelmed. Why? Because the more Love gives of itself, the more it grows. How can you overcome a force that increases both in intensity and quantity the more it gives of itself? People will resist hate but they cannot resist Love. Why? Because it is at the core of their Being. Creations are born through love and are sustained by love. They find it irresistible. The more Love gives of itself the more it grows. That is why Love is for giving and that is why Love forgives.

Tolerance, acceptance and forgiveness are basic characteristics of love. Intolerance, bigotry and the unwillingness to forgive on the other hand are basic characteristic of hate.

Anyone who thinks that God or Allah or the Divine wants everyone and everything to be the same is not living in reality. All one has to do is to look around to realize that the Power, Entity or Circumstance which created the Universe loves variety. We need not even ponder the immense Universe and all the galaxies within it to realize this. All we have to do is observe the myriads of life forms that inhabit the Earth. The Earth itself has so many different species of plants, animals, birds, insects, and fish. Amongst humans, too, there are so many different races; and within each race there are so many different shapes and sizes. To think that the Creator wants everyone and everything to be the same is absurd. The Creator loves diversity.

For this diversity to work, it has to function as a cohesive whole.

A very good example of Unity functioning through Diversity is the human body. There are so many different organs within our body, and millions of different types of cells. Even within each organ there are different types of cells. Yet the body functions as one cohesive whole because the cells function in harmony with the laws of the body. The only time we experience pain or illness is when some cells of the body, for whatever reason, are *not* in harmony with the rest of the body.

The Prophets knew that Love is the only Force that can bring about the cohesiveness in the diversity of manifestation and create a Unified whole. Not hate, but Love. Therefore, the Prophets preached Love and tolerance, understanding and charity.

Thus, to propagate hate, and force one's will and/or limited point of view upon others is certainly not in keeping with the teachings of any Prophet of any religion. Propagating hate and forcing one's will upon others is at best un-Divine and at worst anti-Divine. After all, if God or Allah has chosen to give each one of us a free will, what right does anyone of us have to take it away, by forcing our will upon others? We are allowed to use our free will within the limits of the law, "As you sow, so shall you reap," or what Hindus call the Law of Karma. Under no circumstances can propagating hate and intolerance be justified in the name of God or Allah or whatever names one chooses for the Divine.

There is a very nice story, which I am told is a Native American story that teaches us how to deal with the conflict between love and hate that we all face, especially in today's world after September the 11th.

A Native American grandfather was talking to his grandson about how he felt.

He said, "I feel as if I have two wolves fighting in my heart. One wolf is the vengeful, angry, violent one. The other wolf is the loving, compassionate one."

The grandson asked him, "Which wolf will win the fight in your heart?"

The grandfather answered, "The one I feed."

How many of us prefer to feed the wolf of vengeance and anger?

Instead of fighting over our differences, we should celebrate them. We can only learn from one another if we are different and unique. If we were all identical, or even similar, we would not be able to learn from each other, and the world would stagnate and be very boring indeed. Using the human body as an analogy, the human body could not be the wonderful creation it is if all the cells in the body were identical or even similar.

Everyone's illusion is the reality that they live in, and conversely everyone's reality is the illusion they create. The one inescapable reality though is that we are all part of the one whole. We are all on the same ship, *viz.*, Spaceship Earth. And we all have the same destination. But how many of us experience this oneness, let alone live it like the reality it is?

All religions are an expression of Love that is God through individuals who are incarnations of the Divine. All religions have been founded on the same Spiritual Principles. They differ only in their expressions because they have been revealed at different times in different cultures. Thus, each expression had to be such that the people could understand what was being revealed. Of necessity, the explanations given by the Prophets are in different languages and reveal Spiritual practices that reflected the Spiritual truths based upon the way of life of the society into which the Prophet took birth. The Prophet taught as much as the people of the time could absorb, and a little more. Revealing *much* more than could be absorbed would only cause stress. For instance, the Prophet certainly could not talk about human cells, DNA and genetics in the middle ages. Who would understand such things? This is one reason why the Lord Christ is recorded to have said words to the effect, "I have many things to tell you but you cannot bear them now."

Unfortunately though, the people who claim to be followers of the messenger of God get stuck to their own interpretation of what the Master taught, and forget the basic lesson of Love. In order to serve a recent Master, some people feel compelled to spread his teachings. Others who follow teachings of earlier or different Masters similarly feel compelled to remain loyal to the teachings of the Master they follow. A clash between the new and the old then ensues. Rather than embrace fresh teachings represented by the Living Truth without giving up what is good in the older teachings followers of the old order repudiate the new and cling to ceremonies of the past even if they are no longer practical. Similarly preachers of the new order try to obliterate the old rather than build on valid practices of the old order that reflect Eternal Truths. In this clash the followers of the old and new order both seem to forget the basic lesson of Love and tolerance that all Masters have taught. The followers forget that they should not allow their Love of Truth to blind them to the Truth of Love.

And the sad truth is that if you will take away all the arguments and look beyond the surface, you will find that the real motivation for the conflict is money. Temples, Churches, Mosques and Synagogues get built as houses for worshipping God or Allah who is good and tolerant, the Source of Love and Life. Yet in order to preserve the houses of worship, humankind relies on money, and in the pursuit of money we do most of the things that the Prophets have preached against *i.e.* hating, persecuting and killing our fellow man and forcing him to accept our point of view in the name of Love, compassion and tolerance.

The recent revelations of crimes and infractions committed by a *very small fraction* of Catholic priests shows the fallibility of human beings, no matter how good the Religious Orders are and the Principles upon which they are founded. Rather than deal with the embarrassing issue immediately and in keeping with the Principles of Truth, the leaders of the Catholic Church close to the situation chose to keep it quiet. It appears that they lacked faith in the healing and cleansing powers of Truth and perhaps felt, as many of us do when confronted with a problem, that they and the Church would be better off if they concealed the Truth. They perhaps felt that with silence and time the problem would perhaps go away. Further they may have been afraid that the Church would not look good if they did what was good and right: *i.e.* acknowledge the problem and deal with it according to the Spiritual Principles the Church follows. The Church leaders in question seemed to lack faith in their own Principles. Like our Political leaders it seems that at least some of our Religious leaders also opted to look good rather than be good and therefore do good.

Before we condemn the leaders of the Catholic Church or anyone else, we should remember the injunction given by the Lord Christ, which paraphrased is, "Let he who is sinless amongst us cast the first stone." If we apply the standard suggested by the Lord Christ, I would most certainly have to disqualify myself. During these difficult times, instead of abandoning the Catholic Church as some might want to, the faithful should rally around it and should recommit themselves to living by the Principles espoused by their Church. This is an opportunity to practice love and forgiveness and no one needs it more than those who have erred.

As part of the solution, the Church offered a sum of money to the victims as part of the remedy for the crimes committed by the straying clergy. Here again mammon is seen as a necessary part of the solution to the problem and not as part of the problem.

Over time, many religious orders and their leaders tend to believe that those who accept their particular brand of religious beliefs and support their institutions are in fact serving God. In almost all cases that is not true. Institutionalized religions develop their own needs, which have to be met in order for the institutions to survive. Frequently that has nothing to do with God and His Plan. Try telling them that, though. Rather than relying on Divine Supply to fulfill their missions, as they see them, and meet their needs, religious institutions have increasingly turned to mammon for their supply. To achieve this, they need to increase their membership. This then leads to proselytizing and a lowering of standards. In the extreme it can lead to religious intolerance and bigotry.

The real grievance that the Clergy in question have caused is a violation of Spiritual trust and so the real solution has to be Spiritual. I am sure that the faithful who believe in the Church, the Church leaders as well as the victims would much prefer a Spiritual solution. To provide a Spiritual solution, the Church needs must go through a Spiritual catharsis to cleanse it from inside out at all levels, starting from the top down. Why? An analogy may help.

One drop of dirty water can pollute a whole jug of clean water. To purify the water polluted by one dirty drop, all the water in the jug has to go through the purification process. It is the same with the Church. The entire Church has to go through a cleansing process and recommit itself to faithfully live by the everlasting Spiritual Principles it was built upon and represents. If it does this, as I believe it will, all of us will be much better for it. The leaders failed because in dealing with a difficult situation, they chose to reason with their human mind rather than adhere to the Principles of Truth. As Dr. Mehta repeated so often, if we strictly live by Spiritual Principles, "The Principles will Guide you, The Principles will Guard you and the Master will Grace you."

The Catholic Church is a very good institution and will survive and grow. It is a force for good and the vows of poverty and celibacy that the Catholic Church requires of its Clergy are supported by many other faiths as well. But these are exceedingly hard vows to keep. Therefore all the more reason to adhere to strict standards rather than lowering the standards in order to meet the institutional needs of the Church to increase the number of followers who would then donate more money to support the mammon-based activities of the Church.

There are some religions that are so tolerant of other belief systems that they do not try to convert anyone to their way of thinking. For instance you cannot easily become a convert to Judaism. You have to really *want* to practice the Jewish way of life. There is a waiting period, a probationary period during which you are given a chance to think things over. Only after you have passed through the probationary period that can be anywhere up to three years, only then will a Rabbi begin to instruct you about the religion.

And Buddhists, Sikhs and Jains do not proselytize. They accept converts, but do not actively proselytize.

Between those who strive to convert others to their religion, *i.e.*, belief systems, and those who do not, the Zoroastrians of today (though not those of the past) represent one extreme, and the Hindus the opposite extreme. Due to a trend that took hold in India about 150 years ago, many Zoroastrian priests, refuse to convert anyone. Fortunately not all Zoroastrian priests and lay believers accept this rigid position and a few Zoroastrian priests are inducting non-Zoroastrians who wish to practice the Zoroastrian faith. However, no one is *actively* seeking to convert non-Zoroastrians into the religion.

The Hindus on the other hand do not have, nor do they need, any such thing as conversion at all. Hindus accept all forms of worship as being valid. Since God is in everything and He is everything, it makes sense that you should be able to worship God through everything and in a way that appeals to you, provided of course that it does not harm others including yourself. You should be able to see God in everything. Because the Hindus accept all forms of worship, the author is of the opinion that technically we are all Hindus. We may be Zoroastrian Hindus, Muslim Hindus, Jewish Hindus, Christian Hindus, Buddhist Hindus or Vaishnav Hindus, Shaivite Hindus and any of the other myriads of Hindu creeds. If you will go to a Hindu temple, you will see images of Hindu Deities such as Lord Ram, Lord Krishna, Hanuman, Shiva, Pârvati and Laxmi, alongside those of Jesus, Guru Nanak, Zarathushtra, symbols of Islam and Buddhism, and symbols of any other religion, which the local temple keeper can lay his hands on. Hindus even have room for atheists in their belief system. After all, if we accept the notion that in His Pristine State, God is Limitless and Formless, then any *concept* of God cannot but be incomplete, and thus at least partially false. Most atheists reject all man-made concepts of God as being invalid, in the sense of not adequately or properly representing the Reality—and the Hindu way of thinking accepts that notion, too.

In fact, Hindus also have total compassion for sinners. Many Hindus accept that there is no such thing as a good man and a bad man; there is only the man who is awake and the man who is asleep. The man who does seemingly bad things does so because the God within him is asleep. When the God within the man will awaken, the man will stop doing foolish things. Tolerance is very much a part of the Hindu way of life.

Recent events in India have cast a shadow over this beautiful and tolerant religion. But what has happened recently—and also what happened during the 1947 Hindu-Muslim riots—is and was a *perversion* of the teachings of this religion—and not at all consonant with the *actual* teachings of this religion.

These incidents have more to do with politics than religion and certainly have nothing to do with spirituality and Truth. Ambitious political and religious mis-leaders (one cannot call them leaders) are fanning the flames of hatred in the name of Love.

Whenever someone claims that they believe in Scripture, what is usually left unsaid is that they believe in their *interpretation* of Scripture. We live in a relative world, which is balanced by opposites. We cannot have an up without a down, a front without a back, east without west, hot without cold, *et cetera.* Because we live in a relative world, as soon as anyone takes a position, they immediately create their opposition. You cannot have a right without a wrong, and no matter how right you think you are, there will be people who are equally firmly convinced that you are wrong. On the other hand, Love has no position, but Love surrounds and supports all positions. Love can do this because Love is Universal. It is like Silence that can sustain all sound, surround and contain all sound even though it has no sound.

Many religious people think that their point of view is the only right point of view because they believe and have faith in their beliefs and therefore are convinced that it is the Truth. We have to recognize that Truth Is. Truth can stand on its own and does not need our belief and/or faith to support It. For instance, it is true that the Earth is round. Whether you believe it or not, your belief will not change the fact that the Earth is round; the truth that the Earth is round stands on its own merit. However, if you will also believe it, then by your accepting this truth, the truth will enlighten your mind and your understanding of the Earth, and nature will increase by the light of this truth.

We have to also recognize that our beliefs are based on our opinions and from our discussion on the value of opinions (Chapter 3) we observe how fallacious our opinions are. From this we can get some idea of how unreliable and misleading our beliefs can be.

Truth Is; but belief is optional. Truth will help the believer and not the other way around. Another example may also shed some light on the relationship between Truth, belief and faith. If you believe that God will protect you and have faith in your belief and then decide to jump out of the 50th floor to test your belief and faith, what are the chances that you will survive the jump?

Belief and faith without the support of Truth are meaningless at best and dangerous at worst. It is Truth, and belief and faith in the Truth that will save you and guide you. Belief and faith in falsehoods will only cause pain and confusion. Belief and faith in false gods have caused societies to indulge in paganism and human sacrifice and many other wrong practices to appease the gods of their conception.

The journey toward the Truth is to live with love based upon universal spiritual Principles that include all of creation. It takes wisdom and courage, which are born of and sustained by love.

Love and hate cannot coexist anymore than knowledge and ignorance or light and darkness can coexist. Some people argue that you need darkness to see light and that without this contrast we could not see light. I would recommend that these people should go to the desert where there is no vegetation and face the sun, so they cannot see their own shadow. During midday, when there is no darkness, they will be able to see the light of the sun. Just as we need wisdom to recognize ignorance, so also we need light to see darkness, and not the other way around. You cannot see anything in total darkness. But with the light of a candle you can see the darkness.

Whenever someone disagrees with us, it is a great opportunity to practice the principle of tolerance, understanding and cooperation. Viewed as such, we will not hate people who disagree with us but silently thank them for providing us with the opportunity to exercise the principles we choose to live by.

Have the Taliban succeeded in destroying the Lord Buddha? Not hardly. The Lord Buddha is not confined to a statue anymore than the Prophet Mohammed is confined to the Ka'aba in Mecca, the Lord Christ is confined to a cross, the Lord Moses to Mt. Sinai or Asho Zarathushtra, the Prophet of Iran, is confined to Mt. Damavand. Even though their physical forms are no more their consciousness and teachings are still very much alive. Why? Because these Masters represent Living Truth, and try as we might, we mortals will not be able to eradicate the work that they did and are still doing. Indeed, in spite of the so-called Islamic revolution, many Iranians recognize that their culture and past glory is based upon the enduring teachings of Asho Zarathushtra, who some say was born about 8,500 B.C.

Those who have grown beyond the barrier of the conscious human mind and have realized the higher planes of Supra-consciousness and experienced the Source of all sources commonly called God, will tell you that there is no competition amongst the Prophets. Mohammed will not get upset if you follow the teachings of Buddha, and Jesus will not get upset if you follow the teachings of Zarathushtra, who in turn will not be upset if you follow the teaching of Guru Nanak, *et cetera*. They are all servants of God. All of them taught that it is only the Will of God that should be manifested. Indeed, they all insisted that all credit should be given to God or Allah. But many people who claim to love one or the other of the Prophets will, because of their imagined love for the Prophet they claim to follow, perpetrate hate and heap harm upon their fellow human beings who do not share their beliefs. They do not realize that their hateful behavior is totally against the teachings of the Prophets and indeed soils the good name of their own Prophet's teachings.

The Taliban did not hurt the Buddha in the slightest way. In fact they have caused a backlash in the world and strengthened the support for Buddha and His teachings. They have not even succeeded in eradicating the *form* of the Buddha from this world, which they tried to eliminate in such a dramatic fashion.

According to a CNN report that aired on November 19th and 20th, 2001, Rudi Bakhtiar reported that a movement has started in Switzerland to rebuild the 1800-year-old statues of Buddha that were built *circa* 200 to 400 A.D. in Bamiyan. There was another report that a golden statue of Buddha is being built in China that will be larger than the statues that were destroyed in Bamiyan. Further, in the issue dated December 31, 2001, *The Times of India*, New Delhi—a leading daily newspaper in India—reported that the new regime of President Hamed Karzai, in Afghanistan has committed itself to restoring the statues of Buddha that were destroyed in March of last year by the Taliban.

By destroying the statues of Lord Buddha in Bamiyan, all the Taliban succeeded in doing was destroying Afghanistan's cultural heritage and the contribution made by the Afghanis who lived centuries earlier. Centuries earlier, their ancestors worked painstakingly and with love to carve the impressive icons of the Lord Buddha out of the cliffs in Bamiyan. One of the statues in Bamiyan was 174 feet tall. To carve these statues out of the cliffs of Bamiyan may have taken decades. In about 20 days, the Taliban demolished the work that withstood centuries of erosion. Now where once imposing statues looked across the valley, there are only big cavities in the cliffs of Bamiyan. By this act and many others, the Taliban will surely go down in history as one of the more sorry regimes that ever terrorized a nation.

Can you blame the Taliban for doing what they did? Of course not. We are all products of our environment. The Taliban surely believed—and many of them probably still do—in the righteousness of their cause. Why else would so many of them be willing to die for it? I am certain that the incessant bombing of Afghanistan saddened much of the world and most of us in the USA, including President Bush—notwithstanding the political rhetoric he has to indulge in. We would have preferred to reason with the Taliban. But nothing is more difficult to open than a mind that is closed, and by their actions and words the Taliban demonstrated that they had a closed mind and a total disregard for world opinion, or at least the opinion and/or sentiments of a large segment of the world. President Bush had no choice but to authorize the campaign against the Taliban.

People who are willing to die for a cause seem to think that they are making the ultimate sacrifice. Actually dying for a cause is very easy. It is much more difficult to *live* for a cause. If God wanted us to die for Him why would He give us life? He wants us to *live* for Him. In order to live for God, we have to fight the wrong tendencies in us every minute of every day and kill that aspect within us which is not in keeping with the Will Divine.

This is the real jihad and not the false jihad that many Muslims claim to be engaged in when they decide to fight and kill their fellow human beings who have a God-given right to follow their own will. In order to fight the real jihad, we have to live and die daily, and that is much more difficult than blowing oneself up once and destroying prematurely the life God gave us.

What if anything can be learned from the Taliban Tragedy?

There are many lessons that can be learned. Some of the more important ones seem to be:

- Do unto others, as you would have others do unto you.
- Do not oppress your own citizens, and respect the right of others to disagree with you.
- Any society that thinks their redemption lies in the destruction of others cannot lead the world. A rich country whose leaders indulge their citizens in the belief that they can forever deny others what they claim for themselves, also cannot lead the world for long. This is just restating that we should do unto others as we would have done unto ourselves.
- The world's people cannot give in to terror or shortsighted selfishness.
- We live in a world without walls. In that world, we have no choice but to make a home for all our children. The essence of our effort to see that every child has a chance must be to

assure each an equal opportunity, not to become *equal*, but to become *different*—to realize whatever unique potential of mind, body, and spirit he or she possesses.

- Practice Love. It is both infectious and contagious, and is even effective against those who love to hate. Being out of control and undisciplined, most people *react* and do not *act*. They react to their environment. If we treat them with love and understanding, they will react to us with love and understanding. Love is the only force that can eliminate hate permanently. Just as light transforms darkness, Love will absorb the darts of hate and then eliminate it by transforming hate into Love.

An anonymous author wrote: "Fragrance is the forgiveness that a flower showers with love upon the feet that crush it."

Let us strive to be like a flower.

The next chapter explores how each of us can contribute towards creating a Civilized world.

CHAPTER 8
CREATING A CIVILIZED WORLD

Many people think, "I am so powerless and helpless. Nothing that I can do will help change the Universe in any meaningful way. Therefore I may as well accept the situation and live with it. What else can I do?"

Somewhere in the Bible it is mentioned that God made man in His image. A reflection of this is the fact that in a very real sense each one of us is the god of the individual universe that we create, perceive and live in.

We have to recognize and remind ourselves that our personal Universe, and indeed the entire Universe, revolves around each one of us. Each one of us is the center of our Universe and we create our own universe that is shaped by our attitudes, thoughts and attachments. We are responsible for creating the universe we experience and everything that happens to us in it. Therefore as individuals we are not helpless and weak. We will be helpless and weak only if we choose not to use the power to change and influence the universe that exists within each one of us.

Around any center you can draw an infinite number of circles and spheres. If you make changes in all the circles and spheres it will not affect the center in any way. But if you move the center even a little, all the circles and spheres built around it will literally get shaken and will either have to move with the center or they will collapse.

To change our individual Universe all we have to do is to change ourselves. But this is much more easily said than done. Many people have observed that, "After all is said and done, a lot more is said than done." Let us not make that mistake but rather take advantage of the opportunity life gives us to do what is right by getting in tune with our Source.

To be sure, we all change. We cannot help it. Change is the one constant in all of Creation and is also reflected in the physical universe. We are constantly influencing and are being influenced by the situations, people, environment and experiences to which we are exposed. But do we have any *control* over how we change?

Progress brings change but change does not necessarily bring progress. We need to ensure that all change in our life results in progress. How can we make that a continuous reality? This brings us back to the relationship between control or the lack thereof and the states of chaos and progress. If you will recall, in the chapter entitled *The Journey*, we mentioned that chaos and progress are both dynamic situations. In any dynamic situation, there are only two possibilities: *viz.*, either you have control over the situation and can direct it, or you have no control over the situation and it becomes chaotic. We recognized that life is dynamic and therefore there are only two possibilities, *viz.*, we can either gain control over the primary forces in our lives and thus use them to direct our lives in a chaotic world, or we have no control over the primary forces in our lives and thus become victims of and buffeted by the circumstances created by them.

The chapter also elaborates that the primary mechanism in our life, the medium through which we communicate with and interact with the Universe, are the senses of our physical body and our mind. Of these, the mind has the potential of being the controlling mechanism. Therefore, if you are to gain any control over your life and direct it, it is most crucial to gain control over your mind.

The whole purpose of this book is to identify the Journey of Life Eternal and share Spiritual Principles that will help the reader embark on, and hopefully complete, the journey. To do so, one has to gain control over his/her mind and thus control the senses and take charge of one's individual life in a turbulent world. You cannot control anyone else and therefore you cannot change him or her either. You may be able to inspire a few people by your living example. But here again, it is good to remember that you cannot inspire those who do not aspire. The only person you can ever hope to control and therefore change is yourself. To change the Universe within you, you really do not need to change anything else. All you have to do is change yourself.

But that is hard enough. Most of us would prefer to change the Universe outside ourselves so that it serves our needs, rather than the other way around. It is wishful thinking that one can change the universe outside. That will not happen. If pursued it will only lead to frustration.

The battle with yourself is the ultimate battle. It is the longest, fiercest and loneliest battle in the entire universe. Longest and fiercest because the adversary is your exact equal, *i.e., your-*

self, and loneliest because it is fought within you. And when you are victorious there are no accolades in the physical world and no certificates or awards are given, because no one in the physical world can witness your victory. That is one reason why those who witnessed Jesus on the cross, may have thought that he had lost. Yet even when he was nailed to the cross, it is recorded that He pleaded with God with words to the effect, "Forgive them Father for they know not what they do," and before He gave up his breath, He signaled His victory by saying words to the effect, "It is finished," indicating thereby that He had completed the work that was assigned to him by His Father. Similarly it is recorded that when the Lord Buddha had achieved Nirvâna, Mâra (the Pali word for Satan) appeared before Buddha and challenged Him by asking, "Who can confirm that you achieved Nirvâna? Who is your witness?" Buddha responded to Mara's challenge by pointing to the Earth and said, "Earth is my witness."

Why do we need to fight ourselves? Why the need to discipline ourselves and to what end should we be committed? We need to be disciplined and committed to become free from:

- The deception of our mind and the illusory world it creates for us.
- The confusion and bondage that is a result of being attached to the illusions created by our mind.
- The entrapment of our mind and ego, and thus realize our true identity.

To be free is natural. We were born to be free. But free from what? Such is the complete deception accomplished by our mind that we do not think of ourselves as being trapped in our respective minds or by our ego, nor do we think that our mind is out of control. Our idea of freedom seems to be driven by our desires as expressed in the U.S. Declaration of Independence, which states among other things that we have the inalienable rights to life, liberty and the pursuit of happiness. Rather than look for happiness within ourselves, the words "pursuit of happiness" imply that we should look for happiness *outside* ourselves. I am certain that this is not what the Founding Fathers meant when they signed the Declaration of Independence, but judging from our behavior and that of the great majority of the world, it certainly appears that we are pursuing happiness *outside* ourselves.

If we interpret freedom to mean the right to satisfy our insatiable desires and abandon all sense of discipline, decency and morality and indulge in satisfying our every whim and fancy, then as Dr. Mehta used to say, it will drive us to a state of frenzy which will cause us to be in a state that is closer to being "demon-crazy" than being a state of democracy. Dr. Mehta used to say words to the effect, "Unrestrained freedom of expression and pleasures of the senses will lead to *free doom* and does not reflect the Freedom in the Mind Divine."

In *The Lessons of History*, which they gleaned from four decades of their work on the ten monumental volumes of *The Story of Civilization*, Will and Ariel Durant state, "Since men love freedom, and the freedom of individuals in society requires some regulation of conduct, the first condition of freedom is its limitation; make it absolute and it dies in chaos." We can judge the values of a society and/or culture by studying what they invest in and what is popular with the masses. The preponderance of our activities has to do with escaping what is commonly referred to as the reality of day-to-day existence. The recent phenomenal success of the Harry Potter series of books is a reflection of how much we enjoy fantasy. The popular radio and TV talk shows reveal the values that segments of our society cherish and live by. Entertainments and drugs (which include alcohol) help us escape and relax. Why the need to escape? Escape from what? The idea that true freedom can only be achieved if we are free from desires seems alien to us. After all, life would not be worth living if we could not satisfy our physical desires and our mind. We cannot imagine that striving to satisfy our desires causes us the frustrations we experience. If we examine our lives more closely we will find that is indeed the case.

The Lord Buddha taught that desire is the only cause of suffering. Other Masters, including Jesus Christ, have said similar things. If we accept the observation made by the Lord Buddha and the other Masters, then by constantly fanning the flames of desire, through all the advertising in mass media, modern society is certainly contributing to the suffering of the masses. In the Bhagavad Gîtâ, Lord Krishna explains, "To try and eliminate desires by indulging in them is like trying to put out a fire by adding fuel to it."

In his book *The Story of My Experiments with Truth*, Mahatma Gandhi declared that the following verse from Chapter II of *The Song Celestial* by Sir Edwin Arnold, which is a poetic translation of the Bhagavad Gîtâ, is one of his favorite verses:

> … That man alone is wise
> Who keeps the mastery of himself! If one
> Ponders on objects of the sense, there springs
> Attraction; from attraction grows desire,
> Desire flames to fierce passion, passion breeds
> Recklessness; then the memory- all betrayed-
> Lets noble purpose go, and saps the mind,
> Until purpose, mind, and man are all undone.
> But, if one deals with objects of the sense
> Not loving and not hating, making them
> Serve his free soul, which rests serenely Lord,
> Lo! such a man comes to tranquility;
> And out of that tranquility shall rise
> The end and healing of his earthly pains, …

What is the noble purpose? It is none other than to get in touch with your own true self, your soul and through it to ultimately get in touch with the Will Divine and live according to whatever is revealed to one's inner being.

Most of us do not realize this, but the fact remains that all of us are only channels. Our bodies are nothing but a set of hollow tubes. Food flows in and out of our body, as does water, air, sounds, light, thoughts and other radiations. In fact if, for whatever reason, the flow and circulation of these Five Elementals through our bodies is blocked or disrupted we will fall sick. Our bodies are meant to be channels through which the physical Universe flows and distributes itself.

Our mind is the channel through which thoughts flow. Throughout this book, the author's thoughts are being distributed. Now most of us do not think of ourselves as channels through which the Universe recycles and distributes itself, but the fact remains that that is exactly what happens. When you travel from one city to another, you are distributing parts of the physical universe as surely as the air that disperses seeds or birds and bees that disperse pollen.

We can be channels of either good or other than good. All depends upon the Principles we live by and which we use to

193

make choices that reflect the values we cherish.

If you will take the time to study the issue, you will find that the great majority of people do not have any guiding principles, which they use to make day-to-day decisions. Most people just *react* to situations that occur in their lives. They do not have any real *purpose* in life, a *goal* of life and principles, which they embrace and live by. They live day-to-day, reacting to the situations that arise in their lives. And because their minds are out of control, their lives are out of control. Is it any wonder then that the world is experiencing so much turmoil?

If asked, most people will tell you that they prefer truth to lies. Yet, if you see how many people behave, you will realize that they have more faith in lies than in truth. When caught in a bind, many people will try to lie their way out of a situation rather than tell the truth and face the consequences of their actions. As a result, many people seldom say what they mean and seldom mean what they say. Therefore, it is no surprise that they are confused and their lives are in disarray and full of disharmony. This is reflected in society in general, including our government and business institutions. Notice how many people plead the Fifth Amendment when called before Congress—and many of them are supposed to be our leaders and outstanding citizens. Are they really?

What is the solution to this dilemma? How do we begin to correct the condition? As previously mentioned above, if you move the center of a circle, the entire circle shifts with it. Since you are at the center of your universe, the best place to begin the work of correcting the problems of the universe is to start with yourself. Learn to observe yourself and question your motives. Why do you do what you do? Why do you like what attracts you? Do not try to *force* yourself to change, because that may cause more harm than good. If you will live by the Seven Principles of Right Surrender, then you will *automatically* gain control over your mind and senses and you will change *naturally*. What you want to do is live a life according to Principles that will *naturally* align you with the Source within you.

We all influence and are influenced by the thoughts, things, people and environment to which we are exposed. If you sit by a warm fire, you naturally become warm. The same thing is true if you are exposed to a cold environment. When you live by the

Principles of Right Surrender and are exposed to higher levels of consciousness, your mind will also become more aware naturally. But just as you can shut out the light of the mighty Sun by closing your eyes or pulling a shade over them, similarly you can shut out the Light of your soul by closing your mind and/or keeping it filled by clinging to your own thoughts.

Learn to become *familiar* with your mind and use its natural characteristics to help it grow towards higher levels of consciousness. You cannot change the characteristics of your mind any more than you can change the characteristics of water. As we observed in earlier chapters, all water, whether it is fresh or salty, hot or cold, clean or dirty has one common characteristic: the ability to make things wet.

Now you cannot change this basic characteristic of water. You also know that you need water to drink, cook and wash with. You can also swim in it, sail on it, and drown in it. Water can be useful and also harmful depending upon how you deal with it. However, no matter what you do, you cannot change water. But you can become *familiar* with the characteristics of water and learn to use it to your advantage. The same is true with fire and the other elements. You can cook with fire, it keeps you warm, but it can also kill you. You need air to breathe but a hurricane can destroy both property and life. The same is true of the human mind. You need to become *familiar* with it and how it functions.

The human mind has certain basic characteristics, which have been described in fair detail in the chapter on the Seven Principles of Right Surrender. No matter how hard you try, you will not be able to *change* the characteristics of the human mind. But you can become *familiar* with them and learn to use them to control the mind. Once you gain control of your mind, you can use it to grow to higher levels of consciousness. Most of us are victimized by our mind and remain enslaved by it and are forced to live in a world of illusion created by it for its own satisfaction.

My childhood friend and neighbor Mr. Nariman N. Rabadi once told me that if mankind could control the three T's, then we would all be better off. The three T's are Tongue, Temper and Temptation. Of course, to control the three T's, we have to control our mind. The Principles of Right Surrender will help you gain control over your mind and use it to break free from the shackles of attachment to the physical universe.

Only you can do this for yourself. No one else can do this for you. Is it an easy task? No. It is very hard indeed because what comes in the way is your mind and ego ... the very aspects of your personality with whom you identify and through whom you interact with people in society. So, what to do?

This is where the Lord Buddha has given an injunction to his disciples, which is: The seeker (*i.e.*, Spiritual seeker) should seek the company of his superiors. If he cannot find the company of his superiors, let him keep the company of his equals. If he cannot find the company of his equals, then let him live alone. But let him shun the company of fools.

The above injunction is true not only for Spiritual seekers but seekers of all knowledge. After all, if you want to learn any subject, you seek the company of someone who knows *more* than you. That is what the apprenticeship program of trade unions is all about. In schools and universities, you learn from teachers and professors and keep the company of your fellow students.

The need to remain in constant touch with the Source that is reflected in the above-cited advice given by the Lord Buddha to his disciples is very nicely illustrated in the following story about *The Lonely Ember:*

> A member of a certain church, who previously had been attending services regularly, stopped going.
>
> After a few weeks, the pastor decided to visit him. It was a chilly evening.
>
> The pastor found the man at home alone, sitting before a blazing fire.
>
> Guessing the reason for his pastor's visit, the man welcomed him, led him to a big chair near the fireplace and waited. The pastor made himself comfortable but said nothing. In the grave silence, he contemplated the play of the flames around the burning logs.
>
> After some minutes, the pastor took the fire tongs, carefully picked up a brightly burning ember and placed it to one side of the hearth all alone.
>
> Then he sat back in his chair, still silent. The host watched all this in quiet fascination. As the one lone ember's flame diminished, there was a momentary glow and then its fire was no more. Soon it was cold and "dead as a

doornail."

Not a word had been spoken since the initial greeting.

Just before the pastor was ready to leave, he picked up the cold, dead ember and placed it back in the middle of the fire. Immediately it began to glow once more with the light and warmth of the burning coals around it. As the pastor reached the door to leave, his host said, "Thank you so much for your visit and especially for the fiery sermon. I shall be back in church next Sunday."

Author Unknown

To help his disciples see things clearly from a Spiritual point of view, the Lord Buddha made the following additional remarks about fools:

"The fool thinks: 'This is my wife, this is my wealth, these are my children.' But the fool does not realize that his own life does not belong to him; how then can a wife, wealth or children belong to him?"

If we accept the above definition of a fool from a Spiritual point of view, then we can see that in the Spiritual sense, almost everyone is a fool. The author accepts Buddha's definition stated above as correct. If you do not own the very breath that flows through your lungs and sustains your life, if you do not even own your own *self*, how can you own anything else?

If you have any doubts and think that you own the breath that flows through your lungs, then I suggest that you hold on to it. *Don't* exhale. Do *not* surrender your breath back to the Universe. Of course you know that you cannot do that and live. You *have* to surrender your breath back to the Universe, because it does not belong to you. Your breath flows through your body as part of the process of life, as does water, food, light/heat, and space. Nothing really belongs to us. Paraphrasing Chief Joseph Seattle, "It is all part of the web of life. We have not created the web of life but are merely small links within one of its strands."

The basic insecurity of the mind and its tendency to get attached to various thoughts, people and objects creates the illusion that we can *own* things. This tendency also makes us want to own other people, either as chattel, as in slaves and/or bonded labor, or spouse, children and relatives in the name of love.

197

Many of us know that in reality, we were born with nothing and we are going to take back nothing with us. That is because we own absolutely nothing. Yet how many of us consciously strive to *live* with this reality?

It is very difficult to accept these truths and harder still to live by them. For many people it takes many years of inner struggle to finally recognize that they do not own their spouses or their children. It took centuries for us to end slavery in most of the world. Unfortunately in some parts of the world slavery still exists today. And in all parts of the world people routinely say, and mean it while saying it: "This is *my* wife or husband, these are *my* children or parents."

Very few of us can arrive at a state of being where we can accept and live by the truth that nothing belongs to anyone and everything belongs to the Divine and should be used in serving His Will. Very few of us can accept and live by these realities from the very start. Many religious communes over the centuries have lived and worked by these values. Some exist to this day and new ones are also being formed.

Society at large has to change considerably before it can develop systems of wealth sharing that will nurture Spiritual values. But there is a pressing need to do just that especially after September 11, 2001.

Until such time as societies the world over adopt systems of economics that reflect Spiritual values, those of us who are interested in growing to know the truth have to live by the sacred Principles that have been revealed to humankind by Spiritual Masters who have descended to help us to grow towards the Divine.

Revered Dr. Mehta explained that human beings are born with different kinds of minds, which in general can be described as:

- The mind that wants everything but God,
- The mind that wants everything plus God,
- The mind that wants God plus everything,
- The mind that wants only God, and
- The mind that does not want anything ... not even God.

Of the various minds described above, only the last one has any chance of experiencing the Divine Reality. We have emphasized that it is the human mind with all its insecurities and wants that is the creator of illusion and binds us to the object of attachment. As long as the mind wants this or that, or does not want them, it means that it is attached, either positively or negatively, to objects and results, and is therefore full of desire. All desires are the cause of suffering. If desire can be qualified as good or bad, then desiring God could be classified as a good desire. Yet it will also lead to suffering. It is only when the mind is emptied of *all* desires and is silent that it will automatically experience the vibrations of its soul. Then the mind will do nothing of its own volition, and will merely witness God in Action. When we replace our self-consciousness with God Consciousness, then we become channels for the Divine to work out Its Plan through us. We have then achieved a state of being Godman, *i.e,.* God in human form, because it is God who is working through us. Until we achieve that state of being, our self-consciousness prevents God from working through us. Yet He supports us even if we go against His Will.

Never forget that the battle is *within* you, and the challenge is to gain control of your mind and senses. You have to *empty* your mind, and *eliminate* your ego rather than identify with them and thus become enslaved by them. Living a life striving to satisfy the desires that originate in your human mind and ego will lead only to suffering and bondage. Most of us plan our days around mammon and pray to God to support our effort. Instead we should plan our day around God, and mammon will automatically come as needed. This is reflected in the statements made by Jesus when he said words to the effect: "Look at the birds of the air, they sow not nor do they reap. Yet My Father in Heaven provides for them. Are ye lesser than birds of the air? But seek ye first the Kingdom of God and His Righteousness and all else will be added unto you."

Would you like to be in a vehicle over which you have no control? Of course not. The mind and the body together represent the vehicle through which your soul is journeying through this Universe. Before you can use them, you need to learn to control them.

You cannot give what you do not have. Before you can teach

a subject, you have to learn it yourself. You cannot become what you are not. The Lord Christ taught, "Be ye perfect as your Father in Heaven is perfect." When you *are* perfect, whatever you *do* will be naturally perfect. Perfection flows from perfection naturally. Dr. Mehta said, "Be so ere ye do."

About 400 years ago, the great Iranian Sufi Hazrat Jalaluddin Rumi, whose tomb is in modern day Turkey, is recorded to have said words to the effect, "In the physical world, there is no creation. There is only the becoming of the Being." You can only become what you are.

How many of us focus on our beings and try to change our beings? If you are unwilling and/or unable to pick up the gauntlet now, do not despair. Most of us are not going to be able to gain full control over our minds and bodies and so we will be unable to "Be perfect."

Does that mean that there is no hope for us? Does that mean that we cannot make positive contributions in and for this world? Of course not. Hope's flame is eternal, and each one of us can make positive contributions within the limits of our capability. And the more we strive, the more our capacity will increase. To begin with, at least practice the principle of Humility, and practice being compassionate towards the environment and all who share it with you. The most important environment is the one within you, *i.e.,* your body and mind. Look after your body. Exercise it and eat the right kind of food, and take control of your mind and thoughts.

Let us examine some statistics.

It is estimated that there are about six billion people on earth. Yet, if each of us will examine our own life, we will find that in our entire life, we do not interact on a day-to-day basis with more than about 100 people. Think about it for a moment. Even if you are part of a large family, you are close to only a few of your siblings and relatives. And you do not interact all the time with even the relatives with whom you are close.

Similarly, if you are among the fortunate few who have gone to school and college, you interact with a few teachers and friends. At work you interact with a few colleagues. When you add all the people that you interact with on a one-on-one basis, for most of us the number will be less than 100 in our *entire* life.

One way of looking at this statistic is to accept that out of a total population of six billion, the Universe, Fate, Destiny, call it what you will, has selected these 100 people for you to share your life and experiences with. If you divide the total population of the earth, *i.e.,* 6,000 million people, by 100, then this group of 100 people represents one person out of 60 million people that the Universe has selected for you to grow through life, and help them to do the same. Should you not be nice to them? Should you not be willing to sacrifice for them and support them by sharing your good thoughts, time, resources and such?

And we do not deal with all 100 people at once. Mercifully, to make it easier for us, the Universe has distributed them over our lifetime. At any given stage in our lives we may deal with no more than 10 to 15 people on a day-to-day basis. If each one of us will commit to loving the 100 or so persons that we interact with on a day-to-day basis in our entire life, the world will be much more harmonious and civilized. Then, like the Himalayan nation of Bhutan, each country will be able to measure success in terms of their Gross National Happiness instead of their Gross National Product, and together we will celebrate and learn from our differences and enjoy Global Peace.

We have seen in earlier chapters that the human mind is limited and incapable of experiencing the Limitless. To negotiate its way around and understand the immense universe, the human mind breaks up the Unity into small parts that it can deal with. We can use these very limitations and capacity of the human mind to create a civilized world. To ask the human mind to love all of creation is to make a request that is beyond its capacity. But it is capable of showering 100 people with love especially if the 100 people are broken up into smaller groups that it has to interact over a lifetime. To do so, usually all we have to do is to give up our point of view.

Yet how many of us are prepared to sacrifice our petty point of view for these special people who have been chosen for us and with whom we share our life? The reality is that quite often, older siblings bully their younger brothers and sisters, and most schools have a bully. In the name of freedom and competition, many of us prey upon each other, especially if they are strangers or belong to a different country or culture. Employers and employees abuse each other, and the list goes on and on. The question is, why? The answer is always the same. We human beings are shortsighted, insecure and therefore selfish. We choose to ignore the physical realities of the Universe even though we now have the technological prowess to go into space and clearly see that we are sharing the planet with each other and with the different species of plant and animal life. But our policies and actions do not reflect this new awareness. We are also increasingly aware that cutting down rain forests, polluting our air and water and covering a substantial portion of the earth under cement, asphalt and concrete is causing real damage. Yet we are unable to stop ourselves.

Why is that? Why do we lack the collective political and social will to make the commitment necessary to do what is right? This as discussed earlier is due to the law of inertia. We are *entrenched* in our way of life. The speed with which new technologies are being developed and adopted is so dizzying that a substantial percentage of the people of this world are being left behind. Even in technologically developed nations, the masses are too busy struggling to make ends meet, and depend upon the leaders of their respective nations to solve the problems we all face. Unfortunately many of the leaders have demonstrated that they lack the moral fiber and the strength to make the tough decisions that are necessary to put us on a course that will prevent global catastrophes. Of course, we cannot fault them entirely. Running for political office has become a very expensive proposition. The amount of money spent running for public office defies common sense. Candidates and their parties spend millions of dollars to win the right to a job that pays less than they could earn in the private sector. One would think that people who do this must be real angels and want to work for the public good. However, the public record shows otherwise. Today political leaders do not enjoy the trust and confidence of their own constituents—and this is true all over the world.

Since this is the case, can the citizens of the world rely upon these political leaders to correct the mistakes of the past? The answer is obvious. The problem is so complex and there are so many opposing interests involved that even well intentioned leaders such as President George W. Bush cannot accomplish much. We suffer from the paralysis of analysis. And even if they could, there is always the threat of assassination. What is the solution to the dilemma?

Again the answer is the same. Each one of us has to take responsibility. If each one of us will carry out the small actions needed to help the environment that we live in, then the world will become a better place. One of the Buddha's living instructions to his monks is for each monk to plant a sapling and take care of it for five years and repeat the process throughout their lives. If the public at large followed just this one instruction given by the Lord Buddha, and if each person on earth were to plant a sapling and take care of it until it becomes a tree that will go a long way to purifying the air. "Think globally, act locally."

Proactive citizen groups can come up with many ideas that will help the environment in their own communities. Their actions will encourage like-minded politicians to propose laws and policies that will support such activities.

According to some estimates, three quarters of the world's six billion people live in poverty. Many of these people are desperately trying to survive. Some organizations that provide food aid report that annually about 800 million people are starving. In their struggle to exist, we cannot blame them if they cut down forests or devastate other natural resources. "Solutions to save the forests that don't address the pocket book won't fly," says Randy Curtis, a director of conservations finance with *The Nature Conservancy*, the world's largest private organization. Make preservation *profitable*, and conservation will follow.

This observation recognizes our social values, which give money paramount importance. Until such time as society can develop a value system that recognizes the prime importance of nature and her contribution, and the secondary—if not a still lower ranking—for money as a form of wealth, we will *have* to make preservation profitable to save what is left of our natural environment.

This type of thinking is beginning to take hold in some parts of world. Ecotourism is helping save the wild animal parks in Kenya and South Africa as well as helping save what is left of the rain forests in Brazil and Costa Rica. At the heart of Ecotourism is the notion that people who appreciate nature must be willing to put their money where their values are and pay-to-play, pay-to-see, and pay-to-protect. And the model seems to be working. Among the 425 million international travelers each year, some experts believe more than half partake in some form of nature-based activity.

Concerned citizen groups started many of these conservation activities when they realized that they could not depend upon politicians to save the environment.

It appears that at present political leaders are not *leading* their constituents. Mercifully some of them are trying to *follow* them. Very often before a policy is announced or proposed, sample opinion polls are taken to find out how the public will react. If the reaction is not favorable then the policy is shelved and another trial balloon to test the public's reaction to a particular proposed policy is floated. Rather than make tough choices, controversial issues are placed on the ballots for the citizens' vote. As mentioned above, most of us are struggling to keep our heads above water in the ocean of existence. Most citizens really do not have the time, skills and information necessary to consider the pros and cons of all the issues we are expected to vote on.

Until such time as we have *real* leaders who have a vision for peace and harmony and the courage to communicate that vision and inspire citizens to make the hard choices needed to help societies embrace the right values and grow in the right direction, citizen groups around the world should act to show the political leaders the way. Some political leaders may then develop the courage to *follow* the lead of the citizen groups and challenge their party bosses and propose the right legislative measures and policies and/or block the wrong ones. Many such groups already exist and have contributed immensely to increasing the awareness of the environmental and other global issues threatening all of us.

History has shown that the revolutionaries of today who rebel against and overthrow the tyrants of today become the oppressors of tomorrow, and in turn are the tyrants that are overthrown by the rebels of the future who will themselves become the new oppressors ... and the cycle will repeat itself. After analyzing the lessons of history, Will and Ariel Durant concluded, "The only real revolution is in the enlightenment of the mind and the improvement of character, the only real emancipation is the individual, and the only real revolutionists are philosophers and saints." In the final analysis, the only lasting change that transforms us as individuals, and through us, the society we live in and the world, is the change that occurs within us when our mind is enlightened. That change can be brought about in a controlled manner with disciplined self-restraint leading to the surrender of the small ego self and the mind to the Divine.

Until that happens, all the talk about World Peace, *et cetera*, is just talk and an empty promise. Why? Because war is nothing more than the culmination of the individual fights each one of us has within his/herself. If each one of us cannot control himself/herself and chooses instead to vent his/her frustration on someone else who in turn does the same thing, it starts a chain reaction, which spreads throughout society. Unfortunately this happens in all societies the world over. Sooner or later the pent-up frustrations must have an outlet and explode into war. If frustrated people and/or societies do not explode, they will implode. The incidents of road rage, killings by children in our schools, shootings by postal employees and frustrated employees and investors are symptoms of a very serious underlying problem that our society has. There is a real need for each one of us to discipline ourselves and commit to change ourselves so that we live in harmony with nature. That can only happen if instead of venting our frustrations on each other we surrender them to the Divine. This will also help us to gradually become free from desires that blind us and bind us to the objects our mind is attached to, which in turn shackle us to the cycles of pleasure and pain and the rounds of birth, life and death.

In this book, the author has tried to share the Principles that have helped him. Principles that he learned from Dr. Dinshah K. Mehta after meeting him finally as the culmination of years of groping, searching and finally seeking Spiritual Principles to live by. Hopefully this book will inspire you, the reader, to take charge of your life and strive to become truly free. The sooner you start to battle and take control of yourself, *i.e.*, your mind and ego, the closer you will be to experiencing the state described by the Lord Christ as, "The joy that surpasseth understanding."

Given below is a Script on Freedom and Peace that was received by Rev. Dr. Dinshah K. Mehta in a state of Spiritual samâdhi (meditation) that may help spur you on the quest for your true identity ... the God within us all including those whom we perceive to be our enemies. There are no real enemies. All of us are children of one Creator, one God. The enemies only exist in our mind. We need to get control of our mind and change our point of view.

FREEDOM AND PEACE

Freedom is the Goal and not the means,
Means to the Goal are ever bound,
Bound by the Laws that are writ in unseen,
Given through the chosen in soundless sound.

Known only to the few, others know not,
But Truth that Freedom is, reflects in all,
The unknowing minds mix means with the goal,
Suffering results though happiness is sought.

To be free from such, go to chosen ones who know,
The door and the way unto the Goal,
Obey what they say and step a time grow
Unto the Goal open for all.

Author's Note:
The Seven Principles of Right Surrender are an answer to the appeal made in the ancient Hindu prayer reproduced below.

Asato ma sadgamaya
Tamaso ma jyotir gamaya
Mrityor ma amritam gamaya

From untruth lead me to Truth.
From darkness lead me to Light.
From death lead me to Immortality.

Those who practice these Seven Principles will achieve in due course the Freedom and Peace which is the Goal open to all.

ADDENDUM

In this section we will briefly discuss some of the problems we face as a result of our attitudes and current lifestyle. The modern lifestyle with its urban sprawl, automobiles and highly toxic industrial discharges is threatening to disrupt the very fabric of nature so adequately described by Chief Seattle as the "Web of Life."

Most of the information contained in this chapter was reported on television by popular news channels at prime time.

Rather than being an integral part of nature, Technological man seems to be on a collision course with nature. With the Human Genome Project completed, the cloning of animals a reality, and genetic engineering an accomplished fact modern man has reached a new level vis-à-vis his interaction with nature. Modern man has not yet fully understood the myriad relationships that have been forged in nature through eons of time. If we rush headlong to bioengineer crops we run the risk of creating unforeseen problems that could threaten the very web of life.

It has been reported that about 20% of the corn (*i.e.*, maize) planted in the USA has been genetically altered to resist pests and disease. That may be well and good for man and his plans. But someone forgot to take into consideration the needs of the Monarch butterfly. The Monarch butterfly migrates between Mexico and Canada. It takes three generations of Monarch butterflies to complete the migration over a period of approximately a year. It has been noted that the larvae of the Monarch butterflies do not survive in the genetically engineered corn.

This is quite a red flag if ever one heeds the signals given out by nature.

According to an article that appeared in the Sept 19, 2000 Business Section of the *TriValley Herald*,

> "StarLink is one of several varieties of biotech corn that contains a bacterium gene that makes the plant toxic to the European corn borer. A scientific panel that advises the EPA was unable to decide this summer whether the protein in the corn, Cry9C should be allowed in food. The protein has shown resistance to digestive juices and heat, signs that it might cause allergic reactions. Aventis is required to

have agreements with farmers to make sure that the corn is kept separate from the grain that is approved for food use."

Apparently that did not happen.

On Nov 28, 2000 *ABC Evening News* reported that in Iowa although only 1% of the corn planted was the genetically engineered variety sold as StarLink, yet it managed to contaminate 50% of the natural corn that was planted and harvested. Farmers who were interviewed for the news report stated that the company did not inform them that the genetically engineered corn they planted could contaminate the non-genetically engineered natural corn which they planted, even if the genetically engineered and the natural corn were separated by rows that were 200 feet wide.

Some scientists are of the opinion that the StarLink corn should not be used for animal feed because humans may suffer from allergic reactions if they consume the products of animals that were fed the genetically engineered corn. They reason that the protein known as Cry9C found in the genetically altered corn is known to act as an allergen, and may pass through the animals to humans. Further, if the genetically engineered corn produces an insecticide that kills the larvae of the European corn borer, and if we eat it, in effect the insecticide now has become a part of our diet. Are consumers given any choice? When toxic insecticides, however undesirable, are sprayed on crops we have a chance to rinse them off. We cannot do that with insecticides that are built right into the food and thus become part of our diet.

The StarLink fiasco is not an isolated incident.

According to a July 11, 2002 news release by Friends of the Earth, more than 300 field trials of genetically engineered biopharmaceutical crops were already conducted in secret locations nationwide. "Just one mistake by a biotech company and we'll be eating other people's prescription drugs in our corn flakes," said Larry Bohlen, Director of Health and Environment Programs at Friends of the Earth, a member of the Genetically Engineered Food Alert coalition. For more information on this story and the concerns it raises, kindly visit the URL:

http://www.foe.org/new/releases/702freesereport.html

The Genetically Engineered Food Alert founding members include: Center for Food Safety, Friends of the Earth, Institute for Agriculture and Trade Policy, National Environmental Trust, Organic Consumers Association, Pesticide Action Network North America, and the State Public Interest Research Groups.

The coalition details the threats that biopharm crops pose, the extent to which they have been planted across the U.S., the failure of regulatory agencies to serve the public, and a set of recommendations. The report, entitled, "Manufacturing Drugs and Chemicals in Crops: Biopharming Poses New Threats to Consumers, Farmers, Food Companies and the Environment," may be found at www.gefoodalert.org and at www.foe.org/biopharm

On October 8, 2002 CBS Evening News reported on the risk of contamination associated with "farm-aceutical" corn. Among other items the report states, "Inside ears of corn are the seeds of a brand new growth industry. This year 2002 the USDA has issued 32 field permits for the growing of drugs and drug compounds in barley, rice, tobacco and corn. And the list of what is being grown is revolutionary: plant-based insulin and vaccines for hepatitis B, cholera and diarrhea. There have been greenhouse attempts to grow spermicide. Next year, the biotech firm Epicyte will be the first to start human clinical tests on a gel to treat herpes. That drug, too, is being grown in corn." For the full story, please go to the URL:

http://www.cbsnews.com/stories/2002/10/08/eveningnews/main524766.shtml

In the Health & Science section of USA TODAY dated November 13, 2002 Ms. Elizabeth Weise reported, "A bioengineered food plant had gotten within a hair's breadth of entering the US food supply...The biotech company ProdiGene had grown the corn on a one-acre experimental plot in 2001. Neither the company nor the U.S. Department of Agriculture would say for what pharmaceutical purpose the corn was intended. ProdiGene has several drugs in development, including an insulin-making enzyme and vaccines for hepatitis B and traveler's diarrhea.

In 2002 the field was planted with soybeans. However, stray corn plants left from the year before sprang up in the field. USDA inspectors saw the corn plants and alerted the company. Instead of removing them the company allowed the field to be harvested. It took 12 hours for the USDA officials to track down the beans, which were impounded and will likely be destroyed. ProdiGene is facing possible fines of up to $500,000 ..."

According to another report dated Nov. 13, 2002 by Mr. Randy Fabi of Reuters, on the same issue, Prodigene's corn variety was engineered to make trypsin, a protein used in insulin. The report states that Mr. John Cady, president of the National Food Processors Association, called the incident alarming and said it, "very nearly placed the integrity of the food supply in jeopardy."

Despite assurances by Industry leaders, the risk of and worries of cross contamination between biotech corn and corn used for human consumption persist and for valid reasons. For more information on this subject, kindly visit the following URLs:

http://www.usatoday.com/news/health/2002-11-13-biotech-corn-usat_x.htm

http://www.msnbc.com/news/835455.asp

http://members.tripod.com/~ngin/190302b.htm

In defending bioengineering, some scientists state that genetic engineers are merely doing what occurs naturally and that they are only speeding up natural processes for the benefit of mankind. Although this may be true in many instances it certainly is not true in many other cases. Nature does not take a gene out of one species and put it into another species. In nature, a gene from a rat is not placed in a pig, a horse, and a monkey or *vice versa*, and a gene from a bacterium is not inserted into corn.

On the March 13, 2001 *60 Minutes II*, broadcast a segment entitled, "What have they done to our food?" it was reported that scientists have taken a gene from a flounder and placed into a tomato to allow the tomato to withstand colder temperatures on the vine and also remain fresh in freezers.

The segment also reported that 70% of products in grocery stores have genetically engineered foods. On February 12, 2002, Dan Rather reported on the *CBS Evening News* that scientists are now reinventing pigs to become donors of organs for human transplantation. PPL, the company that cloned Dolly the sheep, has developed a technique to knock out the gene in pigs that would be rejected by humans. By switching off this gene, the human body is tricked into thinking that the pig organ is a human organ. PPL is not the only company that is developing pigs whose organs may be used to save human lives.

In another report, CBS also broadcast a story about goats on a farm in Quebec into whose cells scientists have transplanted the gene from spiders that enables spiders to weave silk. The idea is to have the goats produce spider's silk on a commercial scale so that the silk can be used to make bulletproof vests. The spider's silk is harvested from the milk the goats produce.

To claim that such manipulation of the natural environment is only speeding up natural processes seems to be very suspect. It would seem that if we continue along these lines, we would disrupt natural relationships that have evolved over millions of years. *Our behavior towards the earth and nature is very similar to that of an alien virus or cancer that invades our bodies and interferes with the normal functioning and processes of the body.* With their limited knowledge, scientists are delving into realms that may have consequences that cannot be fully imagined let alone understood. We observe and understand a tiny piece of the puzzle of life and then begin to manipulate it. The scientific community seems to be accepting cloning as a routine technique.

In news broadcasts, clones were presented as being identical to the donor parent. However on February 14, 2002 Dan Rather reported on *CBS Evening News* that at the A&M University in Texas they cloned CC the cat. CC stands for "Cloned Cat."

However CC's color patterns were different from those of the cat whose genetic material was used to clone CC. This shows that clones are not identical to the animal/donor whose genetic material was used to clone them. Yet companies are rushing headlong into bioengineering as if they know what they are doing and are giving us reassurances that it is safe and for the greater good of humanity, if not the earth itself.

The absurdity of scientist's claims that their manipulation of the natural environment is harmless because they have identified one link out of the chain is reflected in the solution recommended by the King in the following children's story:

"There was a kingdom in which the population was not too bright and neither was the King. It was reported to the King that many people missed work because they were intoxicated. The King ordered his Secret Service to find out why the people were getting intoxicated. After a thorough investigation, the Secret Service reported that the people were getting intoxicated because they were drinking soda and rum, soda and whiskey, soda and gin, soda and brandy and so forth. The King concluded that soda was the common ingredient that all the people were drinking, and that therefore soda was obviously the source of the problem. Therefore, to stop his subjects from getting intoxicated, the king passed an edict that no one should be allowed to drink soda."

What is it that motivates these scientists and the companies that finance such projects to subject the rest of us to huge risks, mostly without our consent? Is it the good of mankind or is it monetary gain? The market for organs that can be transplanted into human beings is estimated at $10 billion annually.

We have to be very careful that we do not allow the few who will gain financially from genetic engineering or other processes to destroy the very environment that supports us all. In his ignorance coupled with arrogance and greed modern man may end up disrupting and/or breaking the chain of natural relationships that have evolved over eons of time and which hold us together in the web of life as we experience it, even though we may not fully understand it.

Make sure the price we will have to pay is worth the promised benefits and that the inevitable problems created by the new processes can be contained.

Rachel Carson, author of *Silent Spring*, which was serialized in *The New Yorker* in June 1962, exposed the havoc caused by DDT. Manufacturers of pesticides tried to discredit and suppress her work. Instead they succeeded in drawing attention to it thereby publicizing her work even more. In a CBS interview in 1963, Rachel Carson echoed the words of Chief Joseph Seattle when she said, "Man is a part of nature, and his war against nature is inevitably a war against himself."

Today some of the very companies that criticized Ms. Carson's warnings of the damage caused to the environment by pesticides and chemical fertilizers are pushing to adopt genetic engineering as an answer to our needs and are using their financial and legal might to suppress voices of reason and caution.

Voices that urge scientists to:

- Respect the myriads of natural relationships that currently exist in nature and which have evolved over millions of years.
- Work in harmony with nature and not bioengineer genes across natural boundaries.

Instead of being Clean, Clear and Complete in their communication with society, companies have historically Conspired to Confuse and Challenge community watchdogs and have done all they could to prevent the public at large from knowing the truth about their products and the effect they may have on the environment and the public's health. Some people believe that this practice still continues.

When dealing with legitimate dissent, Corporate America has used the time tested successful techniques of:

- Refusing to acknowledge the problem.
- Throwing up smoke screens by sponsoring studies to justify their point of view thereby delaying action.
- Misinterpreting scientific data to suit their own needs contrary to the conclusions arrived at by the scientists who did the research and reported their findings.
- Relentlessly lobbying politicians to pass legislation in their favor or delay legislation that blocks their activities.
- Sponsor campaigns and ads that support their point of view.
- File a series of lawsuits to bleed the opposition by using up their time, energy and financial resources.
- Use the appeal process to delay paying victims of their wrong doings if the victims win judgments against them.

Years later after they have raked in the profits and it is evident that the environment and/or people have suffered, the argument used to defend their actions is that they did not know any better. Statements are released saying in effect that they cannot be held responsible for any damage they may have caused to the environment or people because at the time they were using state of the art technology for the public good (not profits). To that we can add that they were also using state of the art deception and are continuing to do so today.

Already Bioengineering firms are trying to downplay the impact that genetically engineered corn has on the larvae of the Monarch butterfly and its migration. They claim that the adverse effects have been grossly exaggerated. The risk of bioengineered corn for producing "farm-aceuticals" is also being glossed over or totally ignored. Assurances are given that the methods used to prevent cross contamination of food for human consumption with crops bio-engineered to produce medicines are fool proof.

Big tobacco, large chemical companies including the oil companies, and the automobile industry, all used these tactics successfully for years, and many are still doing so. What big tobacco did and to a certain extent what the oil companies have done has been publicized quite well. What big chemical and big auto companies did is receiving fresh publicity.

In a very nice exposé, entitled *Trade Secrets: A Moyers Report* narrated by Mr. Bill Moyers and produced by Ms Sherry Jones that aired on March 26th, 2001 in the San Francisco Bay Area on PBS Channel 9 at 9 p.m., venerable journalist Mr. Bill Moyers examined the chemical revolution that has taken place in the USA over the past 50 years and the toll it has taken.

According to the news article in the March 26th, 2001 edition of ANG Newspapers, most of the information offered in his report comes from a lawsuit brought about by the widow of Mr. Dan Ross, who died of a rare brain cancer at the age of 46 after working 23 years with vinyl chloride and other toxic chemicals at a plant in Lake Charles, Louisiana. When she sued her husband's former employer, the process of legal discovery led deeper into the inner chambers of the chemical industry and its Washington trade association.

Moyers even rolled up his own sleeve and gave blood for the investigative report. He took part in a pilot study sponsored by Mt. Sinai School of Medicine designed to measure the synthetic chemicals in the human body.

Even though he had never worked in a chemical plant, or to his knowledge even been exposed to chemicals, he learned that his body contains 31 types of PCBs, 13 toxins and pesticides including malathion and DDT.

In the film, Dr. Michael McCally of Mt. Sinai tells Moyers "we do know enough now to know it doesn't make a lot of sense to make chemicals that are carcinogenic and add them to our bodies. ... Suddenly, we find that the industry has put a bunch of chemicals in our body that are not good for us and we didn't have any say in that."

Even before the documentary aired, the chemical companies were on the defensive. Over the years there have been several news stories about entire communities being contaminated by chemical factories. Libby, Montana; Fallon, Nevada; Love Canal, New York and Herculaneum, Missouri are just few of the communities that have been drastically affected by chemical pollution. In the latest in a series of cases brought against manufacturers, on Friday, February 22, 2002 in Gadsden, Alabama, a jury ruled that Monsanto, Inc., polluted an Alabama town with PCBs from a chemical plant over several decades, a verdict that sets the stage for more trials on claims the contamination harmed property and the resident's health. The verdict by the state court jury came in a lawsuit against Monsanto and its spin-off, Solutia, Inc. The verdict also went against Pharmacia Corp., which merged with Monsanto in 2000. The two companies were found liable for claims, including negligence. The Solutia, Inc. plant in West Anniston, Alabama was involved and CBS News Correspondent Mark Strassman reports fear of PCB contamination has caused entire neighborhoods in Anniston to disappear. According to court documents presented in the case, even before PCB's were classified as dangerous, Monsanto's own research showed that PCB's were bad for health but the company chose to release them anyway into the local environment.

On Wednesday, April 23, 200d Health Scout reported a study that ties breast cancer to pesticide exposure. To find the study go to http://www.healthscout.com/static/news/512873.html

On Monday, November 12, 2001, *The Times*, a local newspaper distributed in Alameda and Contra Costa Counties, California, ran a story that the gasoline additive MTBE is polluting the nation's water supplies from coast to coast. The article goes on to explain that MTBE is added to gasoline to make it burn cleaner and cut air pollution. At the same time, however, it pollutes groundwater far more readily than gasoline alone. A mere gallon of gasoline containing MTBE can foul an entire community's water supply. In one of the country's worst cases, the scenic Sierra Nevada town of Glennville, population 300, was devastated from a single underground tank. Water had to be trucked in.

According to an article published in the Saturday, March 16, 2002 issue of *The Valley Times*, Dublin, California, MTBE has been detected in 54 drinking water wells around the state, 19 of which were found to have enough MTBE to raise health concerns according to state officials. Even in extremely low concentrations, MTBE lends a turpentine-like odor to water. Wells have been shut down in San Jose, Sacramento, Lake Tahoe, The Central Coast, Santa Monica and Kern County. In other words wells have been shut down across the entire length and breadth of the state. In spite of such devastating experiences on Friday March 15, 2002, California Governor Gray Davis announced that he was extending the use of MTBE in California gasoline to avoid gasoline prices as high as $3.00 per gallon. Gov. Davis went on to explain that if he did not extend the MTBE ban, the state faced a repeat of the electricity crisis. By the end of the year 2002, MTBE *was supposed to be banned* as an additive to gasoline sold in California. But then 2002 was an election year and so one can surmise that the politics of economics trumped the politics of saving the environment. *Once again our leaders have given more importance to mammon or money than to our own good health and that of the natural environment.* Can you blame them? *As a society, we have repeatedly demonstrated that we vote with our pocket books.*

It has been reported recently that Automobile manufacturers also have been involved in cover-ups of mistakes. Such behavior on the part of industry seems to be the norm rather than the exception.

On Thursday, February 21, at 10 p.m. KQED, a PBS station in the San Francisco Bay Area, aired a *Frontline* documentary entitled *Rollover* that discusses the rollover problem that SUVs have, and the behind the scenes corporate and political manipulations that made decisions that favored corporate profits over the public's safety. How such decisions result in the public good and benefits the corporations in the long run, defies common sense.

To be fair, society cannot on the one hand expect to benefit from the tremendous achievements of our chemical, automobile and other industries and then complain about the pollution caused by the processes used to manufacture the products we have come to appreciate. It seems though that society at large and communities in particular would not bring any action against these companies if they had been forthright. From the internal documents uncovered during the process of discovery, it appears that company executives knowingly either withheld information or gave false information to their employees and community leaders. That is unfortunate. One can surmise that such behavior is generally brought on by insecurity at best and uncontrolled greed at worst.

When the mindset of business leaders is to make a profit at all costs, then at times we get some ludicrous suggestions, such as when tobacco giant Philip Morris suggested that premature deaths caused by smoking can be good for the economy. A report commissioned by the company says that the early deaths of smokers saved the Czech government money in health care, pensions and housing for the elderly. When this was reported in the news, the company issued a statement regretting any impression from their study that the premature death of smokers represents a benefit to society.

When will we get serious about ensuring that we do not destroy the web of life? How can we talk about the quality of life when we are living in such a toxic environment?

Fortunately there are some business leaders who recognize the need to be socially responsible. As reported by *Time Magazine* in their April 9, 2001 issue, "Shortly after Kyoto was signed, BP CEO Sir John Browne set his company's goal of cutting carbon dioxide output 10% below its 1990 levels; four years later, he is halfway there." Says Sir John Browne, "We use compliance with the law as a minimum and then go beyond that."

In October 2,000 some companies like BP, Alcan, DuPont and others joined with Environmental Defense to launch the Partnership for Climate Action, pledging to reduce their greenhouse emissions to levels meeting or exceeding Kyoto's requirements.

Political leaders have begun to take notice of the environmental damage inflicted by modern technology. To his credit, as reported on the news and on MSNBC on December 4th, 2000 at 12:30 p.m., President William Jefferson Clinton decreed that 84 million acres of Hawaii's coral reefs be set aside as a nature preserve. The area of coral reefs set aside as a natural preserve is about 5,000 times larger than San Francisco, and was dubbed as the Yellowstone of coral reefs. This action by President Clinton prohibits dumping of waste and drilling of oil in the area that is part of the preserve. Why did President Clinton take this action? In his news conference announcing the decision, President Clinton acknowledged that 90% of the coral reefs off the coast of

India have died due to pollution. But the question remains, "Why did President Clinton wait to take these decisions towards the end of his administration? Why did he not take these actions soon after taking office?" Although we cannot prove it, one rather suspects that the timing of these decisions had more to do with politics than caring for the environment. Nevertheless, decisions favoring the environment are always welcome.

The action taken by President Clinton is a very good start and hopefully will spur our nation to do more along the same lines and inspire other nations to do likewise individually and the United Nations to act collectively. But will they and we do so? The chances are very slim.

In fact after he took office, President George W. Bush rejected the levels of arsenic acceptable in our water that were established under the Clinton Administration. To his credit, on October 31, 2001 President Bush reversed himself and accepted the tougher standards for arsenic levels in water that were established during the final days of the Clinton Administration. On January 9, 2002, the Bush Administration stated that it was replacing a program to develop high-mileage, gasoline-electric cars with one that promises even more: the end of the internal combustion engine and the start of vehicles driven by pollution-free hydrogen and fuel cells.

But, on the issue of global warming, according to the April 9, 2001 issue of *Time Magazine*, President Bush remarked, "Our economy has slowed down. We also have an energy crisis, and the idea of placing caps on carbon dioxide does not make economic sense."

Once again the need to earn money trumps the need to have a healthy environment. After all, the advice given is that we will be able to use the money to pay the medical bills that we will have to pay should we fall sick due to the pollution. What would we do if we did not have the money and the pollution?

In the same issue of *Time Magazine*, the article on global warming reports that after her February 2001 meeting with European leaders on the subject of climate change, EPA Chief Christie Whitman wrote to President Bush, "The world community ... are all convinced of the seriousness of this issue," and "It is also an issue that is resonating here, at home. We need to appear engaged." Thus, the appearance of doing something seems to be preferred to real action.

Today the USA is the world's greatest power and greatest polluter. We will not always be in this position. Right now, many countries are following our lead and President Bush has the rare privilege of leading the world in the fight against terrorism and pollution. The problem of course is how to balance the many conflicting interests at play both at home and abroad?

President Bush comes across as a very decent and caring person. In keeping with his campaign rhetoric, President Bush is trying to practice Compassionate Conservatism. To do so, he has to consider many valid opposing points of view. Rather than being persuaded by his advisors, if the President will just go by his instincts we will all come out ahead.

President George W. Bush has made some very good moves. On January 11, 2002 the President signed the Brownfields Bill that aims to clean up thousands of polluted industrial sites, a measure he lauded as evidence of what happens "when people decide to cooperate, not bicker" in Congress. Bush traveled to Conshohocken, Pa., to sign the bill, a five-year plan to provide up to $250 million a year to states, local governments and Indian tribes to clean up the sites known as brownfields. The bill was signed at the Millennium Corporate Center, which stands on 30 acres that once was a contaminated site. Before re-development, the land—which sits on the banks of the Schuylkill River and once held a steel plant—was closed off by chain-link fences and littered with abandoned tires and industrial trash.

Skeptics may claim that by signing the bill the President passed on the cost of cleaning up the brownfields to the American taxpayer and rescued the large corporations that caused the brownfields. Such objections are supported by the fact that the Superfund was established on the Principle that those who were responsible for the pollution had to pay for cleaning up the polluted sites. For whatever reason, that did not work, and the President and Congress needed to come up with a workable solution. Before we criticize our leaders, we have to remember that the President and our Congressional leaders also pay taxes. Indeed when President Bush was pushing for the bill to reduce taxes, he pointed out that when he assumed the office of the President, he received a sizeable increase in salary compared to the salary he received as Governor of Texas. If the tax reduction bill were passed, the President would also personally benefit. President Bush and many of our leaders are probably paying more in taxes than most of us private citizens. In order to work cohesively together during these troubled times, we should try and avoid the "us versus them" syndrome and count our leaders also among us as co-taxpayers.

They, our leaders, are not the people who are causing us, the citizens, problems. But we the people are electing our leaders and we are collectively responsible for our current situation. As a society, instead of looking for scapegoats we should strive to accept responsibility for our collective actions. Only then will we stand a chance to clean up the mess we have created. In order to clean up our act, it should be clear that we cannot continue to live and do business as usual. We have to accept that we need to adopt radical changes in our current values and lifestyles. We should support our leaders and other public servants. We should get rid of Partisan bull(ies) and also Bipartisan bull(ies) and climb aboard what Senator John McCain referred to his Straight Talk Express when he ran for the Republican Party's nomination.

But alas, we are not there yet. In its Daily Environment Report, Volume: 2002 Number: 41 dated March 1, 2002 on Air Pollution, www.bna.com states:

> A departing Environmental Protection Agency official left with a broadside attack Feb. 27 on the Bush administration's air quality and environmental enforcement policies.
>
> Eric V. Schaeffer, director of the Office of Regulatory Enforcement, wrote to EPA Administrator Christine Todd Whitman Feb. 27, his last day in office, saying the administration is working to weaken the Clean Air Act and is depriving the agency of needed personnel.
>
> The letter comes as the administration is considering exemptions to the new source review enforcement program and is promoting its Clear Skies initiative to reduce air pollution from power plants.

For the full article as well as the text of Mr. Schaeffer's resignation letter dated February 27, 2002 to Ms. Christine Whit-

man, Administrator, U.S. Environmental Protection Agency please go to the following URL:
http://ehscenter.bna.com/PIC/enspic.nsf/(Index)/B9061C260 31F759585256B6F004FC016?OpenDocument

Most of our business, political and religious leaders are very intelligent and decent people. Why then do our leaders resist making the hard choices they know we have to live with?

There are many reasons, but it seems that the following two are the most basic:

- Their need to stay in office, *i.e.,* personal security, and
- The law of inertia.

Many of us know that the present lifestyle we enjoy in America is not sustainable and that something needs to be done about it soon. But how many of us really stop to analyze whether our current lifestyle is desirable. We are so caught up in the struggle to pay bills and to live up to the values thrust upon us by peer pressure that at the end of the day we do not have the inclination or strength to think differently. This fact of our daily struggle coupled with the momentum of our society prevents us from supporting our leaders who propose innovative solutions, *i.e.,* solutions that are outside the box.

In most urban areas there are bedroom communities and people have to commute to work. My friend Bruce Welinski wisely observed that if the average *round trip* commute from home to work is 50 miles, and the average work year is 230 days, then the average worker travels a distance of 11,750 miles per year just commuting to work. That is almost half the circumference of the earth at it's widest, *i.e.,* 0 degrees latitude or at the equator. No wonder people are tired of commuting. Commuting may be good for the economy because people have to buy cars in order to commute. This supports the automobile industry, oil and tire industries all of which are anchor industries that drive our economy. It also supports the insurance industry, personal injury lawyers and doctors as well as a host of other industries. Commuting by car may be good for the economy but it is a tremendous waste of natural and national resources and the source of so many environmental problems, accidents and all sorts of health problems.

On October 23, 2002 CNN reported that urban expansion and loss of open space have put some 25 percent of North America's bird species in trouble or decline, more than double the number of species at risk five years ago. About 201 birds are on the watch list and 21 of them are in the endangered category said Audubon spokesman John Bianchi.

For the complete story, please visit:
http://www.cnn.com/2002/TECH/science/10/23/audubon.birds.reut/index.html

Urban sprawl has another very serious consequence that has not been widely publicized, *i.e.,* the loss of rainwater. Rain performs some very important functions.

One of the functions of rain is to wash the salts of the earth into the ocean. The ocean is salty because rainwater percolates into the soil dissolve the salts of the earth, drains into rivers, which empty into the sea. This gradual desalination of the soil, allows plants to grow and extract nutrients from the soil through the process of osmosis. Further when rain falls on soil, it collects in wells and lakes and is generally available to plants, animals and man through underground water reservoirs. When the same rain falls in urban areas streets that are paved with cement concrete, it drains down the neighborhood sewers, is then directed to our sewage treatment plants, and is generally discharged into the ocean. Rain that falls onto urban areas is unable to perform the vital functions that it can when it falls on forests and farms. Urban sprawl deprives us of the benefits of rain. When we consider that in order to live on land, creatures generally need fresh water, this is a big loss.

With the unabated expansion of urban sprawl the problem will only become worse and it is bound to adversely affect our climate and health.

What are the alternatives?

Most if not all the choices confronting us are painful. Because we have had so much for so long, we seem to be unwilling to make those painful choices unless they are thrust upon us as on September 11th. Even so, in our personal lives and neighborhoods the great majority of us are unfortunately still unwilling to make the necessary changes in our lifestyle. NIMBY ("Not In My Back Yard") is frequently heard in town meetings when sensitive environmental and growth issues are discussed. We want the benefits but do not wish to pay the price.

President George W. Bush and the Republican Party are very keenly aware that his father, former President Bush, lost his bid to get re-elected primarily because of the economic slowdown that occurred during the last couple of years of his administration. In the final analysis, the fact that President Bush, Sr. is a very decent man and accomplished so many great things during his term in office did not matter to the voters as much as the impact his administration had on their pocket book. Can we then blame our political leaders for not making the hard choices they and we know must be made? How many of us have the moral courage to risk our jobs if we were in their shoes? Besides over the years, many politicians the world over—and our country is no exception—have demonstrated that they are unwilling to do what is in the best interest of the common man. Slick-talking lawyers representing special interest groups promote legislation that favors their clients. Special interest groups offer campaign contributions, which unfortunately have become all too important in the current political scene. Indeed the issue of campaign reform has been debated ever since the Watergate scandal brought down the Nixon administration.

Only now, thanks to the obscenity of the Enron and other scandals have the politicians acknowledged that they are now firing real bullets. What were they doing up to now? Would their job performance enable them to hold onto their jobs in private industry? Even with real bullets, the campaign reform bill passed by Congress on March 20, 2002 reduces unregulated soft money contributions to National political parties. But it doubles the hard money contributions from individuals from $1,000 to $2,000. Under the old rules President Bush raised $100 million in hard money when he campaigned for his first term as President. According to some Pundits, under the new rules, if the same people contributed again, President Bush could raise $200 million. If that is correct, then to call this Campaign Finance Reform is stretching it a bit.

Some of the people who opposed the Campaign Reform Bill said that it would not stop the flow of money but only redistribute it. Senator John McCain, one of the chief proponents of the bill, correctly pointed out that if the bill did not accomplish anything, why did they oppose it for seven years?

In any situation, usually those who have the advantage will strive to maintain the status quo. If their spirit is not completely crushed, it is also only the disadvantaged who will strive to change the status quo so as to improve their lot. Those who strive to maintain the status quo usually claim that they are doing it for the good of the public. They will issue statements that make their actions seem noble, just and altruistic. Some Congressional leaders and members of the administration claim that campaign contributions do not in any way influence their decisions. Really? Why then are they fighting so hard to resist Campaign Finance Reform? Why are Lobbyists so popular, successful and even sought? Ms. Whitman's disclosures are supported by the Pew Oceans Commission's Final Report which is most alarming. The report is based on an in-depth three year study conducted by the Commission. The Pew Oceans Commission report which was released on June 4, 2003 is available at: http://www.pewoceans.com

Even before the bill was being signed into law, plans were underway to challenge it in court. Former Whitewater independent counsel Ken Starr will head up the legal team assembled by Sen. Mitchell McConnell (R-KY) in a legal challenge to the Campaign Finance Reform bill when it is signed into law. Starr is expected to argue that the law is an unconstitutional abridgement of free speech. According to the Associated Press, with McConnell at his side, Starr told a news conference, "These are perilous waters into which the Republic has now sailed. The questions are grave, the questions are serious. It is now time for the courts to speak authoritatively to what the Congress has chosen to do." (President Bush quietly signed the bill into law on March 27, 2002 and the lawsuit challenging it has been filed charging that it restricts Freedom of Speech).

By any standard, these statements are being made by the very best and brightest people our Society has to offer—our leaders. And most of them are very decent human beings ... more so than most. Yet it is hard to believe some, if not many, of the things they say. *The most unfortunate form of deception is self-deception.* Most Americans see through the false statements our leaders make. But before we criticize them, each one of us has to ask himself/herself, "What would I do if I was in their shoes?" Because we are still relatively comfortable, most of us are not motivated to send a message to Congress and the Administration. We lull ourselves into doing nothing with the thought that the problems and issues will sort themselves out. They most assuredly will not.

On April 3, 2002, Mr. Bob Jamieson of ABC News reported that a report released today by the Environmental Protection Agency stated that, "Nearly half of all the waters off the coast of United States are so damaged they cannot fully support aquatic life...The EPA gave poor marks to the Northeast and Great Lakes. The worst coast waters, it said, were in the Gulf of Mexico, where in some places there is no fishing at all. The best marks went to waters off the Southeast and West Coasts, but those were graded only 'fair.'" "It varies around the country," said EPA Administrator Christine Todd Whitman. "It varies up and down the coast. It certainly tells us there are serious problems we need to address."

Tom Doggett and Chis Baltimore of ABC news reported on June 3, 2002 that the Bush Administration acknowledged for the first time that U.S. greenhouse gas emissions will increase significantly over the next two decades mostly due to human activities but again rejected the international treaty to slow global warming. The report released by the Environmental Protection Agency was a surprising endorsement of what many scientists and weather experts have long argued—that human activities such as oil refining, power plants and automobile emissions are important causes of global warming. In a report to the United Nations, the administration forecast that total U.S. greenhouse gas emissions will increase 43% between 2000 and 2020. Yet on July 11, 2002 CNN reported that the Bush Administration pulled out of the Kyoto Accord. It seems the Bush Administration wants to back Science and Technology to solve the problem of greenhouse gas emissions.

As a people we have to stop deceiving ourselves. We need to wake up and clean up our Political and Financial institutions and our environment. We need to act as decisively as we did when we decided to go after the Taliban and the terrorists. Similarly the Religious institutions have to clean themselves up. Instead of surrendering to Truth and God, it seems that almost all of us have surrendered to mammon. If we tarry, we will have to face the consequences and they will not be good. The Wrath of God may visit us.

Those who think they have the advantage should remember that so long as they are holding someone down, they can never rise above them, because some part of them has to remain at the level where they are holding down those they are preventing from rising.

Due to a paucity of political will and their reliance on John Q. Public's apathy and short memory, quite often instead of taking bold decisions, which will give us all a hard time in the short run but provide major long term benefits, our leaders seem to favor projecting the *appearance* of doing good rather than actually *doing* good.

Similarly, on the business front, *Reuters* released a news bulletin dated November 16, 2001 that Philip Morris, Inc. proposed a corporate name change to Altria Group, Inc. Altria—a coined term that comes from *altus*, the Latin word for "high"—was chosen to reflect its "peak performance," the company said. Still, the move is being viewed by many as a clear sign that the company no longer wants to be shrouded in a name synonymous with cigarettes. "We fully expected some criticism," Senior Vice President of Corporate Affairs Steven Parrish said during a Friday conference call with analysts and others. Likewise on February 22, 2002, Dan Rather reported on *CBS Evening News* that Enron's new chief is proposing a name change because the company needs a fresh start. Instead of proposing a name change to get a fresh start, most people would agree that Enron should engage in fresh *thinking* that reflects sound business practices based on good moral principles. On the same day, Dan Rather also reported that we had the warmest November to January since record keeping began more than 100 years ago, with severe drought from Georgia to Maine, and that the water level in the Potomac River in Washington was down 89%.

Just how serious are the problems of Global Warming, Climate Change and Destruction of Habitat? For centuries the aborigines of Australia worshipped Ayers Rock and lived in harmony with the environment. In a documentary called *The Naked Planet* aired by KQED on September 10, 2000 it was reported that within 100 years of Europeans coming to Ayers Rock, fully half of all the species that lived around Ayers Rock, *i.e.,* 30 species, have become extinct in the immediate area around Ayers Rock, and many of these species have become extinct throughout Australia.

This is not surprising. With Technological man's adversarial attitude towards the Universe and his emphasis on exploiting the natural environment for monetary gain, we are rapidly moving towards global disaster. Once limited to discussion among scientists and published in scientific journals, global warming is so much a part of the public dialog that it is discussed in political races and is part of regular news broadcasts and the subject of documentaries and national and international controversy.

But alas, in spite of the serious consequences of global warming, politicians in many developed countries, who follow the lead of the USA are dragging their heels.

In the year 2001 the BBC broadcast a very informative program entitled *Warning from the Wild*. The show explored the devastation that is occurring to our biosphere as a result of global warming. Dr. Alan Pounds, who has been studying natural life forms in the Monteverde Forest Reserve, Costa Rica, reported that due to global warming the ecosystem in this rare cloud forest is changing. The cloud forest is very unique because it offers three major climates all within the preserve. Monteverde rises to about 1,500 meters.

Prevailing trade winds from the Caribbean carry moisture to these forests.

At the lower levels we have the tropical forest, at the middle level of the forest canopy the temperatures are warmer, and are coolest at the top of the canopy. Due to global warming as many as sixteen species have vanished from the forest in the past twenty-odd years. The golden toad, found only in this forest, has vanished and now can be seen only in photographs and video clips taken by Dr. Pounds. Twenty of the 50 amphibian species seem to have become extinct since the 1980s.

The global warming is also causing birds and other creatures that inhabit the middle levels of the canopy to invade the higher regions. The net result of this is that birds such as the lovely Quetzal and other creatures that live up in the colder regions of the forest canopy have no place to go.

Their habitat is threatened and they may become extinct.

Mr. John Campbell, who has kept daily records of the weather data in the Monteverde Forest Preserve for 27 years, reported that the weather patterns are changing.

According to an analysis of his data, Mr. Campbell reported that dry spells lasting five days or more have increased markedly, as have the number of dry years.

According to Michael Falcon, who has studied birds for 20 years, global warming is also contributing to changing migratory patterns of birds. Dr. Stephen Schneider of Stanford University, California used computer models to predict the changes that could result from global warming and Dr. Alan Pounds, John Campbell and Michael Falcon confirm his findings with empirical observations. Dr. Schneider thinks that global warming occurs because we are using our atmosphere as a sewer to dump our gaseous and other waste.

Sandhill cranes that live near Michigan fly down to Florida for the winter and return in summer. It is observed that due to the warmer weather the cranes now leave 20 days earlier in the fall. One would think that the warmer weather would make the cranes stay longer rather than depart earlier. Nevertheless, the change in their behavior illustrates the impact that global warming is having on sophisticated life forms. Such an impact cannot be ignored because it is bound to further exacerbate the ecosystems that are already so severely strained that they have begun to breakdown.

The effects of global warming are truly global. Summer temperatures along the Pacific Coast of California have risen by two degrees since the 1930s.

Between 1931 and 1933 Mr. Charles Baxter of The Hopkins Institute, studied 30 species in the Monterey Bay of California. He recently noted the effects of climate change on the local sea life. His student Mr. Rafe Sagrin conducted a three-year study and noted that along the Pacific Coast of California, southern species that live in warmer waters are now migrating towards the north as temperatures in the north get warmer. The same trend has been observed in the southern hemisphere where movement of species towards the South Pole has been observed.

Dr. Mark Spalding, who is associated with the World Conservation Monitoring Center in Cambridge, reports that as a result of global warming, coral reefs are dying in the Maldives, which is a nation of islands in the Indian Ocean.

Dr. Tom Goreau of the Global Coral Reef Alliance states that half the reefs in the Indian Ocean are already destroyed. This is very significant because coral reefs occupy less than 1% of the earth's oceans but support 95% life in the oceans.

It is further reported that the Arctic and the Antarctic used to absorb the earth's carbon dioxide. As a result of global warming, the ice in these regions is now melting. According to the April 9, 2001 issue of *Time Magazine* the annual melt season in Antarctica has increased up to three weeks in 20 years. This in turn is affecting the plant life there and now these cold regions of the earth are no longer absorbing the carbon dioxide that the rest of the earth is releasing. They are themselves net producers of carbon dioxide and methane gas are thus contributing to global warming. Around March 19, 2002, Mr. Peter Jennings reported on ABC's World News tonight that British Scientists reported that a glacier the size of Rhode Island melted in the Antarctica, within one month, a rate faster than anyone had anticipated.

The glaciers of the Antarctic are not the only ones that are melting.

Venezuelan mountaintops had six glaciers in 1972. Today only two remain. On February 15, 2001, Peter Jennings reported on *World News Tonight* that photographs have been released showing that glaciers in Everest National Park in Nepal are melting and have formed lakes. According to the report, the group of glaciers in Nepal forms the third largest glacier belt in the world. Mount Kilimanjaro, Africa's tallest mountain, has lost 75% of its ice cap since 1912 and could lose all of it in the next 15 years. According to an October 17, 2002 broadcast by CNN the 11,000-year-old ice cap of Mt. Kilimanjaro is expected to disappear completely within 20 years. There are many other examples of melting bodies of ice as a result of global warming.

According to a study conducted by researchers from the Cooperative Institute for Research in Environmental Sciences or CIRES of the University of Colorado at Boulder, the Artic Sea Ice is shrinking and the Greenland Ice Sheet is also melting. The CU-Boulder findings were reported in a press briefing at the annual fall meeting of the American Geophysical Union, held Dec. 6 to Dec. 10, 2002 in San Francisco. According to Mr. Konrad Steffen, one of the researchers, "For every degree (F) in the mean annual temperature near Greenland, the rate of sea level rise increases by about 10%." For more information, the reader can visit the following URL:

http://nsidc.org/news/press/20021207_seaice.html

... or visit the NASA News Archive at:

http://earthobservatory.nasa.gov:81/Newsroom/NasaNews/20
02/2002120710965.html

Global warming is not just changing the climate of the world. *The entire biosphere is changing as a result of global warming.* On October 5, 2000, ABC reported on the evening news that scientists in New Zealand discovered that the hole in the ozone layer over the Antarctic has become three times as big as the USA, and for the first time the hole in the ozone layer has extended beyond all of Antarctica and is over one of the cities in Southern Chile. Through the hole in the ozone layer harmful radiations of the sun enter and increase the incidence of skin cancer and have other unknown effects.

The 1990s are reported to be the warmest decade in the last 1,000 years, and 1998 is the warmest year since records have been kept. According to a CNN news report aired on October 26, 2000, around 2:40 p.m. Pacific Standard Time, in a report issued by the United Nations Intergovernmental Panel, Dr. Michael Oppenheimer of the Environmental Defense Fund estimated that in the next 100 years global warming will increase the average temperature of the earth from between 2.7 to 11 degrees Fahrenheit.

Global warming has been recognized as the international problem that it is. In 1997 the Kyoto Protocol was adopted to try and deal with the problem. The Kyoto Protocol called for each nation to reduce by 5% the total volume of greenhouse gases it released in the year 1990 by the year 2012. As of the year 2000 no industrialized nation had ratified the protocol and none have adopted its recommendations even in the year 2002. The USA's position is unequivocally expressed in the report on Global Warming published by Time Magazine in the issue dated April 9, 2001. According to the article, National Security Advisor Condoleezza Rice stated that Kyoto is dead because it is not acceptable to the Administration or Congress. Indeed, the article goes on to point out that on the issue of global warming, members of both parties realize that it is a long-term problem that carries little short-term political risk. They will be long gone by the time the devastation wrought by global warming becomes apparent. However, if they mess up the economy, they could lose their seat in Congress. Therefore, it appears that decisions are being made in terms of personal priorities as opposed to what is good for the nation and the natural environment—decisions that do not necessarily reflect the personal values of Congressional leaders and members of the administration but are deemed to be politically correct and expedient.

During the week of September 6, 2000 the United Nations held its Millennium Summit in New York, which was attended by approximately 160 Heads of State.

The leader of each nation was given five minutes to address the audience. On ABC's *World News Tonight* Peter Jennings reported that His Excellency President Maumoon Abdul Gayoom, President of the Maldives, the island nation in the Indian Ocean mentioned above, reported that due to global warming most of the coral reefs around his nation have died, and indeed the water level of the ocean is rising with the result that his nation may be swallowed up. The President of one of the island nations of Micronesia reported similar conditions. No one seemed to take serious note of these warnings supposedly because these are small nations with no real economic and political clout in world affairs. In its November 25, 2000 issue, *The Herald* reported that the U.N.'s global warming conference held at The Hague in the Netherlands ended without any concrete plans. "Conference chairman Jan Pronk suggested a compromise plan to break a deadlock over fundamental issues. But both the main negotiating blocs at the U.N. conference rejected this. European Union delegates said Pronk's plan was bad for the environment, allowing countries too much leeway to avoid honoring greenhouse gas reductions they had committed to three years ago in Kyoto, Japan. The United States, which leads the other main negotiating group and was widely seen as the main beneficiary of the new proposal, released a statement saying it considered the plan 'unacceptably imbalanced.'"

To many technocrats it is more important to balance the economic environment which supports our life style than to balance the natural environment, which supports life itself and which is also "unacceptably imbalanced." Thus the article in *The Herald* continues, "The United States along with Canada, Japan and Australia, want no limitations on alternatives such as international trade of pollution allowances and counting farmlands and forests toward reduction targets because they take carbon dioxide out of the air. Opponents say such programs give credit for doing nothing and would mean countries could pollute more than they otherwise would be allowed."

In the meanwhile, as a result of the impasse, it is business as usual to the detriment of the health of the earth and all the creatures that inhabit it.

Much has been written about global warming and due to the size and intensity of the problem, much more continues to be written. According to an article by Mr. Paul Recer of the *Associated Press*, a British satellite study that appears on February 2, 2001 in the journal *Science*, shows that about 7.5 cubic miles of ice have eroded from a key area of the Antarctic ice sheet in just 8 years. But statements made by the lead author of the study cause some people to feel that it may take centuries before oceans rise to dangerous levels. Those who feel that way need to speak to His Excellency President Maumoon Abdul Gayoom, President of the Maldives, the island nation in the Indian Ocean mentioned above and to the people of Kiribati mentioned below.

On July 16, 2001 ITN (World News for Public Television) reported that the ocean threatens Kiribati, an island in the South Pacific. Many coastal areas of the island are already under the ocean, which is rising due to global warming. It is estimated that unless the countries that are contributing to global warming stop doing so by the year 2020 the island may be completely swallowed by the ocean. The island nation of Samoa and the Marshall Islands are also similarly threatened. After World War II the Marshall Islands were used by the USA for testing nuclear bombs. The islands are still trying to recover from the impact of the nuclear blasts.

The threat that Global warming poses to these islands has been very well depicted in a documentary produced by Andrea Torrice. The documentary is entitled *Rising Waters: Global Warming and the Fate of the Pacific Islands. Rising Waters* brings home the point the islanders are trying to make to us all. The film traces Penehuro Lefale, a Pacific Islander climatologist, on a trip to New York City, where he attends a United Nations conference on climate change. While in New York, Penehuro joins Dr. Vivian Gorniz who is a sea-level scientist for the island of Manhattan at the NASA Goddard Institute for Space Studies. Dr. Vivian Gorniz takes Penehuro Lefale and others on a very unusual tour of Manhattan Island—a tour of the areas potentially threatened by sea level rise, the lowest of which is Wall Street. *She reminds her audience of a devastating 1991 Nor'easter, which swamped the Manhattan subway system and flooded the PATH trains to New Jersey, virtually shutting the city down.* The effects of global warming now seem devastatingly close.

Echoing the warning given by Chief Joseph Seattle, Penehuro Lafale of Samoa tells us, "We may be the first victims of this phenomenon, but your turn will come up later whether it be your children or your grandchildren—unless we do something about it."

Ben Graham of the Marshall Islands observes, "It's very difficult for somebody living in the United States to grasp the fact that if the sea level rises just a few feet, a whole nation will disappear."

Through personal stories of Pacific Islanders—fisherman, elders, scientists and farmers—Rising Waters puts a human face on the international climate debate. It can be viewed on http://www.itvs.com and also purchased by calling 1(800) 543-FROG (3464).

While policymakers and scientists argue about how much—or how little—to reduce greenhouse gas emissions over the next decades, the seven million people living on thousands of islands scattered across the Pacific wonder if they have a future at all. For these people, global warming is not something that looms in the distant future. It's a threat whose real effects have already begun. The island of Bikeman, a former landmark to guide fisherman home is now totally submerged at high tide.

The United States, the largest emitter of greenhouse gasses, bears a special responsibility in the debate yet has failed to formulate a consistent government policy on the reduction of emissions. Some U.S. experts have resisted taking action because they fear a global economic slowdown if stringent measures are taken. Meanwhile, in the Pacific Islands—some of which are American protectorates—all eyes turn toward the U.S. for relief from the rising waters. While the policy makers and scientists argue about how much to reduce greenhouse gas emissions over the next 20 years, many Pacific Islanders are wondering whether they will even have a future.

To get some idea about the state of the global environment, the reader is advised to visit the website of the Global Environ-

ment Outlook, *i.e.,* GEO-2000 by going to the URL:
http://www.unep.org/geo2000/english/0026.htm
Like any other area of science, the case for human-induced global warming has uncertainties—and like many pro-business lobbyists President Bush had proclaimed those uncertainties as a reason to study the problem further rather than act now to solve the problem. However according to a Reuters story reported by Tom Doggett and Chris Baltimore and reported by ABC news, on June 3, 2002, "The Bush administration acknowledged for the first time in a new report that U.S. greenhouse emissions will increase significantly over the next two decades due mostly to human activities, *but again rejected* an international treaty to slow global warming ..."

On the same day, all 15 European Union nations ratified the Kyoto pact—the only global framework for reducing emissions of greenhouse gases such as carbon dioxide and soot.

The Science & Technology section of the March 17, 2003 issue of U.S. News & World Report briefly mentions, "...a vast brown cloud that often extends thousands of miles east, from India across China." The cloud is formed by a collection of dust, ash and smoke from fires and industry. Fires from cheap coal, cow dung and wood used for cooking by millions of citizens in India and other Asian countries, industrial furnaces and the like cause this huge cloud that spreads over several thousand square miles. The cloud threatens the health of the billions that live under it and also warm some areas and cool others and may even play a role in El Nino.

Global warming is not the only danger to the earth's biosphere. Cutting down the tropical rainforests, over-fishing, oil spills, *et cetera,* are also major contributing factors. "Empty Oceans, Empty Nets" is a very nice documentary that explores the devastation of the world's fisheries caused by over fishing. Those wishing to view it can order a home video by calling PBS at 1(800)Play-PBS.

Since the Republican Party regained control of the House and Senate, President Bush has moved swiftly to relax environmental regulations to help the economy and some say his supporters. On Nov. 22, 2002 Associated Press Writer Mr. John Heilprin reported: "The Bush Administration relaxed air pollution regulations and proposed other changes Friday to make it easier for

234

older factories, refineries and power plants to modernize without having to install expensive new anti-pollution equipment." For full story, please visit the URL:

http://story.news.yahoo.com/news?tmpl=story2&cid=544&e =4&u=/ap/20021123/ap_on_go_pr_wh/clean_air

CBS News reported on November 27, 2002 that "The Bush administration Wednesday proposed new rules that would allow more logging of federal forests for commercial or recreational activities with less study of potential harm to the environment." The new rules would affect some 190 million acres of forests and grasslands that protect our nation's forests. For the complete story, please visit:

http://www.cbsnews.com/stories/2002/11/27/politics/main5 31046.shtml

However, to be fair to President Bush, CBS news reported on December 2, 2002 that Mr. Bush also signed legislation to continue a program aimed at preserving America's wetlands. In a White House ceremony the President said, "The federal government will continue its partnership with land owners, conservation groups and states to save and improve millions of acres of wetlands," For the full story, please visit:

http://www.cbsnews.com/stories/2002/12/02/politics/main5 31368.shtml

But, in general, the Bush Record on the environment is less than flattering and/or encouraging. To review the Bush record on the environment, please go to the following URL:

http://search.yahoo.com/search?fr=slv1&p=NRDC%20The %20Bush%20Record

Or go to: http://yahoo.com and search for: NRDC The Bush Record.

We talk a lot about our health but we don't seem to care much about it because we are not willing to make sacrifices to achieve good health and protect the environment.

Of course, it is very easy to criticize others. That does not do much, if any, good. We have to face the fact that in all probability, our political leaders will not make the hard decisions needed to set things right for the environment. If the past is any indication, business decisions will largely be made with a total disregard for the environment. Our nation is so focused on business that President Calvin Coolidge said words to the effect, "The business of America is business." Indeed when our troops are sent on a mission, they are often reported to be taking care of business.

In such a situation, how can the average citizen of the world bring about the needed change? ... and where to begin?

Changes will have to be made at the grass roots level and like all change we have to first begin with ourselves. Each one of us can begin to change the world by changing him or herself. The only person that you can ever hope to control and change is yourself. When you will attempt to transform yourself, you will find that it is so difficult to do so that the futility of trying to control and change anyone else will become apparent. Yet many of us do not take the time to discipline and transform ourselves and instead waste a lot of energy trying to control and change others. To that end, our Political leaders legislate new laws. Laws have been passed protecting our rights. There are laws against racism and such. There are laws against drinking and driving, against guns and killing, *et cetera*. Have these laws succeeded in changing people? The record speaks for itself. Surely we have made some progress. But it is very gradual. One cannot legislate morality and/or force people to change. That is against the very basis of Civilized man and it is against the Divine Principle of Free Will.

We have learned from history that use of force will subdue people for a while but eventually they will resist and then those in power will have to change their tactics or they will be overthrown. How much more true is this then that of the environment, of which we are but a small part? How long can we continue to ignore the warning signs and expect that things will naturally change for the better?

Let each one of us strive to live in harmony with ourselves and those we associate with and thus begin to change the environment we live in by first changing the environment within ourselves. This will automatically influence the environment around us. If we do not act now, the Web that supports us may get irreparably damaged. Then as she has done in the past, Earth will create a new web but we may not be a part of it.

In our own interest let us work together to preserve the Web of Life the way it is now.

The young Dinshah around age 5 with his younger sister.
Circa 1908

DISCOBOLO Teenaged Dinshah at age 17 posing on stage by popular demand to inspire Indian youth that were under the thraldom of the British Colonial Rulers.

Circa 1920

FLYING MERCURY

Flying Mercury Dinshah posing as Flying Mercury
Circa 1920

One of many poses of famous statues done by Dr. Dinshah K. Mehta during his teens.

Young Dinshah at about age 21 in typical Parsi attire. The Parsis are devout followers of Zarathustra who immigrated to India from Iran about 1450 years ago. Dr. Dinshah K. Mehta was born into a prominent Parsi Zarathusti family.

A Young Dinshah poses with one of the many marauding panthers that he killed at a request by the local villagers.

Dr. Dinshah K. Mehta, with his future wife Gool and brother-in-law Dr. Jehangir Jussawalla, poses with one of the panthers he killed to protect the villagers. Dr. Jussawalla learned naturopathy under Dr. Mehta and then later on was honored by the Government of India for his contribution to Naturopathy, in particular, and Health Care, in general.

Mrs. Gool Mehta carrying a panther that had been shot by her husband, Dr. Dinshah K. Mehta.

Dr. Dinshah K. Mehta circa 1940

Dr. Dinshah Mehta with his wife Gool, daughter Shirin and son Ardeshir.

Rev. Dr. Dinshah K. Mehta in meditation, receiving a Script from His Guiding Mind.

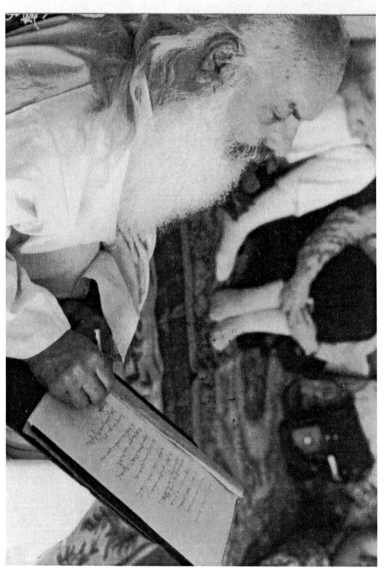

Dr. Mehta writing a Script as it is being revealed to him by his Guiding Mind.

Rev. Dr. Dinshah K. Mehta in attire typical of monks in India.

Rev. Dr. Dinshah K. Mehta in deep thought.

The late Mr. Fakhruddin Ali Ahmed, President of India 1974-77, praised the contribution made by Rev. Dr. Dinshah K. Mehta to India during a function organized to honor him. On the left is Mr. C. Subramaniam, Minister for Defence.

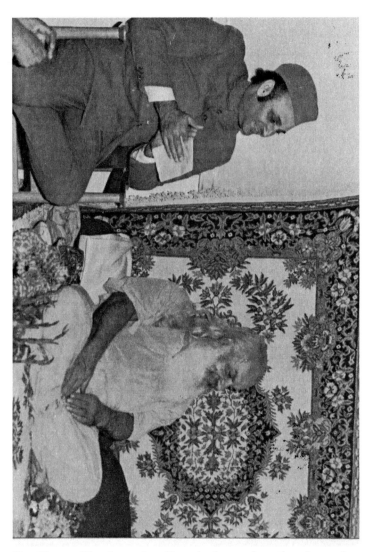

Dr. Karan Singh applauding during a function honoring Dr. Mehta. Dr. Karan Singh is a former Health Minister of India and was also the Indian Ambassador to the United States.

ICONS OF VARIOUS RELIGIONS

For the benefit of the readers, on the following pages, some of the popularly accepted forms of icons of six major world religions have been printed. Anyone of these icons can be used as a Form for one's chosen Entity as recommended by the first aspect of the First Principle of Right Surrender. Icons of Sikhism as well as Jainism and the Baha'i faith may also be used.

Readers should not limit their choice to only the forms reproduced here but are encouraged to select a form of their liking for a Master of their choosing from a wider selection if they so desire.

Zarathustra, the Prophet of Persia

Afarghan containing the Sacred Fire

Another Icon of the Zarathusti Religion

Fravashi (Spiritual Being)

An Icon of the Hindu Religion

Rama

Another Icon of the Hindu Religion

Krishna

Another Icon of the Hindu Religion

Shiva

A Popular Icon of Judaism

Jewish Star (Magen David)

Another Icon of Judaism

The Second Temple in Jerusalem

Another Icon of Judaism

Torah Scroll (Sefer Torah)

An Icon of Buddhism

Buddha

Another Icon of Buddhism

Buddha

Another Icon of Buddhism

Buddha

An Icon of Christianity

Jesus

Another Icon of Christianity

Cross

Another Icon of Christianity

The Crucifixion of Christ

An Icon of Islam

The word, "Allah"

Another Icon of Islam

The Ka'aba

Another Icon of Islam

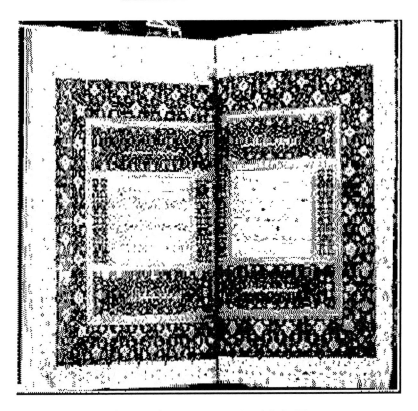

An Eighteenth Century Turkish Koran

A BRIEF EXPLANATION OF THE SOURCE OF THE SCRIPTS RECEIVED BY DR. DINSHAH K. MEHTA

INTRODUCTION to the Source of Scripts as written by Dr. Dinshah K. Mehta in a publication of the Society of Servants of God, a spiritual organization that he was instructed to start by what he calls the Guiding Mind:

It is often felt that only the saints and the sages are capable of hearing the "Inner Voice." This is true, but it is not the whole truth. It is possible for most people, if not all, to hear the "Voice of Silence," provided they remove the hindrances that are inherent, as well as those that have been created in their minds.

There are many ways of being able to hear the "Voice of Silence." It is possible for an average human being to realize this goal if, by any practice, he/she succeeds in stopping the usual thinking mind, the feeling consciousness, the working of the five senses and yet remains wide awake. Until that state is achieved it is essential that during such practices the expression of thoughts, feelings and senses is stopped by the use of will. Once the above conditions are satisfied, a state of "void" results which gradually gives way to experiences from the "Voice of Silence." These experiences differ with individuals according to the degree of evolution of the soul and human consciousness. Even before the experiences begin, one can be guided in one's life in one or the other of the three ways, namely, inspirations in one's human mind from the superconscious planes, guidance through others who are in tune with these planes and guidance through environmental forces, provided one surrenders oneself to the Guiding Force.

When one achieves the state whereby human consciousness stops functioning and the plane of rationality is transcended, one begins to get in tune with one's soul and the Oversoul. In that state of superconsciousness one begins to get spiritual experiences. They take different forms such as audition, vision and awareness. As one descends with these experiences into the usual conscious mind, some of them can be converted into human thought forms and recorded in words. The knowledge gathered thus seems beyond the average human mind and yet it is not new. These are old Truths that have been revealed to us by spiritual Masters from time to time.

"Inner experiences" began spontaneously in my life as early as the year 1936, in spite of the fact that I was an agnostic then. Doubts and resistance followed in their wake. It took me full seventeen years of inner fight to overcome doubts and become a convert to the Truth that is the "Voice of Silence."

For nearly three years it has been my practice to record in writing the experiences received during the spiritual meditations. Not all the experiences can be so recorded, for some are so deep that they defy expression even in thoughts; much less can they be expressed in words. The messages recorded on various subjects range from the highest spiritual experiences such as, origin of the Creator and creation, to the day-to-day affairs of material life.

The Source of Knowledge lies beyond the usual conscious mind. And, in my opinion, the best way to live one's worldly life is to ascend first into the superconscious planes and, descending with the experiences received there, reflect them in thoughts, words and actions in the day-to-day affairs of life.

The messages titled "Scripts" are from the "Voice of Silence." I lay no claim to the authorship of the contents. What is published as "Scripts" has been received *through* me, not *from* me. Nor do I lay any claim to the messages having been recorded in Divine language. In my meditations I have been getting experiences in the form of audition, vision and awareness. Whatever is expressible is transformed into human thought and is scribed in whatever language I have at my command. At times, I also "hear" specific words during the process of conversion of the experiences into thought-forms or during the time of scribing.

In the Scripts, "I" signifies the Guiding Source, and "My Father," as well as "My Father in Heaven," stands for God.

- A doubter converted

LIGHT OF LOVE

Dark is My Light yet brightest of bright
In which arose My Thought TO BE
When day was not nor was there night
Nor were there eyes for the sight to see.

Out of the Thought the Word took birth
That sounded like nought that could be heard
And out of the Sound all took form
And thus was My Universe born.

This I give in terms of the past
But to Me the past is not the last
Nor is there future that shall ever come
For I AM the Eternal Present One.

What I started was not yesterday
Nor is it the morrow that I create today
But the Present that was, is and shall be—
The Eternal Book for My Children to see.

But minds of My dear ones are stuffed with self
That crowds out My Love which alone can help
To know the Eternal now and the Love that I AM
And light My Light in their empty lamp.

From **THE SCRIPTS** May 27, 1956

Bahram Rashid Shahmardaan, Ph.D.

The author Bahram R. Shahmardaan was born

into a Zoroastrian family and grew up in the multi-religious-cultural-ethnic-racial city of Bombay, India while India was still a British colony. For those who are unaware, scholars now acknowledge that the three wise men that brought gifts for the infant Jesus were followers of the Zoroastrian faith. For his high school education, Bahram was enrolled in a catholic school in which 90% of his fellow students were Muslims. Bahram used the unusual opportunity provided by the rich human experience to determine if there is a purpose to life and if so, the principles one can live by to realize it. With the help of many religious teachers and eventually a Spiritual Master in the person of Dr. Dinshah K. Mehta, Bahram sifted through the seemingly conflicting values and customs of the various religions of India, which include but are not limited to Zoroastrianism, Hinduism, Judaism, Buddhism, Jainism, Christianity, Islam, Sikhism, the Baha'i faith and a host of other denominations.

After obtaining a Bachelor's degree in science from Bombay University, Bahram came to the United States in 1968 where he completed his M.B.A. and Ph.D. *However Bahram reminds himself and others that none of the Great Masters through whom the World Religions have been founded had any college education. Nor did most of the Saints who attained sainthood by living according to the teachings of the Masters.*

That a lack of formal education does not prevent one from being great is also reflected in the life of the great American inventor Thomas Alva Edison. It is reported that Mr. Edison had only 3 months of formal schooling. Yet Mr. Edison remains the most prolific American Inventor whose 1,190 patents is still the record for the number of patents issued to any one American.

Bahram feels that much of what is called education blocks and quite often retards Spiritual growth. To grow spiritually, most of us have to first unlearn much of what we have learned. Thus, in a very real sense, on the spiritual path, individuals who have received a formal education can be at a disadvantage than their less educated brethren because the educated ones have more to unlearn than those who have had less or no formal education.

To help those who are unfamiliar about the Goal of Life, Bahram established the "Society of Servants of God" as a church in California. The Society of Servants of God, which started in India through Dr. Dinshah K. Mehta has associates around the world.

Through many years of spiritual practice and teaching spiritual principles Bahram can now explain the spiritual principles that are common to all religions. Bahram clearly demonstrates how the Divine Creative Plan unfolds in nature and how it is also reflected in human activities. To explain difficult spiritual concepts, Bahram has used natural phenomena and everyday occurrences that anyone can verify with their own experiences. Bahram encourages people to not believe what he says unless they can verify it against the backdrop of their own experience.

Due to the simple examples used by Bahram, the difference between religiosity and spirituality is obvious. The book also outlines and explains in detail the spiritual principles that will enable individuals to deal with conflicting value systems, dogmas and different interpretations presented by various world religions about man and his relationship with the Universe and more specifically the Creator.

Anyone who practices the principles explained in the book will be able to reach the highest experiences of which they are capable. These principles are unique and have never been revealed before to the general public.

For more than thirty-five years, Bahram has strived to live by these principles in his daily life. This effort has given him deep insights, which are both unique and highly useful in clarifying the universal issues all of us face in sorting out the conflicts we experience in our daily lives. Bahram's gift of expressing these insights with clarity and simplicity can help us all as we navigate our own journeys through Life Eternal.

NOTES

(It is suggested that you use the following blank pages to make your own notes on your *practice* of the advice given in this book!)

NOTES